PSYCHOANALYSIS
AND
THE LAW

Publication Number 869

AMERICAN LECTURE SERIES®

A Monograph in

The BANNERSTONE DIVISION *of*
AMERICAN LECTURES IN BEHAVIORAL SCIENCE AND LAW

Edited by

RALPH SLOVENKO, B.E., LL.B., M.A., Ph.D.
Wayne State University
Law School
Detroit, Michigan

PSYCHOANALYSIS
AND
THE LAW

By

C. G. SCHOENFELD, B.A., LL.B., LL.M.

CHARLES C THOMAS • PUBLISHER

Springfield • Illinois • U.S.A.

Published and Distributed Throughout the World by
CHARLES C THOMAS • PUBLISHER
BANNERSTONE HOUSE
301–327 East Lawrence Avenue, Springfield, Illinois, U.S.A.

© *1973, by* CHARLES C THOMAS • PUBLISHER
ISBN 0-398-02656-4
Library of Congress Card Catalog Number: 72-87013

Printed in the United States of America
CC-11

FOREWORD

THIS BOOK IS a pioneer effort to synthesize psychoanalysis and the law. It is an attempt to apply the discoveries and concepts of Freud and his followers to the law so as to gain new insights regarding it, facilitate improvements in it, and help to resolve some of its basic problems.

To achieve these goals, fundamental psychoanalytic tenets are described and then applied both to the law and to those who influence and are influenced by it. The facets of the law dealt with in the book are many and varied, ranging from abstruse jurisprudential concepts to "live" courtroom tactics, from a consideration of the theory of the law of negligence to a consideration of the punishments imposed (both now and in earlier—and presumably more savage—times) by the criminal law.

In the beginning of this book, psychoanalytic insights regarding unconscious motivation are employed to help explain the behavior of criminals and the police who seek to apprehend them, clients and the lawyers who try to serve them, legislators and the judges who interpret the laws they pass. Later the book deals with psychoanalytic discoveries concerning unconscious symbolism and their relevance to such seemingly disparate matters as labor law, President Roosevelt's so-called "court packing" plan of 1937, juvenile deliquency and the way in which the law seeks to cope with kleptomania and pyromania.

A large part of the book is devoted to an in-depth psychoanalytic study of four basic perennial problems of constitutional law—problems that (as the text reveals) lawyers, judges and legislators, among others, have wrestled with for almost two hundred years.

Though many very different areas and facets of the law are touched upon in the book, all of them are treated with the goal in mind of helping to facilitate informed and meaningful social changes.

The author, C. G. Schoenfeld, is Secretary-Treasurer of Schoenfeld and Sons, Inc., New York City. He has earned his B.A. degree in 1947 from Yale University; his LL.B. degree in 1950 from Harvard Law School; and his LL.M. (Criminal Justice) degree in 1971 from New York University. He has published articles on applied psychoanalysis and on psychoanalysis and the law in a number of professional psychoanalytic and legal journals.

RALPH SLOVENKO
Editor, American Lectures in
Behavioral Science and the Law

To the memory of Sigmund Freud
and Oliver Wendell Holmes, Jr.

The perfect lawyer, like the perfect orator, must accomplish himself for his duties by familiarity with every study. It may be truly said, that to him nothing, that concerns human nature or human art, is indifferent or useless.

MR. JUSTICE STORY

(Inaugural address, 1829, as Dane Professor of Law, Harvard University)

CONTENTS

PSYCHOANALYSIS
AND
THE LAW

I

INTRODUCTION

IT IS A COMMONPLACE thing that criminals frequently "auto-graph" their crimes by employing a self-identifying mode of operation or by returning afterwards to the scene of the crime. Not as well known, however, is the psychoanalytic discovery that breaking the law in such a self-incriminatory manner or acting afterwards in such a suspicious manner may be less a product of habit or curiosity than of an unconscious desire to caught and punished.[1]

Lawyers may find this psychoanalytic discovery difficult to accept (at least at first sight), for it appears to contradict the traditional assumption of the criminal law that crime is the offspring of a free and vicious will.[2] Yet, as psychoanalysts have learned, criminals are frequently beset by considerable unconscious guilt; and to assuage this guilt, a criminal may unconsciously seek punishment, much as a conscience-stricken person may deliberately impose a penance upon himself. The criminal may commit an offense using a self-identifying mode of operation or return afterwards to the scene of the crime, so as to invite—though without conscious knowledge or intent—capture and punishment.[3]

But if crime is at times the product of an unconscious wish for punishment by the law, then the law may actually function as the unwitting accomplice of certain offenders. That is, by punishing these "criminals from a sense of guilt,"[4] the law may actually encourage—rather than discourage—the commission of crimes by them.

As startling as such a conclusion may be, it is but one of many fascinating, and often unexpected, insights regarding the law that awaits lawyers (for whom this book is primarily intended) and others who may be interested in applying psychoanalytic discoveries to the law. More specifically, this book will

3

attempt to advance an interest in synthesizing psychoanalytic psychology and law by presenting, in Part I, certain basic psychoanalytic tenets and suggesting how they may prove applicable to—and lead to an increased understanding of—the law; and by considering, in Part II, four specific, basic, perennial and hitherto insoluble problems of constitutional law and demonstrating how they may be better understood—and possibly even begin to be resolved—in the light of psychoanalytic doctrines. Requiring attention first, however, are certain preliminary questions.

To begin with, ought modern psychology (especially as it finds expression in psychoanalytic psychology) be applied to the law? A number of lawyers would probably say "no," some of them influenced by the dismal failure of attempts (especially during the 1920's and 1930's) to apply the psychological system known as "behaviorism" to the law,[5] others believing that the law is somehow unique—a discipline that stands apart from sociology, anthropology, psychology or any other discipline.[6] Indisputably however, the law (especially by using such devices as judicial notice and testimony by experts) has traditionally made use of knowledge acquired in other fields, and surely, attempts by great legal thinkers during the past century or two (Jeremy Bentham and Roscoe Pound, for example) to apply extralegal knowledge and concepts to the law have had a salutary effect upon the law.[7]

As the noted psychologist Edward S. Robinson once pointed out, the law—concerned as it is with the regulation, mitigation and composition of disputes—almost inevitably treats of matters dealt with by psychology,[8] and if so, does not the conscientiousness about their profession that so frequently characterizes lawyers require them to learn what modern psychology has to offer concerning the resolution of disputes? Further, lawyers might consider Robinson's warning that "men who resolve to think about human affairs without recourse to psychology never actually succeed in avoiding psychology; they simply make up a crude, uncritical psychology of their own."[9]

If then it may be suggested that lawyers need to have at

least *some* familiarity with modern psychology, a further question arises: Why ought they pay particular attention to, and try to apply to the law, that special form of psychology known as psychoanalytic psychology?

In reply, it might be pointed out that significant advances in knowledge have resulted from the application of psychoanalytic tools and insights to the social sciences: to history, anthropology, sociology and the like.[10] Moreover, many students of psychology believe that psychoanalytic concepts and doctrines constitute by far the most valuable part of modern psychology.[11] As the well-known psychologist John Dollard once, in effect, observed, "Let's face it, Freud has won."[12] Even more to the point, however, many psychoanalytic theories, as well as many of the topics dealt with by psychoanalysts, seem to be particularly relevant to the law. In Robinson's words, a lawyer is "likely to conclude that of all contemporary psychologists, the Freudian is the one whose interests are most nearly identical with his own."[13]

But even lawyers greatly interested in psychoanalysis and convinced of the desirability of applying it to the law have been concerned about what has sometimes been termed "the principal focus of tension between psychoanalysis and the law."[14] That is, the law has traditionally assumed that most men are endowed with a significant degree of free will; and hence, they are free to choose between lawful and unlawful behavior. Psychoanalysis, on the other hand, is usually regarded by its practitioners as based upon Freud's view that free will is an illusion that "must give ground before the claims of a determinism which governs even mental life."[15]

Yet despite this seeming conflict, the law has traditionally recognized the possibility of situations arising in which free will is absent. According to a well-settled common law doctrine, for example, "if a woman commits larceny, burglary, 'or other civil offenses against the laws of society,' by the coercion of her husband, she is considered as acting under compulsion and not of her own will, and is not guilty of any crime."[16] Also when the law exonerates an insane man on the grounds that his otherwise criminal acts were the result of an irresistible impulse, the law is, in effect, recognizing that he lacked the free will needed to be held responsible for his acts.[17]

By the same token, psychoanalytic discoveries—contrary to the usual view of psychoanalysts—fail to require a belief in complete mental determinism. Admittedly, psychoanalytic discoveries reveal that *more* behavior is determined than had previously been supposed, that dreams and a number of other psychic events are *often* determined. By no means, however, have these discoveries shown that *all* behavior is determined or even that dreams (or other psychic events) are *always* determined. Further, certain major psychoanalytic tenets—for instance, Freud's theories concerning the healthy "ego" (the "I" of the personality)—are incompatible with determinism and imply the existence of some degree of free will. Thus, when discussing the relationship between the ego and the "id" (the "it" of the personality—the instincts), Freud suggests that "One might compare the relation of the ego to the id with that between a rider and his horse. The horse provides the locomotive energy, and the rider has the prerogative of determining the goal and of guiding the movements of his powerful mount towards it."[18]

In short, despite the assumption made by many persons that psychoanalysis and the law contain irreconcilable attitudes concerning free will and determinism,[19] the fact is that both psychoanalysis and law are consistent with the existence of partial free will and partial determinism. Both are in accordance with the view that most men possess "some spark of capacity for consciously and creatively guiding their conduct in conformity with legal sanctions."[20]

Even if the free will–determinism problem fails to stand in the way of combining law and psychoanalytic psychology, lawyers may be deterred from synthesizing these disciplines by still other considerations. For instance, can law—which, after all, is essentially a social product largely concerned with societal or group needs—be analyzed in terms of a discipline like psychoanalytic psychology, which is focused upon and grounded in discoveries regarding individuals?

In reply, it might be contended that since psychoanalytic discoveries are based in part upon psychoanalyses of lawyers, judges and others who have helped to mold the law,[21] the law ought to prove examinable in the light of such discoveries, at least to the extent that these persons and others like them have influenced the law. A more incisive (though related) answer would be, however that insofar as laws "are made by men, for men, they cannot help having the nature of men in them"[22]; and for this reason, psychoanalytic discoveries deduced from the study of individuals are likely to prove useful in understanding that social product known as the law.

However, despite advantages that may result from applying psychoanalytic psychology to the law, care must be taken never to assume that psychoanalytic discoveries *alone* can lead to a complete understanding of law. Psychoanalytic explanations, certainly of anything as complex as law, are at best *partial* explanations: they cannot reveal what only a knowledge of history, or sociology, or anthropology, or philosophy—or, indeed, of law itself—can reveal about law. For example, it may well be true that some of the unconscious motives described by Freud play a part in molding the decisions rendered by judges. Yet it hardly follows, as one psychoanalytic enthusiast has contended, that judicial decisions are little more than special pleas made in defense of unconscious motives.[23] Rather, as Mr. Justice Cardozo took care to point out in his classic work *The Nature of the Judicial Process*,[24] the influences that help to mold judicial decisions are many and varied: unconscious motives may have a role to be sure, but so do logic, reason, precedent, social desiderata, and so on. To waive aside all such influences except unconscious motivation in trying to explain a judicial decision is to be naively simplistic. By the same token, is it not equally naive to assume *a priori* (as have some lawyers) that only logic, reason and the like play a significant role in judicial decisions and that unconscious motives can therefore be disregarded completely?[25]

Perhaps lawyers who object to considering the possible effect of unconscious motivation upon judicial decisions have in mind a more general objection to applying psychoanalytic psychology to law: the objection that any conclusions deduced from combining psychoanalysis and law are unlikely to be based upon scientifically definitive evidence and are, indeed, likely to be highly speculative.

To contend that the evidence available to support the conclusions advanced in this book is in any way comparable to the evidence usually adduced in the physical or exact sciences would be folly, as would a failure to admit that some of the conclusions reached in this book are speculative. Yet clearly, neither psychoanalysis nor law can (certainly as they exist today) be considered to be exact sciences,[26] and if for no other reason, it would be highly unrealistic to expect a synthesis of psychoanalysis and law to be based upon the type of evidence available in chemistry or physics—or even in biology or physiology. Admittedly, any synthesis of psychoanalysis and law could be put off until psychoanalytic psychology and the law become more scientific. But is this not to court a harmful, and perhaps indefinite, delay? To continue to delay applying modern psychological principles to the law is, in the words of Robert M. Hutchins, to increasingly run the risk that "we may wake up some day to find ourselves promulgating in court . . . rules of human behavior which have no more relation to the way humans behave than the old rule that one having a financial interest in a suit could not possibly tell the truth on the witness stand. . . . We have not progressed so far since *Jarndyce v. Jarndyce* and *Bardell v. Pickwick* that we can afford to be sure of ourselves."[27] Further, examining the law in the light of psychoanalytic and other modern psychological principles may well be a prerequisite for obtaining the theoretical knowledge needed to make the law more scientific than it is now. If so, then to put off applying psychoanalysis to law until the law becomes more scientific would be, in effect, to delay this synthesis indefinitely. Criminologists especially have learned that advances in theoretical scientific knowledge are often dependent upon the initiation of practical programs, so that if "practical programs wait until theoretical knowledge is complete, they will wait for eternity."[28]

Finally (and despite the numerous changes in law effected by the Supreme Court during the 1950's and the 1960's under Mr. Chief Justice Warren), many areas and aspects of the law (for instance, rules concerning alimony and divorce, the treatment of criminals and juvenile offenders, and the administration of laws regarding labor relations) are still in great need of reform. It is still true that "the sores in our legal system are many and grievous—all the more grievous because many of them have been repeatedly pointed out at least as far back as Bentham."[29] The sooner psychoanalytic discoveries are applied to the law, the sooner ways may be found to heal some of these old and grievous sores. Admittedly, some of the law's faults are probably endemic. For example, the development of cumbersome legal procedures (and the concomitant need for periodic procedural reforms) may be inevitable by-products of the case-by-case, instance-by-instance common law method of building substantive law[30]; and as Roscoe Pound pointed out in his celebrated essay *The Causes of Popular Dissatisfaction with the Administration of Justice*,[31] there may well be an unavoidable time lag between a society's mores and its laws, with the result that "law is often in very truth a government of the living by the dead."[32] Nevertheless, as this book will attempt to demonstrate, viewing the law in the light of psychoanalytic psychology not only ought to lead to a greater understanding of the law but may also point the way to needed changes in the law— changes that may well help the law become more effective and mature than now.

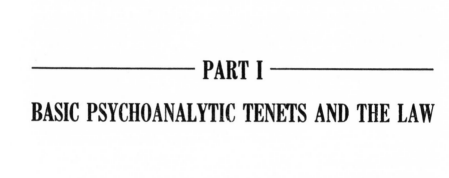

PART I

BASIC PSYCHOANALYTIC TENETS AND THE LAW

II

UNCONSCIOUS MOTIVES
AND THE LAW

Discoveries concerning unconscious motives constitute the essence of psychoanalytic psychology. This chapter will describe some of these discoveries and will attempt to suggest wherein unconscious motivation has influenced the law (and those who affect and are affected by the law).

SIGMUND FREUD began to write about unconscious motives in the early 1890's. Yet even before this, references to unconscious mentation had begun to appear in law books; for example, in *Ancient Law*, Henry S. Maine's pioneer volume on the early history of the law, published in 1861, and in *The Common Law*, Oliver Wendell Holmes, Jr.'s seminal work, published in 1881. By no means is this to say that Maine, Holmes or any other legal scholar anticipated Freud's discoveries concerning unconscious motives—or even thought of unconscious motivation in the same manner as did Freud. When Maine and Holmes wrote their great legal works, references to unconscious mental activity could already be found in books by a host of renowned thinkers: Spinoza, Fichte, Herder, Goethe, Schiller, Schopenhauer and Herbart, to mention but a few.[1] What is arresting in the attitude of Maine and Holmes towards unconscious mentation, however, is their unhesitating acceptance of its existence and relevance to the law, an attitude later found in the writings of Benjamin Cardozo, Felix Frankfurter and Jerome Frank. In fact, in *The Nature of the Judicial Process*, Mr. Justice Cardozo speaks openly of "forces so far beneath the surface that they cannot be classified as other than subconscious" and goes on to declare that "it is often through these subconscious forces that judges are kept consistent with themselves and inconsistent with one another."[2]

Despite the accepting attitude towards unconscious mentation described above, there can be no doubt that some legal scholars still find it hard to believe that lawyers and judges are really "tainted" with "an 'unconscious' or a 'subconscious.' "[3] Yet this disbelief flies in the face of psychoanalytic discoveries which, indisputably, have refuted the one prevalent notion that consciousness and mental activity are synonymous and instead have revealed that mental processes are largely unconscious—and, indeed, that most of the mind's contents are unconscious. Admittedly, some of this unconscious material can be made conscious by an attempt to remember. Such an attempt may, for example, be successful in bringing to mind the temporarily forgotten name of a book or perhaps the face of a childhood sweetheart. Certain unconscious thoughts and feelings, however, resist even the most determined efforts at recall. Many of these unconscious ideas and emotions have been "repressed" (that is, excluded from consciousness—or indeed never even permitted to enter consciousness—by powerful unconscious forces) and may succeed in gaining access to consciousness only after a prolonged psychoanalysis.

Sometimes repressed ideas are strikingly similar to consciously espoused views. The ultranationalist who preaches the desirability of keeping his country free from "foreign" influences may, for instance, have repressed a profound hatred of foreigners.[4] More frequently, though, repressed ideas and impulses are likely to differ from consciously held views. These repressed wishes—particularly if they are deeply repressed—are often irrational, savage, primitive and extreme. It becomes understandable that such unconscious desires should have such characteristics once it is learned that these desires are largely those of the first few years of life—of infancy and early childhood. Further (and contrary to what one might expect), unconscious ideas "are timeless; that is, they are not ordered temporally . . . [and] are not altered by the passage of time."[5]

Though unconscious ideas and impulses may, at times, have comparatively little influence upon conscious thoughts and urges; the contrary, so psychoanalysts have found, frequently proves to be the case. In fact, psychoanalysts have learned that not only in neurotics and psychotics, but in presumably normal persons as well, unconscious desires may (and often do) have the most profound effect upon behavior. Unconscious desires repeatedly seem to play a vital role, for example, in such diverse and significant matters as religious observances, choosing a spouse, selecting political leaders and determining one's life's work.[6]

Men differ as to the universality of certain unconscious urges (for instance, cultural anthropologists differ with psychoanalysts regarding the ubiquity of certain incestuous and parenticidal impulses).[7] There can be no doubt, however, that unconscious thoughts and feelings per se are universal and hence inevitably affect all persons who influence or are influenced by the law.

Psychoanalytic studies reveal, for example, that criminals are frequently motivated by unconscious wishes: for instance, that when men steal, rape, burn and murder, they are often governed by powerful, and primitive, unconscious wishes.[8] Paradoxically perhaps, those persons whose function it is to apprehend, prosecute, judge and punish criminals may also be moved at times by powerful unconscious motives in so doing.[9] One would have to be extraordinarily imperceptive or insensitive not to sense the aggression and sadism—conscious and unconscious—that sometimes governs policemen, prison guards, district attorneys and judges when they presumably seek to carry out their role of protecting society against its criminals.[10]

Not only criminals and the public officials who try to cope with them, but also lawyers and the civil clients they represent may be motivated at times in their law-oriented activities by strong unconscious forces. For example, powerful unconscious urges may well play a determinative role in the behavior of clients who seek to obtain legal intervention in emotion-laden family squabbles.[11] There can be little doubt that many clients who seek a lawyer's help in obtaining what they describe as "justice" (in a dispute between an employer and an ex-employee, for instance) may actually be driven by aggressive and hostile wishes of which they may be partially or even wholly unaware.[12]

This is not to suggest that a lawyer ought to pay less attention to the contents of what his clients tell him and instead busy himself searching for his clients' presumed hidden motives. Rather it is to suggest that a lawyer ought to keep in mind the possibility that the goals his clients seek may be, in part or in whole, irrational and unconscious. As a result, a lawyer may, for example, find himself in the future better able to recognize members of that difficult-to-detect group known as litigious paranoiacs who try to use the law (in a pathetically futile attempt) to thrash out inner conflicts.[13] Of course, lawyers who keep in mind the possibility that clients may unconsciously seek irrational goals may help to prevent these clients from making very serious—and sometimes tragic—mistakes. Lawyers are, after all, not only advocates but also—(and more especially) counsellors as well.

"Many lawyers," in the words of psychiatrist Herbert C. Modlin, "have taken their turn on the psychoanalytic couch and have been shown to be affected at times by 'the ubiquitous unconscious.' "[14] A lawyer's unconscious feelings and reactions may, for example, interfere with his ability to elicit a sufficiently complete statement of facts from clients, with the result that he may render premature—and incorrect—judgments regarding the legal rights of these clients.[15] More specifically, a lawyer may unconsciously identify himself with his clients and, as a result, may fail not only to elicit needed facts from these clients (especially facts damaging to their legal position) but may also lose his objectivity in evaluating these facts and in forming a proper conclusion as to their legal consequences.[16] Admittedly, the loss of this much needed objectivity can have other unconscious (and conscious) determinants: a lawyer's unconscious (and conscious) aggressive and hostile desires may, for instance, overcome his objectivity—indeed, to such an extent, as to render him willing to employ in the courtroom such disgraceful tactics as discrediting honest witnesses, blocking the introduction of vital evidence and employing outrageously partisan, and even perjured, testimony.[17]

When a lawyer becomes a judge or a legislator, unconscious forces within him would still presumably affect his conduct as they had before his elevation to the bench or his election to the legislature. As Theodore Schroeder insisted more than fifty years ago, unconscious wishes and reactions "are not altered when one assumes the judicial function."[18] In fact, the likelihood of unconscious wishes affecting the behavior of judges so concerned Judge Jerome Frank that in his book *Courts On Trial* he suggested that every judge "should undergo something like a psychoanalysis."[19] Extreme and possibly unacceptable this suggestion may well be, if for no other reason than carrying it out would presumably destroy the typicalness (in certain respects) that men usually hope to find in those whose function it is to judge them. Still if, as psychoanalysts have learned, unconscious forces sometimes cause judges to react improperly in cases brought before them,[20] would it really be so extreme to ask judges, and legislators as well, to "come to grips with the human nature operative in themselves"?[21]

If it may be assumed that the behavior of legislators and judges, lawyers and the clients they serve, criminals and those who arrest, prosecute, judge and punish them—indeed, the behavior of all persons who influence or are influenced by the law—is affected by the unconscious ideas and urges within them, then insofar as legal procedures and substantive law truly reflect man, these procedures and substantive law would also presumably reflect, certainly to some extent, such unconscious ideas and urges. Trials may well provide a number of useful examples.

As psychoanalysts have pointed out, trials offer many opportunities for unconscious ideas and reactions to find expression.[22] For example, to the extent that a judge is unconsciously regarded as a parent figure, parent-oriented unconscious feelings are likely to be aroused in regard to him.[23]

Thus the reverential awe exhibited by some persons towards judges—and conversely, the angry defiance displayed towards judges by others—may well reflect the influence of parent-oriented feelings.[24] In like manner, the all-too-frequent (and at times, shameful) squabbles between attorneys in court may well be, in part, the product of unconscious feelings of sibling rivalry that are aroused in these attorneys when they compete in court for the favor of their unconscious parent substitute—the judge.[25] Further, and this is a matter to which investigators have given considerable attention, unconscious thoughts and emotions may distort perception and hence may result in inaccurate (and sometimes completely false) testimony.[26] As studies (especially by Edwin M. Borchard and Barbara and Jerome Frank) have shown, distorted perception and erroneous testimony based upon it have frequently caused grave miscarriages of justice—including the conviction of innocent persons accused of heinous crimes.[27]

Not only perception but memory as well may be distorted by unconscious forces. Hence, it is not at all surprising to learn that courtroom testimony may be greatly affected by what has been termed "unconscious rearrangement of memories in accuser and accused."[28] A possible motive for this unconscious distortion of memory may be found in Nietzsche's celebrated aphorism concerning memory and pride:

> "I have done that," says my Memory. "I could not have done that," says my Pride, and remains inexorable. Finally, my Memory yields.[29]

Still, there can be little doubt that the "unconscious rearrangement of memories" which results in erroneous testimony by accuser and accused is all too likely to be a product of aggressive and hostile urges, both conscious and unconscious, which seem to be able to find in trials many opportunities to gain expression.[30] Indeed, it may prove helpful to note here that trials not only provide opportunities to express hostility, conscious and unconscious, but may also be *instigated* at times by this hostility. Litigation, in the words of Hubert W. Smith, "has psychological connotations running deeper than self-vindication of one's cause by valor or might. It expresses the animosity factor . . . the desire to be at one's assailant and 'have it out.' "[31]

Not only trials (or other legal procedures) but substantive law as well—and particularly the criminal law—may reveal the influence of unconscious desires and feelings. In fact, Paul Reiwald (a Swiss attorney who attempted to apply psychoanalytic insights to the criminal law) has contended that "Without the acceptance of unconscious drives and of their determining influence, the history of the criminal law must remain incomprehensible even in present times."[32]

One much discussed psychoanalytic insight pertaining to the effect of unconscious forces upon the criminal law is the view that certain sexual acts are labeled "crimes" and are punished as such by the criminal law, because this procedure lends support to the insistent unconscious need of the public to disown the urge to commit such acts themselves (be the urge repressed or even conscious). In the words of Law Professor Henry Weihofen, "Consciously or unconsciously we fear that we might do what the sex offender has done. This disturbing thought we exorcise by publicly repudiating the wicked wretch and piously calling for his punishment."[33] Though no attempt will be made here to evaluate in detail the punishments that the criminal law inflicts upon sex offenders, mention ought to be made, albeit in passing, of the strangely contradictory and self-defeating procedure followed in many states of sending persons convicted of having committed homosexual or related acts prohibited by the criminal law to monosexual penal institutions where, as criminologists have repeatedly pointed out, even sexually normal persons are changed into "homosexual and otherwise perverted wrecks."[34] Indeed, this and related practices have caused Karl Menninger and other psychoanalysts to suggest that society—albeit unconsciously or secretly—"*wants* crime, *needs* crime, and gains definite satisfactions from the present mishandling of it!"[35]

Another way in which unconscious ideas and urges may influence the criminal law pertains to the effect upon it of *lex talionis*: the retaliatory "law" (expressed in the phraseology of the Old Testament) of "eye for eye, tooth for tooth, hand for hand, foot for foot."[36] That is, psychoanalysts have learned that the talion reaction—the desire to retaliate in kind and the fear of such retaliation—is a deep-rooted unconscious reaction (which, for example, is expressed in particularly dramatic fashion in the male infant's fear that his genitals will be cut off because of his desire to appropriate his father's larger genitals).[37] Psychoanalysts believe that unconscious talion wishes have found reflection not only in the Old Testament and in various legal codes of the past such as the extraordinarily ancient Code of Hammurabi (which contains such provision as "If a man destroy the eye of another man, they shall destroy his eye"; "If he break a man's bone, they shall break his bone"; and "If a man knock out a tooth of a man of his own rank, they shall knock out his tooth,"[38]), but in addition, that inner talion urges have continued to influence the "civil and criminal law up to our time."[39] The first example of the influence of talion wishes upon the criminal law that immediately comes to mind is, of course, the practice of executing murderers, a practice still sanctioned in a number of the states.[40] Yet man's unconscious talion wishes may also express themselves in the criminal law in more subtle fashion; for instance, in laws permitting the sterilization (unconsciously equated with the castration) of rapists and other sex criminals.[41]

Related to the criminal law's reflection of man's inner talion urges is its ability to enable man to express conscious and unconscious aggressive feelings. The criminal law, in the words of Paul Reiwald, enables "people to release their own repressed aggression"[42]; or, to quote psychoanalyst Fritz Wittels, it provides "an outlet for conscious and unconscious feelings of revenge."[43]

Probably the most obvious way in which the criminal law reflects man's conscious and unconscious urges is in the punishments it imposes. Historically, one of the prime functions of the punishments imposed by the criminal law was to help to induce the public to abandon the once prevalent practice of obtaining private vengeance against alleged criminals and to substitute instead vengeance by society.[44] There can be no doubt that some of the punishments once enforced by the criminal law—flaying, disemboweling, tearing with red hot pincers, breaking on the wheel, and so on *ad nauseam*[45]— would satisfy even the cruelest of conscious and unconscious private vengeful desires. Today, fines, imprisonment and occasional "painless" executions (in gas chambers and in electric chairs, for instance) have largely replaced the older and more openly vengeful and cruel punishments sanctioned by the criminal law. As a result, it may sometimes seem as if the punishments sanctioned by the criminal law no longer serve man's inner aggressive and hostile urgencies to any great extent. As penologists have repeatedly pointed out, however, imprisonment (today's most usual punishment for serious crimes) frequently proves to be extremely destructive to those who undergo it: the endless monotony, absence of privacy, incredibly minute regimentation and abnormal deprivations (especially sexual deprivations) in even the best of prisons all too often turn men into what Ralph S. Banay has termed "deadly human explosives"—men who are likely, after their release from prison, to " 'explode' . . . against the society that has imprisoned them."[46]

By no means does it follow, however, that the imprisonment of criminals ought, as some psychoanalysts almost seem to suggest, to be abolished forthwith.[47] For one thing, a society's very existence may well be dependent upon its ability to isolate and protect itself against those who would prey upon it. But even more to the point, the behavior of criminals often arouses in the general public powerful conscious and unconscious emotions—feelings of indignation, anger, fury and revulsion that all too readily call forth a wish for retributive vengeance.[48] If this wish for vengeance and the feelings (conscious and unconscious) that contribute to it are ignored by the criminal law, men may revert to private vengeance against criminals, a state of affairs that no viable modern industrial state could possibly tolerate for long.[49] To quote the well-known legal philosopher Morris R. Cohen, "The sentiment that injuries should be avenged . . . cannot be ignored within the life of any community. . . . If the natural desire for vengeance is not met and satisfied by the orderly procedure of the criminal law we shall revert to the more bloody private vengeance of the feud and of the vendetta."[50]

III

THE SUPEREGO AND THE LAW

*Freud divided the psyche into three parts: "id," "ego"
and "superego." This chapter will detail certain psychoanalytic findings concerning the superego (the "judicial"
part of the personality) and will try to point out wherein
the superego has affected the law.*

SOME PSYCHOANALYSTS BELIEVE that man's moral faculty or
superego is "the decisive part of the personality,"[1] the
"real master of the personality."[2] Whether or not this is so,[3]
there can be no doubt that the superego (which includes what
is ordinarily meant by the term "conscience," but which is
in large part unconscious) performs such functions as setting
moral and ethical standards,[4] evaluating thought and actions
in the light of these standards, granting rewards (self-praise,
for example) for moral conduct and demanding repentance
and punishment for unprincipled behavior.[5]

Contrary to what one might expect, the superego does not
exist at birth. It is "not introduced into the . . . [mind] at
birth as a steering gear is fitted into a car."[6] Rather, the
superego develops very slowly and tentatively during the first
four or five years of life, consisting largely of parental prohibitions that are alternately internalized and externalized.[7]
When a child reaches the age of six or so, however, a qualitative
and quantitative change ordinarily occurs in his supergo. At
this time, the child internalizes, on a more or less "permanent"
basis, much of the image he has formed of his parents (and
especially of the parent of the same sex). This internalized
parent image then becomes his superego, which rules him from
within as his parents once ruled him from without.[8]

Though created in the image of a child's parents, the child's
superego is also partly a product of his *own* desires and feelings
(many of which, so psychoanalysts have concluded, reflect
mankind's savage racial past).[9] Psychoanalysts believe, for

example, that the severity of a child's superego may reflect not only the severity exhibited by his parents but also his own aggressive and hostile impulses (which he externalized onto his parents and then internalized as part of the parent image that became his more or less stable superego at the age of six or so). In the words of the well-known psychoanalyst J. C. Flugel, "It is clear that the parent-figure . . . thus introjected is a figure . . . different from the real parent, inasmuch as it is endowed with all the crude and primitive aggressiveness of the young child himself."[10]

Not only is the superego likely to reflect a child's own primitive desires and feelings, but it is also likely to reflect the way in which the child (acting under the spur of environmental frustrations) has attempted to control these desires and feelings. Freud pointed out, for example, that the demand for equality that so often constitutes a major element of the superego's concept of justice is, paradoxically, rooted in the child's original demand for exclusive possession of his parents; that is, when a child learns that (contrary to his fervent wishes) he cannot have his parents to himself but must share them with others (and especially with his brothers and sisters), he often makes a virtue of necessity by renouncing his wish for such exclusive possession—but on condition that nobody else gets more parental time, attention and love than he. For him—and later for his superego—justice means (among other things) that what he cannot have, nobody else can have: that in certain things "everyone must be the same and have the same."[11]

Another typical and significant characteristic of the superego's concept of justice (at least when the superego first appears in somewhat stable form at approximately the age of six) is the demand for retributive—in fact, talion—punishments.[12] This demand of the superego for retributive justice may become muted, however, and may even begin to disappear, if (as is normal in a psychically healthy person) the superego continues to develop and change somewhat after the age of six (though at an increasingly slow pace), most usually by taking over "contributions from later successors and substitutes of . . . parents, such as teachers, admired figures in public life, or high social ideals."[13] Indeed, the superego of an emotionally healthy and mature person often tends to be far less rigid and severe than it was during childhood and frequently differs to a noteworthy degree from the parent images upon which it was originally based. These and related facts have found expression in the existential view of the superego— the view (stated in the words of Erich Fromm) that the superego in its ideal sense "is not the internalized voice of an authority who we are eager to please and afraid of displeasing . . . but rather it is our own voice . . . the voice of our true selves which summons us back to ourselves, to live productively, to develop fully and harmoniously . . . to become what we potentially are."[14]

By no means is all this to deny that the superego of even the most mature of persons would tend, at least in certain basic respects (for example, as a bar to cannibalistic, incestuous or parricidal impulses), to remain as it was at about the age of six. As psychoanalysts have learned, if a person's superego is unhealthy and improperly formed, it may fail completely to develop or change in any significant way after this time of life. Needless to say, perhaps, insofar as the superego fails to grow and mature after childhood, it is likely to cause difficulties: it may, for example (as in the case of many juvenile delinquents and criminals), lack the strength and breadth needed to provide sufficient moral guidance and control[15]; on the other hand, it may, throughout life, adhere to the rigid, primitive and unrealistic behavioral standards of early childhood and, in so doing, block worthwhile development and change.

As John Austin sought ever so painstakingly to demonstrate in his *Lectures On Jurisprudence* (and as legal positivists such as Oliver Wendell Holmes, Jr. and Hans Kelsen have insisted ever since), law and morality are by no means synonymous.[16] Yet it is undeniable that moral ideas and feelings have had a deep and pervasive effect upon the law. In the words of one of the most influential legal thinkers of the past

decade, H. L. A. Hart, "it cannot seriously be disputed that
the development of law, at all times and places, has in fact
been profoundly influenced both by the conventional morality
and ideals of particular social groups, and also by forms of
enlightened moral criticism urged by individuals, whose moral
horizon has transcended the morality currently accepted." [17]
To employ psychoanalytic terminology, there can be little
doubt that men's moral faculty—their superego—has had a
profound influence upon the law.

Equity jurisprudence would appear to provide an endless
number of examples of the influence of men's superego upon
the law, if only because courts of equity (which apply principles elaborated over a number of centuries in the Court of
Chancery—England's "Court of Conscience") [18] have traditionally, and quite openly, attempted to infuse moral concepts
into the law. This concern of courts of equity with moral
considerations has, for instance, expressed itself in such maxims
of equity jurisprudence as "He who seeks equity must do
equity"; "Equity regards substance rather than form"; "Equity
regards that as done which ought to be done"; and "He who
comes into equity must come with clean hands." [19]   More
specifically, if a court of equity is asked by a plaintiff to
rescind a contract (for example, on the grounds of mistake or
fraud), it will usually refuse to do so unless the plaintiff is
first willing to return to the defendant any benefit received
under the contract[20]; or if a mortgagor fails to pay his mortgage
debt on the due date, a court of equity will not permit his
interest in the mortgaged property to be forfeited—provided
that he pays the amount due (plus interest) within a reasonable time thereafter[21]; or if a trustee fails to invest properly
monies entrusted to him, a court of equity may well charge
him with interest on the monies, even though he may not have
actually received such interest[22]; or if the owner of a trademark is guilty of misrepresentation regarding it or if a person
employs his patent so as to create a monopoly or to restrain
competition, a court of equity may fail to grant to the owner
of the trademark or the patent relief against infringement.[23]
In short, courts of equity have traditionally attempted to re-

flect "the requirements of conscience"[24]—the requirements (in psychoanalytic terminology) of the superego.

More perhaps than even equity jurisprudence, the criminal law reveals the imprint of the superego. Such recognized defenses to criminal liability as *coercion* and *mistake of fact*, for instance, would certainly seem to reflect the influence of ethical concepts upon the criminal law.[25] Thus it would surely prove offensive to man's moral sense if a person forced to steal at gunpoint could, as a result, be found guilty of larceny or if a person who mistakenly restrained someone whom he honestly and reasonably believed was committing a serious felony could be convicted of assault for having so behaved. Further, at the common law, homicides committed in sudden passion or heat of blood were considered to be not murder, but manslaughter[26] (on the grounds that "a man is not so much to blame for an act done under the disturbance of great excitement . . . as when he is calm")[27]; and at the common law, a homicide was considered to be morally justifiable and therefore not punishable when committed by someone who was "feloniously assaulted, being without fault himself, and necessarily . . . to save himself from death or great bodily harm."[28]

During the past thirty years or so, one of the most widely discussed, morally based defenses to criminal liability has been the plea of insanity.[29] Though at the early common law, judges refused to allow a plea of insanity to bar criminal liability,[30] this view was ultimately repudiated, and certainly since 1843 when *M'Naghten's Case* was decided in England, insanity has been recognized as a complete defense to criminal liability—at least if the insanity claimed meets the tests promulgated in this case, the main one of which is the following:

> . . . to establish a defense on the ground of insanity, it must be clearly proved that, at the time of the committing of the act, the party accused was labouring under such a defect of reason, from disease of the mind, as not to know the nature and quality of the act he was doing; or, if he did know it, that he did not know he was doing what was wrong.[31]

As legal scholars have pointed out, this test reflects the traditional principle of Anglo-American criminal law that legal responsibility depends upon moral responsibility, that if it can be demonstrated that a person is morally blameless, he ought not to be punished by the criminal law.[32] More specifically, it has traditionally been regarded as unconscionable for the criminal law to impose liability upon a person who lacks the capacity to distinguish right from wrong and to conform his behavior to what is right[33] (though "the necessity of restraining such a person in the interest of public safety would seem clear").[34]

Even more than the plea of insanity or other aspects of the criminal law, certain basic (yet infrequently discussed) principles of law—principles that the well-known legal philosopher Lon L. Fuller has termed "demands of the law's inner morality"[35]—clearly reflect the influence of man's moral faculty or superego. One of these requirements of the law's inner morality stressed by Professor Fuller—a demand that is expressed in part in the Constitution's prohibition against *ex post facto* laws (art. I, § 9)—is that laws be prospective rather than retroactive. Though Professor Fuller himself notes that retroactive legislation may be necessary at times as a curative measure (for example, as a means of validating marriages that are discovered to be technically invalid years after having been performed), he points out that retroactive laws may produce unconscionable results.[36] Commanding a man today, to do something yesterday and then punishing him for his failing to so act could readily have brutally absurd (indeed, monstrous) consequences.

Other "demands of the law's inner morality" identified by Professor Fuller that appear to reflect the influence of man's moral faculty or superego are that laws be understandable, that they not contradict one another, that they not require conduct beyond the powers of the persons affected by them, that they not be changed so often that men cannot orient their actions by them, that they be publicized or at least made available to the persons affected by them, and that there be some congruence between these laws as announced and as they are enforced.[37]

More basic perhaps than even these principles is what

Professor Fuller has identified as the primary or first demand of the law's inner morality: the requirement of generality, the requirement "that, at the very minimum, there must be rules of some kind."[38] Admittedly, there are times when, as in the operation of certain administrative agencies, the law seems to be not an ordered series of general rules but rather an *ad hoc* and patternless exercise of political power and as such to conform to John Austin's classic analytic description of the law as "the command of a sovereign."[39] Yet even Austin (who, it will be recalled, tried to draw a sharp line between law and morality) insisted that laws are "general commands";[40] and the great modern exponent of analytic jurisprudence H. L. A. Hart declared in his most influential work, *The Concept of Law*, that general rules constitute the essence of the law.[41] Hence, it is little wonder that when as in the operation of certain administrative agencies, general rules are almost conspicuous by their absence, the actions and rulings of these agencies have been denounced as (among other things) arbitrary, illegal and immoral[42] and as such, offensive to man's superego.

By no means ought it be inferred from the preceding discussion of the law's inner morality (or, indeed, from any of the materials presented so far in this chapter) that the superego's influence upon the law is always desirable. On the contrary, if the superego of those who affect the law is immature, then the law may well reflect this immaturity. For example, the failure of efforts to abolish timeworn and counterproductive retributive punishments in certain states may well reflect in part the disinclination of the immature and undeveloped superego to abandon its demand for talion vengeance (a demand which, as pointed out earlier in this chapter, is normal at the age of six, but which becomes less and less normal thereafter).[43] In fact, the immature and undeveloped superego may seek at times to block all innovations in the law; not simply because these changes or reforms in the law may be contrary to this superego's primitive demands but also because legal innovations may be viewed at times by the immature and undeveloped superego as a threat to the stability and certainty of laws that it relies upon to provide the firmness, strength and comprehensiveness that it, unfortunately, lacks.[44]

Though the immature superego may help to delay, and sometimes block, needed legal innovations, there can be no doubt that change and reform have frequently taken place in the law. Also there can be no doubt that the impetus for much of this change and reform has been supplied by powerful moral feelings, presumably including moral imperatives engendered by the healthy, mature superego when its sense of justice has been outraged. Reforms in legal procedures accomplished during the past century or so would appear to provide a helpful illustration.

By the late 1820's, legal procedure here and in England was, for a number of historical reasons, governed by "a confused agglomeration of precedents, rules of court, fictions, and statutes."[45] Indeed, Anglo-American legal procedures had become so artificial, cumbersome and complex by this time, that—notably in the English Court of Chancery—"the length of time taken to decide even uncontested cases amounted to a denial of justice."[46] To quote a celebrated passage from Charles Dickens's *Bleak House* regarding the effect of delays in the Court of Chancery:

> This is the Court of Chancery; which has its decaying houses and its blighted lands in every shire; which has its worn-out lunatic in every madhouse, and its dead in every churchyard; which has its ruined suitor, with his slipshod heels and threadbare dress, borrowing and begging through the round of every man's acquaintance; which gives to monied might the means abundantly of wearying out the right; which so exhausts finances, patience, courage, hope; so overthrows the brain and breaks the heart; that there is not an honorable man among its practitioners who would not give—who does not often give—the warning, "Suffer any wrong that can be done you, rather than come here!" [47]

This situation described so vividly by Dickens began to arouse moral indignation among members of the general public (though perhaps not among most members of the English Bar).[48] The conscience of the general public was offended—in fact, outraged—by such abuses as the extraordinary technicalities of pleading, the astronomical cost of litigation, the disgraceful use of judicial patronage, and so on. As a result, the public (led by such crusading newspapers as the *Westminster Review*) demanded and finally got from Parliament a series of reform bills that, by the end of the nineteenth century, succeeded in doing away with most of the procedural abuses that had discredited English justice.[49]

In the United States, as in England, "procedure was [certainly in the view of Roscoe Pound] the spot at which the law in . . . the nineteenth century was conspicuously most in need of reform."[50] Fortunately, a law reformer equal to the task appeared in the person of David Dudley Field ("a man of genius in a family of geniuses").[51] Appalled by the horrendously complex and absurdly technical legal procedures of the day—procedures that helped to father an incalculable number of delays and injustices—Field drew up a revolutionary Code of Civil Procedure, which was first adopted in 1848 by the New York legislature. This code sought, among other things, to achieve such fundamental procedural changes as abolishing the many distinctions between actions at law and suits in equity, reducing pleadings from a theoretically interminable series to only three—complaint, answer and reply—and substituting one cause of action for the numerous "forms of action" known to the common law.[52]

Field's Code of Civil Procedure proved to be enormously influential. It was adopted in whole or in part by a majority of the states[53] and became "the model for the fundamentals of civil procedure" in most of the remaining states.[54] Admittedly, it was eventually amended beyond recognition in New York and other jurisdictions (for example, it was expanded from 393 to 3441 sections in New York within two generations).[55] Nevertheless, Field's basic concepts and the moral feelings that had led to the adoption of his procedural code never really died out. They ultimately joined forces again and found reflection in what has, to date, proven to be the most significant American procedural reform of this century: the Federal Rules of Civil Procedure.[56]

The essential objective of these rules (promulgated by the Supreme Court in 1937) was—and still is—(in the words of Rule 1) "to secure the just, speedy, and inexpensive determination of every action." This objective was amplified in the Federal Rules of Criminal Procedure (adopted seven years later), which sought (in the words of Rule 2) "to secure simplicity in procedure, fairness in administration, and the elimination of unjustifiable expense and delay."

Clearly the most important innovation embodied in the Federal Rules of Civil Procedure is the emphasis upon, and the extraordinarily free availability of, such pretrial devices as interrogatories, inspections, depositions and examinations. These pretrial mechanisms (coupled with the pretrial conference provided for in Rule 16) ought, so it is believed, to enable a party to a suit to force his opponent to disclose all pertinent facts and sources of information before trial. As a result, these mechanisms ought to help greatly to eliminate the influence of surprise and chance during the trial that follows and thus help to minimize the possibility of a party securing a judgment that disregards the merits of the controversy.[57]

Mechanisms that reduce the influence of surprise and chance during a trial by facilitating the pretrial disclosure of relevant data would certainly seem to be of considerable value in making a lawsuit what it presumably ought to be: a rational investigation of the factual basis of a controversy.[58] Hence, it seems reasonable to assume that the mature superego (presumably appalled by the blatant trickery, surprise and chicane that have marked—and still mark—so many trials)[59] may have helped to devise—or, at the very least, have welcomed and been a strong advocate of—the pretrial disclosure devices listed above.

To suggest reasons why it took so long for the pretrial disclosure mechanisms embodied in the Federal Rules of Civil Procedure to be made a part of federal procedural law or why it took so long for the other procedural reforms described above to gain acceptance in the law is not at all difficult. For example, one can point to the proverbial conservatism of lawyers and contend that their preference for precedents rather than innovations (what might be termed their "trust in the past") may have helped to block the adoption of these procedural reforms.[60] Or, one may note that historically trials began as "substitutes for private out-of-court brawls":[61] substitutes in which justice was expected to triumph not as the result of a rational investigation of the relevant facts by the court but rather—as in trial by battle (one of the precursors of courtroom trials)—as a result at times of a court-supervised fight between the parties or their champions.[62] One may go on to speculate that a major reason why pretrial and trial procedures of the past have been reformed so very slowly, especially those procedures which emphasize the historic role of a trial as a sublimated court-supervised fight, is that the immature superego may find in procedures of the past which stress the "combat aspect of litigation"[63] manifold opportunities for venting aggression and hostility: for venting powerful aggressive and hostile feelings that (as was pointed out early in this chapter) tend to characterize the immature superego.

Whether or not the reasons suggested above help to explain the slow pace of procedural reform in the law, there can be little doubt that justice is best served when procedural laws are adopted that make trials not so much "sublimation mechanisms for combat feelings and the expression of grudges,"[64] as rational investigations of the factual bases of controversies. Hopefully, the mature superego will help to supply the impetus needed to achieve this goal and, in so doing, help to narrow the gap between man's moral strivings and the law.

IV

UNCONSCIOUS SYMBOLISM
AND THE LAW

The findings of psychoanalysts concerning unconscious symbolism have produced more determined opposition and have led to more startling discoveries than perhaps any other aspect of psychoanalytic psychology. This chapter will present some of these psychoanalytic findings and will try to suggest how they may prove applicable to the law.

ONE OF SIGMUND FREUD's most significant discoveries was that the dreams of his patients were "written" in an unconscious symbolic primordial "language"[1] (described in Erich Fromm's book *The Forgotten Language* as mankind's one universal dialect or tongue—"the same for all cultures and throughout history").[2] As psychoanalytically oriented scholars have repeatedly stressed, the "words" or symbols (and other elements) of this unconscious "language" appear not only in dreams but also in such diverse creations as poetry, folklore, humor and myths.[3]

A symbol may be defined most simply as "something that stands for something else." Thus the American flag is a symbol, in that it stands for the United States. The word "hat" is a symbol, in that it stands for a shaped covering (usually with a crown and a brim) for the head. Like the vast majority of symbols, the American flag and the word "hat" are *conventional* symbols, for the relationship between these symbols and what they represent is not intrinsic but rather is simply a matter of convention or agreement. The United States could, for example, be symbolized by a flag without stars or stripes: by the red and white flag now used by the American Red Cross or by a flag with any other design, including a yellow flag with the picture of a snake and containing the words "Don't tread on me." Similarly, a hat could be symbolized (as it is in

33

French) by the letters C-H-A-P-E-A-U or (as it is in Spanish) by the letters S-O-M-B-R-E-R-O or, indeed, by any combination of letters, long or short, harmonious or dissonant.

Unlike conventional symbols, the special symbols studied by psychoanalysts are related to what they stand for or represent not by convention or agreement but rather by *an unconscious bond*.

This unconscious bond between a symbol and its referent may be at times entirely individual. Thus someone grievously injured in a certain city may, on an unconscious level, equate the city with great danger, or even death; and as a result, any mention of the name of the city may cause this person (for whom the city now symbolizes danger or death) to become quite apprehensive and fearful. Also, there are times when a comparatively small group or limited number of persons may unconsciously symbolize something in the same way. For instance, what kleptomaniacs steal is often unconsciously regarded by them as a symbol of affection and love[4]; and for pyromaniacs, the setting of a fire often symbolizes on an unconscious level an attempt to achieve sexual gratification.[5]

The unconscious symbols of greatest interest to psychoanalysts are the basic "words" of the primordial "language" referred to at the beginning of this chapter. These symbols are often called *universal*, in that they seem to have the same unconscious meaning for practically everybody and in addition appear to have played a considerable role in the poetry, folklore, humor and myths of many very different cultures since earliest times.[6] The earth, for example, is a universal unconscious mother symbol; and emerging from water is a ubiquitous unconscious method of symbolizing birth. A serpent is perhaps the most used unconscious symbol of the male phallus; and starting out on a trip is a universal unconscious symbol of death.[7]

Though there are literally thousands of unconscious symbols, the ideas or topics that they, and especially universal unconscious symbols, represent are extraordinarily limited. In fact, with rare exceptions, unconscious symbols have to do mainly with such matters as birth, love (sex) and death and with ideas of the self and of close blood relatives (or sub-stitutes for them).[8]

Of particular interest for this chapter's purposes are un-conscious parent symbols—of which, it might be added, ex-amples abound. The rulers of countries (kings, queens, dictators, presidents, prime ministers and the like)—in fact, the countries themselves—often serve as unconscious parent substitutes.[9] Similarly, judges, the courts on which they sit and even the law itself may function as unconscious parent symbols (as may religious leaders, employers, physicians and others who act *in loco parentis*).[10]

Persons who may serve as unconscious parent symbols (kings, judges, employers and so on) often have displaced onto them repressed parent-oriented feelings that have re-mained in the unconscious since early childhood; and because, as psychoanalysts have discovered, a child's early feelings towards his parents usually range from primitive love to savage hatred,[11] the repressed emotions of early childhood displaced onto parent substitutes are frequently not only affectionate and loving but also angry and hostile. In addition it ought to be noted here that a young child may well feel extremely angry and hostile towards his brothers and sisters (with whom he must share his parents)[12]; and if some of this anger and hostility is repressed and remains trapped in the unconscious, there is a very good chance that unconscious sibling sub-stitutes—classmates, colleagues and the like—will be its targets.

To suggest possible connections between unconscious sym-bolism and the law is not at all difficult. Thus it might be contended that if persons who act *in loco parentis* (guardians, trustees and the like) tend to be regarded unconsciously as parent symbols or substitutes, then unconscious parent-oriented ideas and feelings may well find reflection in laws concerning the duties and responsibilities of these persons. Or, if it may be assumed that a universal unconscious symbolic bond exists between the idea of birth and that of water—a bond regarded by psychoanalysts as deep-rooted and archaic[13]—then it is conceivable that some of the very strange and blatantly archaic concepts that still characterize Admiralty

Law (concepts that Holmes described as "peculiar" almost a hundred years ago) [14] may well reflect the influence of primitive unconscious thoughts and feelings concerning birth.

Unfortunately, these and other possible connections between unconscious symbolism and the law have, to date, remained largely unexplored. Yet, as will now be seen, some basis does exist for considering, though preliminarily, the relationship between unconscious symbolism and the law in a few diverse areas.

To begin with, psychoanalysts have learned that certain people commit crimes mainly because of the unconscious symbolic meaning these crimes have. Kleptomaniacs, for example, usually steal not so much for monetary gain but rather to satisfy an imperious inner need for what the articles they steal symbolize on an unconscious level. [15] As was pointed out earlier, psychoanalysts have discovered that these articles often prove to be symbolic substitutes for love and affection for the kleptomaniacs who steal them. [16] In like manner, pyromaniacs are ordinarily motivated to set fires not so much by a desire for pecuniary gain but rather by an insistent inner need for what the fires symbolize on an unconscious level. [17] As was noted earlier, psychoanalysts have learned that these fires are often unconscious symbolic substitutes for sexual activity: they frequently provide the pyromaniac with a "substitute for a sexual thrill." [18]

However if kleptomaniacs and pyromaniacs (and presumably certain other criminals as well) [19] are so motivated, how then is society to deal with them? Imprisoning them (the usual modern punishment for serious offenses) would appear to be futile if not counterproductive, for a prison is hardly the place where a kleptomaniac or a pyromaniac (or anybody else except, perhaps, an overt homosexual) is likely to receive the love, affection and sexual gratification that he craves. On the contrary, imprisonment will probably exacerbate such cravings, if only because being imprisoned is likely to be interpreted by a kleptomaniac or a pyromaniac as a rejection [20]; and being rejected by society is an extraordinarily painful psychic experience, especially for kleptomaniacs and pyromaniacs who have acute unsatisfied needs for love and the like. In short, punishing a kleptomaniac or a pyromaniac by sending him to prison would probably intensify his unsatisfied needs for love, affection and sexual gratification and, in so doing, make him that much more likely to try to satisfy these needs by stealing or by setting fires when he is released from prison.

But if so, what ought society do to protect itself against kleptomaniacs and pyromaniacs or, indeed, against other persons who also commit crimes mainly because of the inner symbolic meaning these crimes have?

"Treatment" is the answer proposed by many reformers today; that is, kleptomaniacs, pyromaniacs and other similarly motivated criminals are to be sent to state institutions not for punishment but rather for rehabilitative treatment. Since (according to this view) treatment differs greatly from punishment, treatment (unlike punishment) would presumably not only fail to magnify the unsatisfied unconscious cravings of these criminals (which, in the past, led so often to crime) but would also reduce the frequency and intensity of these cravings, change the way in which they seek to express themselves symbolically and thus minimize the likelihood that they will continue to find symbolic expression in theft, arson and other antisocial acts.[21]

Unfortunately, however, it is anything but clear that society has the knowledge, the means and (perhaps most important) the will to treat successfully kleptomaniacs, pyromaniacs and other criminals who commit crimes largely because of the unconscious symbolic meaning these crimes have for them.[22] It is hardly comforting to learn that even when society appears willing to treat rather than to punish persons convicted under the criminal law (for instance, persons convicted under statutes pertaining to so-called "sexual psychopaths") or even when society is presumably attempting to treat rather than to punish ordinary noncriminal mentally disturbed patients in state mental institutions, the results achieved are far from satisfactory.[23] In fact, Thomas Szasz (a psychoanalyst who has written extensively on the dangers inherent in the so-called "treatment" of the mentally ill in state institutions) has contended that state hospitals are "notorious for their neglect, and indeed abuse, of the mental patient" and that "there is evidence that incarceration in a mental hospital may be more harmful for the personality than incarceration in a prison."[24]

Not only the behavior of kleptomaniacs or pyromaniacs (or others whose crimes may symbolize unconscious goals) but the behavior of noncriminal normal persons as well may be greatly influenced at times by unconscious symbolism. As will now be seen, certain reactions of employees towards their employers would appear to provide a case in point.

Employers, as was noted earlier in this chapter, may sometimes function as unconscious parent symbols. As a result, their employees may displace repressed parent-oriented ideas and feelings onto them—ideas and feelings that, as was also pointed out earlier, may be warm and affectionate or angry and hostile.[25] If the repressed parent-oriented thoughts and emotions displaced onto employers by their employees are warm and affectionate, then industrial peace is likely to prevail (unless, of course, employers attempt to take undue advantage of their "parental" role vis-à-vis their employees or do something else to arouse the ire of these employees). On the other hand, if the repressed parent-oriented thoughts and emotions directed towards employers by their employees are angry and hostile, then industrial strife may well result. Indeed, as one psychoanalytically oriented student of labor relations has pointed out, not only may such parent-oriented ideas and feelings "trip off a strike,"[26] but they may be responsible in part for much of the irrationality, emotionalism and violence that all too often have tended to characterize labor relations in the United States.[27]

Yet if angry and hostile parent-oriented feelings are likely at times to affect the reactions of employees to their employers (if, for example, a protracted and violent strike may unconsciously and symbolically constitute "a revolt of the sons against the father"[28]), then—as experience has certainly demonstrated—one can hardly assume that the parties involved in a labor dispute will act with wisdom, maturity and restraint.

On the contrary, if the employer-employee relationship is equated on an unconscious level with the parent-child relationship, then one can almost count on the presence of some emotionalism, irrationality and perhaps even violence at times when a serious rupture occurs between employer and employees, especially if the rupture finds expression in a strike.[29] Hence, if it may be assumed that (as was observed in the Introduction) the law is concerned with the regulation, mitigation and composition of disputes,[30] would it not be wise for the law to undertake a more active role in labor disputes than at present— at least to the extent of employing or making available for use mechanisms that would minimize the possibility of these disputes serving as an outlet for (or, indeed, being provoked by) the parent-oriented aggression and hostility of childhood?

Admittedly, these views are, in a sense, quite general— in fact, so general, that men may well agree with them and yet disagree as to how they ought to be implemented.[31] For instance, it is not at all clear whether these views require the availability or use of such devices as mediation, fact-finding, "cooling-off" periods and ultimately arbitration in labor disputes; or whether, for example, these views require the further step of giving back to the federal courts the injunctive powers in labor disputes denied to them under the Norris-LaGuardia Act of 1932.[32] In addition, it ought to be noted that as experience has shown, there is a very real limit to what the force of law—as opposed to freely negotiated agreements—can accomplish regarding the employer-employee relationship, especially when a very powerful union is involved (unless, of course, one is willing to have the government go much further in imposing settlements upon employer and employee than has been traditional in democratic societies).[33] Still, if the employer-employee relationship is likely (particularly when a rupture occurs in the form of a strike) to reflect the influence of angry and hostile parent-oriented feelings of childhood, would it not be better for the law to face up to these facts and to try to find ways of minimizing the influence of the emotions of childhood upon the employer-employee relationship (especially when a vital and vulnerable area of the economy is involved), than for the law to stand by passively and allow parent-oriented emotionalism, irrationalism and violence to gain ascendancy in labor relations?

Just as employers may be regarded on an unconscious level as parent substitutes, so (as was pointed out earlier in this chapter) may judges and the courts on which they serve. Indeed, in view of the central role played by judges and courts in American law, it is conceivable that judges and the courts on which they sit may well constitute the law's most important unconscious parent symbols.

Though there are literally thousands of courts in the United States, not one of them appears to have a symbolic hold upon the American public comparable to that of the Supreme Court of the United States. In fact, there are students of American history and government who believe that the Supreme Court is, and for many years has been, America's single most important symbol of government.[34] Whether or not this is so, the assumption that the Supreme Court functions as an unconscious parent symbol may help to explain such things as the inordinate if not morbid preoccupation of the public at times with what the Court may or may not do and the extraordinary intensity and range of emotions that the Court seems capable of engendering in the public. That is, if the Supreme Court is regarded on an unconscious level as a parent substitute, then the public's preoccupation at times with what the Court will or will not do may well express, in part, an unconscious preoccupation with parental reactions and judgments; and the extraordinarily intense and varied emotional reactions of the public to the Court—reactions which (like the parent-oriented ideas and emotions of early childhood) range from veneration and awe to fury and hatred—may well reflect, in part, repressed parent-oriented thoughts and feelings of childhood that have been displaced onto the Court.[35] Indeed, if it may be assumed that the Supreme Court serves as an unconscious parent symbol for many Americans, then it may be possible to shed some new light here upon what is probably the most traumatic episode in the Court's history since the post–Civil-War era:

President Franklin D. Roosevelt's attempt in 1937 to induce Congress to pass his so-called "court packing" plan.

When President Roosevelt proposed this plan (under which he asked for congressional authorization to appoint an extra Supreme Court Justice for each member of the Court who failed to retire at the age of seventy), the United States was in the midst of the worst economic depression in its history— a depression that after more than seven years had begun to seem endless and that appeared to be getting progressively worse. Yet, despite these facts, the Supreme Court had invalidated (and was continuing to invalidate) economic legislation that President Roosevelt and most members of Congress believed to be indispensable if total economic collapse was to be prevented and a possible political revolution avoided.[36] Further, President Roosevelt and his advisors feared that any similar economic legislation that he proposed and that Congress enacted would also be invalidated by the Court—which, as Professor Bernard Schwartz has pointed out, had come to regard itself as "the Supreme Censor of all legislation:" a sort of half-court, half-legislature that acted as though it had the right to strike down laws not only because it regarded them as unconstitutional but also because it regarded them as unwise.[37]

In view of these facts, it is far from obvious why President Roosevelt's request for the right to add additional Justices to the Supreme Court (a maximum of six new Justices was envisioned) should have aroused opposition that was so immediate, so highly emotional, so widespread and—as things turned out—so decisive.[38] Certainly no such opposition had been anticipated by the Administration, which just two months before (with a majority in the electoral college of 523 to 8 and a plurality of more than ten million votes) had won a tremendous victory at the polls.[39]

Writing a few years after the Court packing fight, the noted social historian Ralph Gabriel suggested that the furious opposition which had been aroused by (and which defeated) President Roosevelt's plan to reorganize the Supreme Court may have been traceable to the symbolic importance of the Court.[40] To follow the lead offered by this suggestion, can it be that partly because of the parent symbolism which, it has been assumed, is inherent in the Supreme Court, many members of the public unconsciously reacted to the Court packing plan as though it were an attack upon their parents, an attempt to limit and render their parents impotent? If so, then the immediacy and emotionalism of the public's reaction to the plan become readily understandable, as do the rapidity and fury with which the plan was defeated. After all, to attack a person's parents is often to attack—particularly on an unconscious level—the very foundation of the person's security and hence is almost certain to arouse the strongest of feelings and the most powerful of reactions.

Though this clearly incomplete explanation[41] of the public's reaction to President Roosevelt's Court packing plan is admittedly open to challenge, there can be little doubt that the judges who sit on the Supreme Court, and on many other courts as well, frequently symbolize parents on an unconscious level.[42] Perhaps judges function so readily as unconscious parent symbols because, as M. Hancock once put it, "Each of us once stood, a prisoner at the bar of the parental court, where father or mother sat as judge."[43] That is, possibly because a child's parents are, in a sense, the first "judges" that he knows (it is they, after all, who first reward him when he is good and punish him when he is bad); and possibly because the unconscious is to a considerable extent a sort of "timeless" repository of the ideas and feelings of early childhood,[44] a close relationship exists on an unconscious level between parents and judges—and as a consequence, unconscious parent-oriented ideas and feelings tend to be displaced with great frequency upon judges.

To suggest how the attitudes of litigants and lawyers towards a judge may reflect the displacement of unconscious parent-oriented ideas and feelings onto this judge requires little perspicacity. For instance, if a litigant or a lawyer directs towards a judge unconscious parent-oriented feelings of admiration and awe, these feelings may well find reflection in an attitude of deference and respect towards the judge and his judicial rulings—an attitude that offhand would seem to be highly desirable. Yet it ought to be kept in mind that if, for example, the repressed parent-oriented feelings of admiration and awe displaced onto a judge by a lawyer are unduly strong, they may well engender in the lawyer a discinclination (or even an inability) to oppose the judge's rulings when these rulings ought to be opposed. It is of interest to note here that although the Code of Professional Responsibility (which presumably governs the professional conduct of lawyers) declares that "Respect for judicial rulings is essential to the proper administration of justice. . . .",[45] the very same section of the Code also declares that lawyers may "in good faith and within the framework of the law, take steps to test the correctness of a ruling of a tribunal."[46]

Just as unconscious parent-oriented feelings of admiration and awe may be displaced onto a judge, so may repressed hostile and aggressive parent-oriented ideas and emotions be directed towards him. When, for example, litigants—apparently without just cause—become disrespectful towards a judge or behave in the courtroom in a seriously contumacious manner, they may be motivated by repressed parent-oriented anger and rage which they have unconsciously displaced onto the judge. In most cases, a judge can control litigants who may be moved by displaced anger and rage by threatening to invoke or indeed by actually invoking his power to punish for contempt of court.[47] (In such cases, the judge would, in a symbolic sense, be acting like a parent who seeks to control an unruly child.) The judge may find, however, that his power to punish for contempt of court is insufficient to control determinedly contumacious litigants who may, for instance, disrupt the contempt proceedings in the same manner as they disrupted the original courtroom proceedings. When faced with such a challenge, judges (like parents during childhood) have both the authority and the power to meet it: in the well-known case of *Illinois v. Allen*, for example, Mr. Justice Black (speaking for the Supreme Court) declared that when courtroom proceedings are disrupted by a "contumacious, stubbornly defiant" defendant, judges may not only invoke their power to punish such a defendant for contempt of court but may also order him to be bound and gagged or even removed from the courtroom during the course of the trial "until he promises to conduct himself properly."[48]

Not only may litigants and lawyers unconsciously react to the judge before whom they appear as though he were a parent substitute, but they may also unconsciously react to the opposing litigant or lawyer as though he were a *sibling* substitute. A lawyer, for example—especially if he unconsciously regards the judges before whom he appears as parent symbols—may on an unconscious level equate the counsel who opposes him with the brother or sister who once competed with him for parental love during childhood.[49] If so, then the likelihood is that angry and hostile feelings of sibling rivalry concerning this brother or sister that he may have repressed during childhood will be displaced onto the opposing counsel; and as a result, he may provoke and actively engage in undignified and unnecessary squabbles with this counsel. In fact, it may be on this basis that it is possible to understand, in part, why undignified and at times, disgraceful squabbles between attorneys are so frequent in court; and why, for example, the American Bar Association has found it necessary to insist in the Code Of Professional Responsibility that "a lawyer should be courteous to opposing counsel"[50] and that he "should not make unfair or derogatory personal reference to opposing counsel."[51]

The final unconscious symbol to be considered here is the law itself. As was pointed out earlier in this chapter (and as Judge Jerome Frank sought to demonstrate at length in his most original work, *Law and the Modern Mind*) the law itself often functions as an unconscious parent symbol.[52] Indeed, it was Jerome Frank's belief that many of the public's mistaken ideas and exaggerated expectations concerning the law— including the idea that the law is or ought to be completely definite, entirely predictable and capable of coping with practically every conceivable controversy—mirrored the displacement of unconscious ideas and expectations of childhood regarding the father onto the law.[53] By the same token, Frank believed that attacks upon the law by certain criminals and rebels (including the rejection of the law by some of them) reflected the unconscious directing of father-oriented hostility and disappointment onto the law.[54] In fact, psychoanalytic studies suggest that the insistence of many of the early Communists that the State—and with it, all law—be abolished, may have mirrored and helped to express powerful unconscious father-oriented hatreds born in childhood that had been displaced from the father onto the State and the law.[55]

Traditional Anglo-American law provides a number of examples of how law may function in a "parental" capacity; how, for instance, it may help to protect a person against himself. A classic illustration of this attempt by the law to protect someone against himself is provided by the concept of "statutory rape": the presumption that a female below a certain age "is incapable of consenting to sexual intercourse, and that it is rape . . . for a man to have intercourse with her [*even*] *with her consent*."[56] In the main, however, Anglo-American law has, at least historically, attempted to eschew a parental role, preferring instead to regard and treat persons subject to the law as though they had at least average intelligence and knowledge and were reasonably prudent, rational and responsible. This concept of the ordinary citizen as a person of some intelligence, knowledge and prudence, rational and fully responsible for his acts and omissions finds particularly clear expression in traditional Anglo-American tort law, especially in the doctrine that liability for negligent conduct is governed not by an inner or "subjective" standard but rather by an outer or "objective" standard. As Holmes put it in *The Common Law*

> The law [regarding negligent acts] takes no account of the infinite varieties of temperament, intellect, and education which make the internal character of a given act so different in different men. . . . If, for instance, a man is born hasty and awkward, is always having accidents and hurting himself or his neighbors, no doubt his congenital defects will be allowed for in the courts of Heaven, but his slips are no less troublesome to his neighbors than if they sprang from guilty neglect. His neighbors accordingly require him, at his proper peril, to come up to their stan-

dard, and the courts which they establish decline to take his personal equation into account. . . .The law considers, in other words, what would be blameworthy in the average man, the man of ordinary intelligence and prudence, and determines liability by that.[57]

Contrary to traditional Anglo-American law (and indeed to early Communist dogma), Soviet law has, especially in recent times, tended to picture the relationship between the law's molders or administrators on the one hand and the ordinary citizen on the other hand, as a sort of parent-child relationship. As Professor Harold J. Berman has observed, "The Soviet legislator, administrator, or judge plays the part of a parent or guardian or teacher; the individual before the law . . . is treated as a child or youth to be guided and trained and made to behave."[58] In like manner, "the parental orientation . . . [appears to be] steadily gaining ground" in certain areas of American law.[59] An example that comes to mind is the rapidly growing practice of requiring persons seeking a divorce to attend and seek marriage counseling at court-supervised reconciliation hearings.[60] Similarly, the past few years have witnessed a growing tendency by the courts to adopt a paternal stance in regard to the treatment of prisoners, for instance, by abandoning the old "hands off" doctrine concerning prison conditions and substituting for it a willingness to investigate and (where need be) to enjoin objectionable prison practices.[61] In fact, even tort law—certainly as exemplified by absolute (strict) liability statutes such as the now almost-traditional workmen's compensation statutes (which make an employer liable for injuries incurred by his employees in the course of their employment, even though the employer may have been blameless and the injured employees grossly negligent)— reveals an increasing tendency of the law to act *in loco parentis* concerning certain classes of persons.[62] It is in the treatment of juvenile offenders, however—especially insofar as the treatment of these youngsters has been influenced by the juvenile court movement—that American law has acted most openly in a "parental" manner during the past number of years.

The juvenile court movement "grew out of the conviction

that youthful offenders should not receive the same treatment as adults. The fundamental idea [which later found reflection in statutes regarding juvenile offenders] ... was that the state, with a judge acting in the role of a parent, should extend its protective arm to children in order to 'cure' and 'save' rather than to punish."[63] As the Supreme Court put it in the leading case of *In re Gault*, "The early conception of the juvenile court proceeding was one in which a fatherly judge touched the heart and conscience of the erring youth by talking over his problems, by paternal advice and admonition, and in which, in extreme situations, benevolent and wise institutions of the State provided guidance and help. . . ."[64] In furtherance of these openly parental objectives concerning youthful offenders, juvenile courts were established in every state of the Union and the statutes that created these courts typically provided for such basic features of juvenile court justice as private hearings, informal courtroom procedures, regular and extensive probation services, separate juvenile detention facilities, mental and physical examinations (where necessary) and the keeping of adequate records free from indiscriminate public inspection.[65]

Unfortunately, however, despite the clearly good intentions of the champions of the juvenile court movement and the honest attempts of many juvenile court justices to act *in loco parentis* regarding the youths brought before them, the juvenile court (in the words of the President's Task Force Report on juvenile delinquency) "has not succeeded significantly in rehabilitating delinquent youth, in reducing or even stemming the tide of juvenile criminality, or in bringing justice and compassion to the child offender."[66] Indeed, critics of the juvenile court have charged that "it contributes to juvenile crime or inaugurates delinquent careers by imposition of the stigma of wardship, unwise detention, and incarceration of children in institutions which don't reform and often corrupt."[67] Further, recent Supreme Court decisions have revealed a growing revulsion against (and have declared unconstitutional) presumably "well intentioned," but unduly informal juvenile court procedures which deny to juveniles basic constitutional protections given to adults in regular adult courts (the right to cross-examine witnesses, the right to engage competent counsel, the right to receive timely notice of charges, and so on).[68]

Other reasons usually given for what the President's Task Force Report on juvenile delinquency has labeled the "failure" of juvenile court justice and the juvenile court movement include the moral confusion frequently aroused in delinquent youths by the stated desire of juvenile courts to "treat" or "cure" them rather than to punish them, a grossly unrealistic and overoptimistic view of what juvenile courts can accomplish in regard to juvenile delinquency, the refusal of communities to provide juvenile courts with adequate resources to carry out their statutory functions, and the related refusal of communities to provide adequate rehabilitation facilities for juveniles.[69]

A further reason for the lack of success of juvenile court law and the juvenile court movement in combating juvenile delinquency that is totally different from those mentioned above is suggested, in a general way, by the material that has been presented in this chapter regarding unconscious symbolism and specifically by the readiness with which the law administered by juvenile courts may serve as an unconscious parent symbol. That is, if (as was noted earlier in this chapter and as Jerome Frank repeatedly observed in his book *Law and the Modern Mind*) law may, in general, function as an unconscious parent symbol; and if (as was also pointed out earlier) juvenile court law has greatly emphasized the parental role of law vis-à-vis juvenile offenders, then it is certainly conceivable that unconscious parent-oriented ideas and feelings of childhood may be attracted to and displaced onto the law administered by juvenile courts (at least, insofar as the actions of these courts have accentuated the law's parental attitudes and responsibilities). Further, to the extent that the repressed parent-directed thoughts and emotions of childhood are displaced onto and influence juvenile court law, this law would presumably be less adult, mature and reality-oriented than would other branches of the law that fail to emphasize parental functions (and, as a result, are presumably less likely to attract and to be affected by what are frequently immature and irrational unconscious parent-oriented desires and urgencies of childhood). Thus, by being in large measure responsible for the adoption of juvenile court legislation that accentuated greatly the parental role of law in regard to the treatment of juvenile offenders—and in so doing, almost inevitably inviting the massive displacement of repressed and often immature and irrational parent-directed ideas and feelings of childhood upon juvenile courts and the law they administer—the juvenile court movement may, in effect, have ensured its own failure.

Speculative this hypothesis surely is, as any preliminary discussion would be regarding whether or not and to what extent a branch of the law that stresses the law's parental attributes is likely to be unduly influenced by unconscious parent-oriented thoughts and emotions of childhood. Still, knowing of the possibility that undue stress upon the parental functions of law may result in distortions of the law by the displacement onto it of repressed childhood parent-directed desires and urgencies may help to give pause to those who seem willing to embrace the view in the legislation they propose (a view which, as has been noted, now appears to characterize Soviet law) that the proper relationship between the law and the ordinary citizen is that of parent and child. In fact, insofar as it is true that the more parentally-oriented the law is, the more likely it is to serve as a magnet for the often irrational and immature repressed parent-oriented ideas and feelings of childhood, the more attractive the traditional Anglo-American view would appear to be that the law ought to treat the ordinary citizen not as a parent would treat a child but rather as one would treat a rational and reasonably knowledgeable responsible person.

V

AGGRESSION AND THE LAW

This chapter will detail certain basic psychoanalytic insights concerning aggression and will try to suggest how they may prove applicable to the law.

WHEN MEN SEEK a respite after a particularly brutal or prolonged war, they often find appealing the notions that human beings are essentially kind and peace loving and that if injustice (social, economic, political, etcetera) were somehow done away with, they and their fellows would be able to live together without rancor and without war. Akin to and frequently cited as the "scientific" basis of this hopeful view of mankind are two doctrines: the concept that "aggressive behavior always presupposes the existence of frustration"[1] and the related doctrine that if frustration and its causes were somehow eliminated, men would reveal themselves to be not aggressive, destructive and "evil" but peace loving, creative and "good."[2] These doctrines are indeed implicit in classical Marxist dogma, which envisions the ultimate emergence of a conflict-free and "therefore" aggression-free classless society, in which both law and the State would "wither away" because they would no longer be needed.[3]

As the comprehensive investigations of Konrad Lorenz and his associates in regard to aggression reveal, however, "the theory that aggression is nothing but a response to frustration is no longer tenable in the light of biological research"[4]; and it is most unlikely that a society completely free from competition and strife will ever emerge—"unless some biological mutation alters the whole character of man as a species."[5] The point is that man appears to be endowed with much of the same instinctual aggressiveness, rapaciousness and cruelty that his ancestors had when they overran and conquered the earth. As William James once put it: "Our ancestors have bred pugnacity into our bone and marrow, and thousands of years of peace won't breed it out of us."[6]

In view of all this, it can hardly be regarded as surprising that psychoanalysts, following Freud's lead, have postulated the existence of an innate aggressive drive or that psychoanalytic studies of early childhood have revealed that even tiny infants are moved at times by what can only be described as a desire to cause pain and suffering—to hurt.[7] So pronounced are such hostile tendencies during early childhood that psychoanalysts have identified an "anal-sadistic" period of infancy.[8]

As for the aggressiveness and cruelty of adults, it hardly seems necessary to quote chapter and verse. When World War II ended and the monstrous Nazi regime was finally defeated, many men believed that the world would never again witness such blatant crueltes as those which resulted in the death of six million Jews at the hands of the rulers of Nazi Germany. Yet less than a decade later, what is probably the greatest blood bath of all time (untold millions are reputed to have been massacred) took place in China under the aegis of leaders who openly proclaimed that "only with guns" could the enemies of Communism be defeated and that only "by war" could the Communist millenium be achieved.[9] Surely further examples are unnecessary to lend support to Freud's celebrated description of what he termed mankind's "lust for aggression and destruction."[10] In Freud's words

> men are not gentle, friendly creatures wishing for love, who simply defend themselves if they are attacked, but. . . .a powerful measure of desire for aggression has to be reckoned as part of their instinctual endowment. The result is that their neighbour is to them not only a possible helper or sexual object, but also a temptation to them to gratify their aggressiveness on him, to exploit his capacity to work without recompense, to use him sexually without his consent, to seize his possessions, to humiliate him, to cause him pain, to torture and to kill him. *Homo homini lupus*; who has the courage to dispute it in the face of all the evidence in his own life and in history? [11]

By no means does it follow from all this that aggressiveness and hostility necessarily lead to undesirable results. For example, the "space race" between the United States and the Soviet Union provides an excellent illustration of how competitiveness and hostility may sometimes result in the most magnificent of achievements. In fact, psychoanalysts believe that aggressive energy is in large measure responsible for much of the work that men do in field and factory and also for much that men have accomplished in the age-old war against ignorance, crime, disease and poverty.[12]

The aggressiveness and hostility that men exhibit are, perhaps more often than not, open, obvious and consciously intended. Psychoanalysts have discovered, however, that a considerable amount of man's aggression and hostility is unconscious; and as such, frequently finds expression in subtle, covert and self-deceptive ways. Indeed, man's aggressiveness may be exceeded at times only by his ability to deceive himself as to how and when it expresses itself. To illustrate these statements: those who engage in such body-contact sports as hockey, football, wrestling and boxing may ventilate and be very much aware of ventilating aggression in so doing. Yet it is most unlikely that a participant in a chess game would be aware that this seemingly "innocent" game may serve at times as an outlet for unconscious urges of murderous intensity.[13] Nor is it so obvious that as psychoanalytic studies of gambling have shown, games of chance may sometimes help those who participate in them to express unconscious aggression: not simply against their families (who may become impoverished as a result of their gambling), for instance, but also against themselves—especially if, as is very frequently the case, they are motivated not so much by a desire to win, but rather by what psychoanalysts have identified as a neurotic "*unconscious wish to lose.*"[14]

Man's unconscious aggression and hostility may seek expression not only in games and sports but also in a variety of other more significant matters. For example, the unduly strict discipline enforced in the classroom by some teachers may reflect not so much the requisites of good education as the unconscious aggression and sadism of these teachers; and as a result, considerable psychic damage may be done by these teachers to the children in their charge.[15] In fact, it is tempting to speculate that the abusive and sarcastic manner in which, at least traditionally, law has sometimes been taught may have expressed not the necessities of legal education but rather the unconscious hostility and oral sadism of certain teachers of law.[16]

Admittedly, the damage inflicted by unduly aggressive and hostile teachers need not be permanent and may often be repaired in the classrooms of healthier teachers. Yet there are times when the results of unconsciously motivated aggression may prove to be irreversible. For instance, there is reason to believe that statutes authorizing the castration or sterilization of so-called habitual criminals may reflect not so much the "eugenic" purposes the supporters of these statutes stress but rather deep-rooted unconscious aggression and sadism.[17] If so, then a habitual criminal who is castrated or permanently sterilized would be marked by this aggression and sadism for the rest of his life. Such a person would, in the words of the court in *Mickle v. Hendricks*, "carry to his grave, a mutilation which, as punishment, is a brand of infamy."[18]

Unconscious aggression and hostility (like conscious aggression and hostility) may result not only in undesirable and unfortunate conduct but in desirable and socially useful conduct as well. When a surgeon performs an operation, for example, he may be motivated not only by a conscious desire to help an ailing patient but also by unconscious sadism and cruelty.[19] This transmutation of primitive or unconscious wishes into socially useful acts is labeled "sublimation" by psychoanalysts and appears to play a significant role in a variety of activities.[20] Frequently cited as illustrations of sublimation are such activities as painting and sculpturing—processes which, so psychoanalysts have discovered, may reflect in part the influence of the repressed desires of early childhood to smear and play with one's natural bodily products.[21]

Some of the most arresting psychoanalytic discoveries concerning aggression pertain to the frequency and the variety of ways with which a man may turn his aggressiveness and hostility against himself. Psychoanalysts have learned, for example, that many physical ills—high blood pressure, ulcers, goiters, arthritis and cardiac ailments, to mention but a few of these ills—often reflect the influence of a man's hostility and aggressiveness that has somehow been turned back against himself.[22] Similarly, it has been discovered that many of the accidents that befall the so-called accident-prone are all too frequently the product of self-directed aggression by such persons.[23] As Manfred S. Guttmacher and Henry Weihofen point out when discussing the problem of compensating victims of industrial accidents, mere chance or physical clumsiness fail to explain why, for instance, "an extensive accident survey in industrial plants showed that 90% of all accidents occurred to 15% of the workers."[24]

Offhand, suicide would seem to be the ultimate example of aggression turned against the self. Yet by no means is suicide so simply explained. Rather, psychoanalytic investigations reveal that suicide is often, at least on an unconscious level, an act of murder directed against someone with whom the person who tries to commit suicide has unconsciously identified himself. As the psychoanalyst Edmund Bergler has put it, "It is known, since Freud's studies on 'Mourning and Melancholia' (1916) that the suicide kills, not himself, but a person who deeply disappointed the suicide candidate and with whom the latter has subsequently unconsciously identified himself."[25] In addition, it may prove of interest here to note that in certain primitive communities, men who find themselves unable to obtain justice against powerful adversaries may commit suicide and thereby expose these adversaries to the vengeance of surviving relatives and friends.[26] In such cases, the offended person (in the words of Karl Menninger) "kills himself for the express purpose of taking revenge upon the offender."[27]

If man is the aggressive creature pictured in the preceding pages, then clearly he needs all the aid that the law can give to him in helping him to control (and, hopefully, in helping him to transmute into socially useful activities) his hostile and often violent urges. In fact, it has been contended that *"The prime operative duty of law is the control of human aggressiveness."*[28] If the restraints imposed by the law upon man's aggressiveness were removed, life might well be (to use the classic phraseology of Thomas Hobbes) "solitary, poor, nasty, brutish and short."[29]

On the other hand, too much law—especially insofar as such law may conflict with society's mores—is likely to exacerbate (rather than to tame) man's aggressive and hostile wishes. During the 1920's, for example, laws prohibiting the manufacture, sale and transportation of intoxicating beverages bred far more lawlessness than they helped to prevent; and it has been argued that current laws which seek to stamp out the use of marihuana may have at times the paradoxical effect of encouraging rather than discouraging the use of this drug.[30] Further, minimizing the restraints imposed by the law upon man's freedom is a time-tested American ideal: Americans traditionally believed (certainly until the New Deal era of the 1930's) that the fewer the laws, the healthier the State.

Still, even if there were neither too much law, nor too little, the law—by itself—could hardly be expected to control man's powerful aggressive desires. For the law to be effective in helping men to curb their hostility and destructiveness—in aiding men (in the words of Ranyard West) to "remedy . . . [their] inability to control . . . [their] own aggressive selves"[31]—it needs all the support it can get from so-called "extra-legal" sources: from conscience, religion, custom and morality, for example.

Unfortunately, the dependence of the law upon conscience, religion, custom and morality, etcetera, in seeking to curb man's hostility and destructiveness and, in addition, the need for a measure of consistency between the law and the values promoted by these "extra-legal" agencies have been obscured by attempts of Austin, Holmes, Kelsen and other legal positivists to draw too sharp a distinction between the law and such extra-legal agencies, morality especially. Typically, the legal positivist poses the question "What is law?" and having done so, goes on to demonstrate to his own satisfaction that the law is completely separate and distinct from such matters as conscience, religion, custom and morality. In so doing, however, the legal positivist tends to forget (as Holmes appears to have forgotten when he suggested that to really know the law one ought to view it through the eyes of a "bad man"— a man presumably unaffected by morality and so forth)[32] that the judges who interpret the law are almost inevitably affected to some extent by conscience, religion, custom and morality; and that as a result, the decisions rendered by these judges interpreting the law will almost inevitably reflect the presence of such "extra-legal" influences (or, as Professor Lon L. Fuller has put it, Holmes's "bad man, if he is effectively to look after his own interests, will have to learn to look at the law through the eyes of a good man"[33]—a man presumably affected by morality, etcetera). A more general or "philosophical" way of saying all this perhaps would be to point out that the very question "What is law?" contains an unproven assumption: the assumption that the law is describable as an *is*—as something that, at any given moment of time, is fully apprehensible. Suppose, however, that instead of being an *is*, the law, at least in part, is a process: something that is always *becoming*, something that is always *about to be*. If so, then to fail (as have legal positivists) to consider what the law is about to be *and what the influences are that will probably play a part in this becoming* is, in effect, to fail to understand properly what the law "is."

If the law's dependence upon conscience, religion and other "extra-legal" agencies in seeking to control man's hostility and destructiveness were more fully understood, then perhaps less time would be spent in what are often vain attempts to manipulate the law so as to control subtle and unconscious forms of antisocial aggression; and instead, more attention would be given to the possibility of employing certain "extra-legal" approaches in regard to this aggression. For example, as was pointed out earlier in this chapter, the accidents that befall the so-called accident-prone are often the result not of mere chance or of physical clumsiness but rather of unconscious self-directed aggression. To cope with

this self-directed aggression, one can (as certain scholars
have suggested) manipulate the tort doctrine of contributory
negligence by declaring that "the standard for contributory
negligence . . . [should] be subjective and [should] take the
victim's accident proneness into account."[34] Such an approach
would, however, not only violate traditional tort doctrine
(which, as was pointed out in Chapter IV, ordinarily employs
an objective rather than a subjective standard in determining
whether conduct is to be considered negligent), but would
also be contrary to the increasingly accepted modern view
which seeks to minimize the role of fault in determining tort
liability and to substitute for it, especially in industry, the
concept that tort losses should be borne (with the help of
appropriate insurance) by the enterprise where they occur.[35]
Hence, instead of trying to manipulate traditional tort law
so as to cope with the unconscious self-directed aggression
of the accident-prone, those who mold the law might expend
their energies more effectively by seeking the assistance of
psychiatrists and other members of the medical profession
in devising ways of identifying and helping to cure (or, at
least, of helping to ameliorate the aggressiveness and destructiveness of) the accident-prone. If this course of action were
followed, it might well result in a much needed and long
overdue start being made not only in the task of reducing
the huge economic cost of "accidents" involving the accident-
prone but also in the even more urgent task of protecting the
public against this group of persons who, indisputably, pose
a very great danger both to themselves and to those around
them. As Manfred S. Guttmacher and Henry Weihofen note
in the discussion of accident proneness in their book on psychiatry and law, "the Atlanta cab-driver who ran down and
killed Margaret Mitchell, the author of *Gone with the Wind,*
had had twenty-one accidents."[36]

Like the self-directed aggression implicit in accident proneness, the aggression inherent in suicide (an act which, as has
been noted, is often interpreted by psychoanalysts as an unconscious attempt by the person seeking to commit suicide
to kill someone with whom he has unconsciously identified him-

self) may be difficult if not impossible to cope with by traditional legal means alone. At the common law, an effort was made to discourage suicide, first by stigmatizing it as a heinous felony (Blackstone declared that suicide was "among the highest crimes," an offense against both God and man)[37] and then by employing such punitive devices as forfeiture of the suicide's chattels, escheat of his lands, dishonoring of his corpse and denial to him of normal burial rites (the bodies of persons who had committed suicide were often buried late at night in a public highway, with a stake driven through them).[38] Yet despite the use of such devices, there can be little doubt that this condemnatory and punitive approach of the common law—and later of the criminal law—in regard to suicide has proven (certainly in the view of many scholars) to be largely an exercise in futility.[39] In the words of Norman St. John-Stevas (a well-known legal scholar who has analyzed the condemnatory-punitive attitude of the criminal law towards suicide): "However different the approach of research workers investigating the suicide problem, their work leads ineluctably to one conclusion, the irrelevance of the criminal law to its solution."[40] If so, then the time may well have come (especially since suicide continues to be "a grave social problem"[41]) for the law to deemphasize (or at least to supplement) its traditional attitude towards suicide by revealing a willingness to employ "extra-legal" approaches to the problem that appear to hold out some hope of success. To quote Norman St. John-Stevas once again:

> Psychiatric treatment should be made more easily available through local hospitals and health services. Research into the causes of suicide should be intensified. . . .The public should be better educated on the subject so that suicidal symptoms would be more often recognized. . . .Priests and ministers should be given some elementary training so as to be able to cope better with suicidal cases they come across in the course of their ministry. Doctors also might be made more alert in diagnosing illness, to the symptoms of suicide, such as insomnia, loss of appetite, interest in life, and drive, which are present in many cases. The indiscriminate prescription of barbiturates, which puts an easy way of ending life in individual's hands, and addiction to which may cause depression, might well be checked. Care should be

taken that patients admitted to hospital for attempted suicide are not discharged prematurely. . . .The Swedish experiment of an emergency clinic for depression, which has been set up in Stockholm, might be imitated in other cities.[42]

What complicates and may at times frustrate completely the law's ability to control man's aggressiveness is the law's role as an instrument of this aggressiveness. Legal scholars believe that one of the major ways in which the law has been able to help maintain public order is by serving as a much used conduit for man's vengefulness: indeed, as the prime social agency through which man's tendency to retaliate for actual or imagined injuries has been able to find expression.[43] When, for example, a woman is raped or a man is murdered, the law tries, on the one hand, to help to preserve public order by attempting to prevent relatives of the victim from seeking out and wrecking vengeance upon the alleged culprit; but, on the other hand, the law (acting through officials of society) undertakes to determine who the culprit is and having done so, helps to express the vengeful feelings of both the victim's relatives and the public by imprisoning or executing the culprit.[44] In fact, legal historians believe that certainly in tort law and in the criminal law, revenge is the original source of most forms of legal redress.[45]

When helping to ventilate man's revengeful feelings, the law historically (and if for no other reason than to forestall the development of feuds and other disorder-producing forms of private warfare) has usually tried to mute and restrain these feelings and to express them in as civilized a manner as possible. Many ancient systems of law, for example, helped to soften and to "civilize" man's retaliatory urges by expressing them in the form of "compositions" (legally-stipulated money payments by wrongdoers to their victims or to the families of their victims). The ancient Laws of Aethelberht, for instance, provided for such compositions as

34. If a bone is laid bare, 3 shillings shall be paid as compensation.

44. If the mouth or an eye is disfigured, 12 shillings shall be paid as compensation.

57. If one man strikes another on the nose with his fist, 3 shillings.[46]

Unlike the money damages awarded in modern lawsuits, however, these compositions were ordinarily determined not so much by the extent of the injury to the victim as by the measure of vengeance that the victim (or his family) were likely to exact from the wrongdoer. For this reason, ancient laws frequently imposed much harsher penalties upon offenders caught while committing or right after committing a wrongful act, than upon those offenders caught after a considerable delay, when the desire of the victim (or his family) for vengeance had presumably cooled down.[47]

Though, as indicated above, the law has traditionally helped to secure public order by calming man's vengeful urges and expressing them in a reasonably civilized fashion, the danger exists that these urges will, at times, escape restraint and transmutation by the law and will, indeed, come to dominate the law. If so, then (as has happened so frequently in the past when vengeance has unduly influenced or controlled the law for a time) the law may well engender not justice and with it order and peace but injustice and ultimately, disorder and violence. In fact, so ever present is the risk of aggressive and vengeful desires subverting and dominating the law, that the remainder of this chapter will treat of this danger in regard to the conduct of public officials—policemen, district attorneys, judges and legislators—whose aggressive and hostile feelings are most likely to affect the law.

To suggest that hostility and sadism (conscious and unconscious) may at times dominate the behavior of policemen and cause them to act unlawfully is hardly to advance a novel thesis. In 1931, for example, the National Commission on Law Observance and Enforcement (the Wickersham Commission) reported that it had found widespread evidence of police brutality,[48] evidence of police practices "so appalling and sadistic as to pose no intellectual issue for civilized men."[49] Partly as a result of the report of this commission and of the reports of later presidential commissions regarding the behavior of the police[50] and more particularly, perhaps, as a result of Supreme Court decisions during the 1950's and the 1960's curbing the powers of the police in regard to suspects and limiting drastically the admissibility in court of evidence obtained illegally by the police,[51] there appears to be far less police brutality today than in the past.[52]

Clearly, any diminution in the likelihood of hostility and sadism dominating the conduct of the police is highly desirable, if only because illegal behavior by policemen tends, almost inevitably, to engender bad community feelings and to lead to disorder, violence and crime.[53] Yet, on the other hand, undue concentration upon the problem of preventing hostility and sadism from ever affecting the behavior of policemen may result in so many restrictions being placed upon the police as to make it difficult if not impossible for policemen to carry out their prime (or, at least, original) function of maintaining public order.[54] In fact, there is reason to suspect that some of the persons who today cry "police brutality" most quickly and most loudly do so not so much out of concern for the victims of police brutality, as out of a secret wish to so hamstring the police as to prevent them from coping successfully with the violence created by society's enemies.

Like policemen, district attorneys may be ruled at times by unduly aggressive and vengeful urges; and these urges may so affect the judgment of district attorneys as to cause them to forget that they have a duty not only to try to convict the guilty but to protect the innocent as well. In the much quoted words of the Court in *Commonwealth v. Nicely*: "The district attorney is a *quasi* judicial officer. He represents the commonwealth, and the commonwealth demands no victims. It seeks justice only, equal and impartial justice, and it is as much the duty of the district attorney to see that no innocent man suffers, as it is to see that no guilty man escapes."[55]

Unfortunately, however—and possibly in large measure because the district attorney's prosecutory functions provide the public with an all-too-tempting (though vicarious) outlet for hostile and vengeful feelings—district attorneys often tend to act towards suspects with undue hostility and vengefulness.

In fact, back in 1942, Judge Jerome Frank charged that literally "hundreds of prosecutors" not only condoned but sometimes actually participated in the then widespread, and clearly unconscionable, practice of extracting confessions from suspects by employing "third degree" methods.[56]

To help discourage district attorneys from acting towards suspects in an unduly aggressive and vengeful manner, the courts have not only refused to admit into evidence other than completely voluntary confessions[57] but have reversed convictions when prosecutors have employed such disgraceful tactics as knowingly using perjured testimony, suppressing facts or concealing witnesses capable of establishing a defendant's innocence, and appealing to a jury's preexisting prejudices concerning the race, nationality or religious beliefs of a defendant.[58] The powers given to district attorneys are often so broad, however, that it is doubtful whether these or similar judicial safeguards can effectively prevent aggressive and hostile urges from subverting and sometimes dominating the official conduct of district attorneys. Indeed, it ought perhaps be noted here that the powers granted to public prosecutors in the United States are often, quite literally, "awesome."[59]

> Under the statutory design of government in New York, the district attorney in his sole discretion and judgment may initiate criminal prosecutions or refrain from doing so. He can order the arrest of anyone suspected of violating the penal law. By exercising the subpoena power of the grand jury, his right to investigate is virtually unlimited, for not only may he seize and examine books and records, but command the appearance of any person, whether public official or private citizen, who is a resident or physically present in the state. It is his prerogative to grant complete immunity from prosecution to any person he so chooses to exempt, regardless of the crime that individual has committed. By mutual statutory provisions with some other states, subpoenas issued to residents thereof must be obeyed. With the filing of an indictment, a district attorney can demand the extradition of a named defendant from any state in the Union and from most foreign countries. After a suspect is finally indicted, every New York district attorney determines and controls the course of the case by expeditiously proceeding to trial or refrain-

ing from doing so. His failure to place the action on the calendar
for trial may end the prosecution. For good reason or none at
all, he may move to dismiss the indictment or to discharge the
defendant on his own recognizance.[60]

In view of the extraordinary breadth of these powers so often
granted to prosecutors in the United States, one can only
wonder whether it might be wise to divide and distribute the
powers—with appropriate checks and balances—among a *number* of public officials (as has been done, in effect, in such
countries as France and West Germany).[61] Then, at the
very least, there would appear to be less danger than now
that a district attorney whose official conduct has been sub-
verted by aggressive and revengeful desires would be able
to cause the injustice and social harm that so many prosecutors
are now all too capable of causing and that, unfortunately,
some of them have caused in the past.

Not only district attorneys (and policemen), but judges
as well may be motivated by hostility and vengefulness (both
conscious and unconscious). This hostility and vengefulness
of judges may find expression in the courtroom in a variety
of ways, ranging from the showing of disrespect to litigants
and attorneys to the imposition of severe and, at times,
egregiously cruel sentences upon defendants.[62]

In an attempt perhaps to control (among other things)
the hostile and vengeful urges of judges, the Canons of Judicial
Ethics provide that judges should be courteous and considerate
to the litigants and attorneys that appear before them[63] and
that when imposing sentences upon defendants, judges should
seek not to be "extreme"[64] but rather to apply "a reasonable
standard of punishment."[65] Despite these well-meant admonitions in the Canons of Judicial Ethics, however, the fact is
that (as is all too apparent even to a casual visitor in the
courts) judges are often blatantly discourteous and disrespectful to the litigants and attorneys that appear before them;
and as psychoanalysts and lawyers alike have noted, judges
continue to impose what are sometimes openly vengeful and
sadistic sentences upon defendants.[66]

To suggest reasons why judges may so act is not at all

difficult. One may point out, for example, that judges "are
not transformed psychically when they don judicial robes"[67]
and hence, like other human beings, are likely to behave at
times in an unduly aggressive and hostile manner. One may
also emphasize the very broad (and often unsupervised) powers
that judges wield (the power of judges to punish offenders
for contempt of court immediately comes to mind)[68]; and
one may then, with reference to the behavior of judges, go
on to suggest the possible applicability of Lord Acton's celebrated aphorism: "Power tends to corrupt; absolute power
corrupts absolutely." In addition, however, it might prove
useful to remember here that (as was mentioned briefly in
an earlier chapter): "Law suits are fights. They are legal
battles fought in a court room. They are historically (and
contemporaneously) substitutes for private gun-fights and
knife-fights."[69] If so, then it certainly seems likely that trials
would, among other things, tend to arouse—not only in par-
ticipants but in spectators and in presumably "neutral" judges
as well—angry and hostile feelings. Indeed, a contrary result
is hard to imagine, once it is recalled that trials (both theoretically and actually) are "adversary" proceedings[70]—proceedings that all too often transform the courtroom into "a
genteel battle ground."[71] In fact, it might prove of interest
to note here that historically trials undoubtedly aroused and
provided an outlet for hostile and vengeful feelings; for, in
early times, a "courtroom" was frequently an *actual* battle-
ground where the parties to a suit (or their champions) engaged
in deadly combat.

> One. . .method of proof. . .introduced into England by the
> Normans. . .was trial by battle. In civil cases it was not fought
> between the parties themselves but between their respective
> champions. The ancient formula suggests that the champion
> was originally a witness who was a tenant bound by bondage to
> defend his lord's title, and that a judicial duel between contra-
> dictory witnesses was allowed to decide the rights of the parties
> . . . .But in criminal cases battle was a much more serious affair.
> It lay when a private person brought a criminal charge against
> another, and was fought by the accuser and accused in person.
> It was deadly; if the defeated defendant was not already slain

in the battle he was immediately hanged on the gallows which stood ready.[72]

In view of the foregoing facts, it hardly seems likely that admonitions alone (in the Canons of Judicial Ethics or elsewhere) are likely to curb effectively the hostile and vengeful urges of judges. But what then ought to be done to minimize the likelihood of these urges affecting unduly the attitudes and decisions of judges?

One seemingly obvious suggestion that immediately comes to mind (a suggestion advanced forty or so years ago by the noted psychoanalyst Fritz Wittels) is that judges be made aware of the possibility that their aggressive and hostile feelings may well subvert their official conduct and that each judge then make an effort (hopefully a studied and sustained effort) to "bridle his own feelings."[73] A related, though admittedly more extreme, course of action that also comes to mind (action suggested by Judge Jerome Frank and mentioned in an earlier chapter) is that each judge seek to gain control over his own conscious and unconscious aggression, hostility and destructiveness by agreeing to undergo (in Judge Frank's words) "something like a psychoanalysis."[74] In addition, however, the likelihood of the hostility and destructiveness of judges subverting their attitudes and decisions might well be considerably reduced if their official conduct were subjected to far more scrutiny, especially by their peers, than is usual in the United States under current methods of appellate review (or that is even employed in the very occasional disciplinary hearings that are held concerning possible instances of judicial misconduct). It is noteworthy that the practice of subjecting the official behavior of judges to considerable scrutiny and supervision by their peers is traditional in very many nations—certainly in France, Italy and other Western democracies that have "a career service for judges, with specialized training and promotion from within the service."[75]

Whether or not any of the suggestions advanced above are adopted in regard to the problem of reducing the presumed deleterious effects of the hostile and vengeful wishes of judges upon their own official judgments and decisions, there can be little doubt that improving the caliber of judges and of the work that they do is likely to contribute to such a reduction. Admittedly, determining how the caliber of judges ought to be assessed or improved is a highly debatable matter (clearly no litmus paper test exist to test the ability of a judge or the validity of his decisions). Yet, it seems most unlikely that the present system of using appointments to the bench as a means of paying political debts and as a means of rewarding friends has resulted in the best possible men becoming judges and in judicial decisions being rendered that are as sound and as just as they could be. It may well be that unless and until better men are chosen to staff the courts, no significant reduction can realistically be expected in the influence of the aggression and vengefulness of judges upon their official opinions and decisions.

Like judges (and district attorneys and policemen), legislators may be influenced greatly at times by their own aggression and vengefulness, conscious and unconscious. The laws formulated and passed by these legislators may reflect the influence of such aggression and vengefulness, particularly insofar as these feelings may, in turn, reflect the strong passions that often move the electorate.

The men who drafted the American Constitution—like their intellectual godfather John Locke, upon whose writings they leaned quite heavily—were very much aware of the danger that the passions which often affected the public might influence unduly the actions of legislators.[76] In fact, one of the main reasons why these Founding Fathers insisted on a government of "checks and balances" was to try to guard against legislative excesses.[77]

The devices employed by the Founding Fathers in the Constitution to help minimize legislative excesses are many and varied, and range in obviousness from the right granted to the President of the United States to veto congressional legislation, to the far more subtle device of dividing the federal legislature into two, and possibly competing, co-equal parts: the Senate and the House of Representatives. Of all these restrictions upon legislative powers in the Constitution, however, two that perhaps most obviously help to limit the effect of the aggression and vengefulness of legislators upon the laws they formulate are the prohibitions against *ex post facto* laws and against bills of attainder.[78]

As was pointed out in Chapter III, laws that operate retroactively—*ex post facto* laws—may have unconscionable results: it would surely be unconscionable, for example, for a legislature to command men today to do something yesterday and then to punish these men for having failed to so act. As was also pointed out, however, the passage of *ex post facto* laws may be necessary at times to prevent injustice: to prevent, for instance, the invalidation of marriages (and other socially desirable relationships and transactions) that, years after having been entered into and relied upon, are discovered to have been technically invalid. The judges on the Supreme Court of the United States may conceivably have taken considerations such as these into account when, in 1798 in the landmark case of *Calder v. Bull*, they restricted the constitutional prohibition against *ex post facto* laws to retroactive *penal* legislation.[79] Whether or not this is so, the Supreme Court's decision in *Calder v. Bull* does appear to have succeeded to some extent in limiting the possible influence upon legislation of the aggression and hostility of legislators, for openly and unequivocally it prohibits (in the words of the majority opinion by Mr. Justice Chase):

1st. Every law that makes an action done before the passing of the law; and which was innocent when done, criminal; and punishes such action. 2d. Every law that aggravates a crime, or makes it greater than it was, when committed. 3d. Every law that changes the punishment, and inflicts a greater punishment, than the law annexed to the crime, when committed. 4th. Every law that alters the legal rules of evidence, and receives less, or different, testimony, than the law required at the time of the commission of the offense, in order to convict the offender.[80]

Like the prohibitions against *ex post facto* laws, the prohibitions in the Constitution against bills of attainder ("legislative acts . . . that apply either to named individuals or to easily ascertainable members of a group in such a way as to inflict punishment on them without a judicial trial")[81] also appear to help to limit the possible effect of the aggression and hostility of legislators upon the laws these legislators might pass. When the Founding Fathers declared in the Constitution that neither Congress nor the legislatures of the states could pass bills of attainder, they undoubtedly had in mind the deplorable abuses that had developed in England, where men were able to deprive their enemies of life, liberty and property by getting Parliament to pass a law declaring that these enemies were guilty of certain crimes.[82] In accordance with the clear desire of the Founding Fathers to prevent such legislative "trials" in the United States, the courts have, to a considerable extent, been vigilant in enforcing the constitutional prohibitions against bills of attainder. During the so-called Reconstruction period following the Civil War, for example, when the Radical Republicans under the leadership of the fiercely vindictive Thaddeus Stevens sought to wreck vengeance upon the defeated southerners, the Supreme Court of the United States held that laws requiring persons who sought to practice certain callings to swear that they had never taken up arms against the United States were actually bills of attainder and therefore null and void.[83] In the years following World War II when the duplicity of the Communists became too obvious to be ignored, the Supreme Court (for good or ill) succeeded in limiting the effect of the vengefulness and fury felt by the public and its representatives in Congress in regard to possible Communist sympathizers in government, by holding in *United States v. Lovett* that a congressional act which, in effect, prohibited the payment of any salary by the government to three named federal employees was a bill of attainder and therefore unconstitutional.[84]

Despite the prohibitions in the Constitution against bills of attainder and against *ex post facto* laws—indeed, despite all of the devices employed in the Constitution to help minimize legislative excesses—there can be no doubt that laws formulated and passed by legislators may still reflect the conscious and unconscious aggression, hostility and vengefulness of these legislators (and of the public that these legislators presumably represent). It is patent, for example, that laws regarding such matters as race relations, the rights of big business and of labor unions, and particularly the threat of subversion[85] may help to express the anger and hostility of legislators. However a moment's reflection soon reveals that legislative hostility and vengefulness may find reflection in laws having to do with a hundred and one other matters: for instance, in laws that dole out in niggardly fashion monies desperately needed for better schools; or in zoning laws that, in effect, prevent certain classes of people from living in specified communities; or in tax laws that place so very harsh a burden upon some groups that one is reminded of the celebrated remark by Mr. Chief Justice John Marshall that "the power to tax involves the power to destroy."[86]

Most obviously affected by the aggression and vengefulness of legislators, however, have been laws specifying the punishments to be inflicted upon criminals. In fact, if one considers the punishments of criminals that presumably civilized nations have sanctioned at different times—hanging, drowning, starving, burning, garroting, burying alive, crushing, branding, electrocuting, poisoning, beheading, scourging, shooting, castrating, dismembering, gassing, impaling on spikes, breaking on the wheel, stretching on the rack, drawing and quartering, disembowling while still alive, and on and on[87]—one can only conclude that, at least historically, aggression, hostility and vengeance have greatly influenced (if not dominated) the law's treatment of criminals. Indeed, it is the view of many persons who have analyzed the punishments decreed by the criminal law that, to this very day, aggressive and vengeful feelings still affect such punishments greatly.[88]

By no means does it follow from all this, however, that an attempt ought to be made to eliminate completely the possible influence of the hostility and vengefulness of legislators upon the legislation (and particularly upon the legislation pertaining to the punishment of criminals) that they pass. For one thing, laws that reflect the influence of the aggressive and hostile urges of legislators may serve as much needed, socially acceptable outlets for the ventilation of the aggressive and hostile

urges of these legislators and of the general public these legislators represent. In fact, the public's needed to ventilate
aggressive and vengeful wishes and to find socially acceptable
targets upon whom these wishes may be displaced is so very
great, that psychoanalysts have even suggested the possibility
that society may actually seduce certain persons into a life
of crime so as to help make sure that a sufficient number
of people exist in regard to whom it is socially acceptable to
express aggression and vengefulness.[89] Further, those who seek
to eliminate the influence upon legislation of aggression, hostility and vengeance would do well to call to mind the warning
sounded by Holmes in *The Common Law*:

> The first requirement of a sound body of law is, that it should
> correspond with the actual feelings and demands of the com-
> munity, whether right or wrong. If people would gratify the
> passion of revenge outside of the law, if the law did not help
> them, the law has no choice but to satisfy the craving itself, and
> thus avoid the greater evil of private retribution.[90]

Despite these considerations, however, there can be little
doubt that preventing the aggression, hostility and vengefulness of legislators from dominating and subverting legislation
is a worthwhile goal. To this end then, existing limitations
upon legislative excesses—constitutional prohibitions against
bills of attainder and against *ex post facto* laws, for example—
ought to be rigorously enforced by an alert, active and indus-
trious judiciary. Indeed, contrary perhaps to what the Founding
Fathers may have believed when they drafted the Constitution,
judicial review of legislation has, at least in the United States,
proven to be a very effective means of limiting legislative excesses.[91] Further, new checks upon legislative excesses might
be devised (perhaps in the form of amendments to the Constitution), though exactly what form these possible new checks
upon legislators ought to take is a matter that time and future
circumstance may be best able to determine. In the final analysis, however, *it may be that only legislators themselves can
effectively prevent their aggression and vengefulness from
dominating and subverting the legislation that they pass.* If
so, then knowing this may help to induce legislators to analyze

the laws they formulate over and over again in an effort to reduce the possible influence upon these laws of such feelings. If legislators make a determined effort to reduce the possible effect of their aggressiveness, hostility and vengefulness upon the laws that they pass, then these laws may—far more than formerly—reflect not so much the angry feelings and passions of these legislators (and of the electorate), as their intelligence and reason.

VI

UNCONSCIOUS MENTAL MECHANISMS AND THE LAW

Unconscious "thinking" tends to find expression in certain stereotyped modes or patterns which psychoanalysts refer to as "unconscious mental mechanisms." This chapter will consider three of the most frequently used of these unconscious mental mechanisms—rationalization, projection and identification—and will try to show how they are likely to prove applicable to the law.

Rationalization—"the inventing of a reason for an attitude or action the motive of which is not recognized." [1]

O NE OF THE MOST frequently used patterns of unconscious "thinking" that psychoanalysts have studied is the mental mechanism known as rationalization. In essence, rationalization is an unconscious and self-deceptive process by which a person—in response to unrecognized motives—forms an attitude or performs an act and then invents certain seemingly rational reasons for this attitude or act.

For example, when a dehypnotized individual obeys a command received under hypnosis and of which he is not consciously aware, and then proceeds to give a specious explanation for his act, he resorts to rationalization. Let us assume that he has been commanded to remove his shoes when there was no reason for the removal. When the hypnotic state is ended and he begins to take off his shoes, he explains that the shoes are too tight, or there are pebbles in them or he gives some explanation that has the appearance of rationality. [2]

Rationalization may consist, however, not only in the self-deceptive invention of spurious reasons for one's attitudes and acts, but in addition it may consist in the self-deceptive *overemphasis* of certain actual and valid motives for these attitudes and acts and the consequent deemphasis, or exclusion from consideration, of other relevant and operative motives. For instance, persons who engage in violent demonstrations for peace (a not so unusual occurrence during recent years) may well be motivated by the idealistic motives they frequently espouse. Yet it is certainly possible, if not probable, that this violent conduct is at times not so much a product of these idealistic motives as of powerful, though unconscious, aggressive and hostile urgencies within these persons—urgencies that are as foreign to idealism as violence is to peace. Psychoanalytic studies reveal, for example, that pacifism, and especially militant pacifism, may reflect at times not so much intellectual certitude as a Herculean and self-deceptive attempt to exercise control over very strong unconscious aggressive urges.[3]

The tendency of men to rationalize appears to have been understood (in a nontechnical sense) by lawyers and others long before psychoanalysts began to stress it. In *The Common Law* for example, published in 1881, Holmes contended that the widely held belief that it was fit and proper for wrongdoing to be followed by punishment—a belief that had found penultimate expression in Immanuel Kant's well-known dogma: "Even if a Civil Society resolved to dissolve itself with the consent of all its members. . . . the last Murderer lying in prison ought to·be executed before the resolution was carried out"[4]—functioned at times as a self-deceptive disguise for vengeful urges. To quote from *The Common Law*

> . . . this feeling of fitness [that punishment ought to follow wrongdoing] is absolute and unconditional only in the case of our neighbors. It does not seem to me that any one who has satisfied himself that an act of his was wrong, and that he will never do it again, would feel the least need or propriety, as between himself and an earthly punishing power alone, of his being made to suffer for what he had done. . . . But when our neighbors do wrong, we sometimes feel the fitness of making them smart for it, whether they have repented or not. The feeling of fitness seems to me to be only vengeance in disguise. . . .[5]

Not only have lawyers and others seemed, almost instinctively, to recognize man's tendency to rationalize (indeed, lawyers themselves have frequently been accused of being "professional rationalizers")[6]; but, in addition, a considerable number of statutes and judicial decisions appear to take this all too human tendency (or something akin to it) into account, particularly insofar as these statutes and judicial decisions seek to implement the ancient legal maxim that "no man shall be a judge in his own cause."[7]

Under the Administrative Procedure Act of 1946,[8] for example, persons who take part in investigating or prosecuting a matter are prohibited from serving as judges in the matter. To quote from Section 5 (c) of the Act: "No officer, employee, or agent engaged in the performance of investigative or prosecuting functions for any agency in any case shall, in that or a factually related case, participate or advise in the decision, recommended decision, or agency review. . . ." Similarly, Section 825 (d) (2) of the Uniform Code of Military Justice of 1950 provides that "No member of an armed force is eligible to serve as a member of a general or special court-martial when he is the accuser or a witness for the prosecution or has acted as an investigating officer or as counsel in the same case."[9] In thus attempting under the Uniform Code of Military Justice and the Administrative Procedure Act to prevent men who are involved in some way in the investigation or prosecution of a matter from acting as judges in it and thus, in effect, attempting to prevent such men from acting as judges in what, at least unconsciously, may well have become their own causes, Congress may have recognized that regardless of how honest or impartial an investigator or prosecutor may be, he is "psychologically prone to take sides"[10]; and hence, he is likely to resort to rationalization or worse if after acting as an investigator or a prosecutor in a matter, he is then permitted or called upon to act as a judge in it.[11]

Attempts to prevent men from judging their own causes have found expression not only in legislation but also (and perhaps more especially) in decisions rendered by the courts. For example, in the leading case of *Wong Yang Sung v. McGrath*,[12] the United States Supreme Court cited with approval (and acted in accordance with) a report of the Secretary of Labor's Committee on Administrative Procedure that condemned the practice of permitting the presiding officer in an administrative hearing to be the same person who had collected the evidence against the accused. To quote from the Court's decision: "A genuinely impartial hearing, conducted with critical detachment, is psychologically improbable if not impossible, when the presiding officer has at once the responsibility of appraising the strength of the case and of seeking to make it as strong as possible."[13] In the leading case of *In Re Murchison*[14] (in which a judge who had sat as a "one-man grand jury" and who had cited the defendant for contempt for what the judge believed were false answers to questions he had put to the defendant, then proceeded to try to convict the defendant on this very contempt charge), the Supreme Court held that "It would be very strange if our system of law permitted a judge to act as a grand jury and then try the very persons accused as a result of his investigations. . . . A single 'judge-grand jury' is even more a part of the accusatory process than an ordinary lay grand juror. Having been a part of that process a judge cannot be, in the nature of things, wholly disinterested in the conviction or acquittal of those accused."[15] These decisions by the Supreme Court would certainly appear to be consistent with and to provide support for the view that to permit even the most upright and disinterested of men to act, in effect, as judges in their own causes is to open the doors to rationalization—and probably to far worse.

Admittedly, there are a number of decisions by the Supreme Court pertaining to the use by judges of their power to punish for contempt of court which seem to disregard the principle that no man should be a judge in his own cause.[16] For example, the Supreme Court has in many instances sustained the rulings of lower courts in cases in which persons have been tried, convicted and sentenced for contempt of court by the very judges towards whom these persons have been accused of acting in an abusive, defiant or threatening manner.[17] In such cases, as legal scholars have pointed out, the presiding judge not only acts as a judge in what is psychologically his own cause, but in addition acts as "prosecutor. . . . jury and executioner."[18]

There are, of course, times when holding disruptive persons in contempt of court and summarily trying and sentencing them may be the only way in which a judge can maintain order in the courtroom and prevent the judicial process from being successfully sabotaged. As Mr. Justice Black put it in *Illinois v. Allen*: "The flagrant disregard in the courtroom of elementary standards of proper conduct should not and cannot be tolerated. . . . trial judges confronted with disruptive, contumacious, stubbornly defiant defendants must be given sufficient discretion to meet the circumstances of each case. . . . our courts, palladiums of liberty as they are, cannot be treated disrespectfully with impunity."[19] Still, as Edmond Cahn has noted, it is anomalous (to say the least) to demand, on the one hand, that a judge disqualify himself in cases in which he may have a minor or remote pecuniary interest and yet, on the other hand, to permit him to preside (as he frequently does today) in contempt cases in which he himself has been the target of the contempt charged—cases which, as a result, are likely to stir up in him deep and powerful emotions.[20] Further, it ought to be noted here that, as Cromwell Thomas pointed out almost forty years ago in his study *Problems of Contempt of Court*, the exercise of the contempt power by a judge may, at times, "invade five of the customary constitutional guarantees: trial by jury, freedom from self-incrimination, double jeopardy, excessive punishments, and in some cases, freedom of speech and press."[21] In view of these facts, it would certainly seem wise for the courts to follow the lead of Section 42 (b) of the Federal Rules of Criminal Procedure, which provides that when "the contempt charged involves disrespect to or criticism of a judge, that judge is disqualified from presiding at the trial or hearing except with the defendant's consent." If the lead indicated by this section of the Federal Rules of Criminal Procedure were followed (and, where possible, enlarged upon) and as a result the number of contempt cases in which men were permitted to act as judges in their own causes were minimized, the danger of judges resorting to rationalization or worse in contempt cases would probably be greatly reduced. To this extent, at least, courts would approximate more closely than now the "palladiums of liberty" that Mr. Justice Black, quite rightly, believed they ought to be.

By no means is all this to suggest that if judges never act as judges in their own causes, they will never resort to rationalization. On the contrary, as studies of the judicial process by such paladins of the bench as Jerome Frank and Benjamin Cardozo appear to reveal, judges may well resort to rationalization when judging the causes of others. In *The Nature of the Judicial Process*, for example, Mr. Justice Cardozo points out that the decisions of judges when judging the causes of others may reflect not only the influence of logic, reason and other conscious operations of the mind but also the influence of nonconscious "predilections . . . prejudices . . . instincts and emotions."[22] In *Law and the Modern Mind*, Judge Frank asserts that the judicial opinions rendered by judges often consist in part of rationalizations of unacknowledged and unconscious ideas, feelings, traits, biases and habits.[23] Indeed, Judge Frank quotes with approval the views of Judge Joseph C. Hutcheson, Jr., who believed that judges often decided cases "by feelings and not by judgment, by hunching and not by ratiocination" and that the judicial opinions written by such judges sometimes failed completely to reveal the real basis for the decisions reached.[24]

It is, of course, one thing to say that rationalization may play *some* part in the judicial process and quite another thing to declare (as has Theodore Schroeder, for example) that the judicial opinions rendered by judges are *nothing but* rationalizations of the unconscious urges of these judges. In Schroeder's words: "[E]very judicial opinion necessarily is . . . . a mere intellectualization or justification of the judge's desires . . . . a special plea made in defense of impulses which are largely unconscious."[25] To so argue is to say, in effect, that logic, reason and other conscious operations of the mind have little or no effect upon the opinions judges render and that persons who believe otherwise (including judges themselves) deceive themselves. But surely such a highly atypical view of the judicial process cannot be accepted in the absence of convincing proof.

For one thing, the contention by Schroeder that the decisions judges reach are essentially products not of conscious processes and motives but rather of unconscious and unacknowledged wishes is contrary to the way in which most legal scholars, lawyers and judges regard the judicial process[26]— including certain eminent jurists who have revealed a willingness to accept the possibility that nonconscious ideas and feelings may play a role in the judicial process. Mr. Justice Cardozo, for example, was (as has been pointed out) very much aware that nonconscious ideas and feelings might have an effect upon the opinions judges write. Yet despite this, he continued to stress in his writings the influence, if not the primacy, of logic and reason in the judicial process.[27] Similarly, Mr. Justice Holmes startled the legal world in 1881 with the statement that "the life of the law has not been logic"; and he went on to emphasize such influences upon the judicial process as "the felt necessities of the time . . . intuitions of public policy, *avowed or unconscious* . . . [and] the prejudices which judges share with their fellow-men."[28] Yet even so, Holmes never asserted in more than fifty years on the bench that judicial decisions (including his own judicial decisions, of course) were simply rationalizations of unacknowledged or unconscious wishes and feelings. In fact, a reading of Holmes's judicial opinions and other writings reveals "a profound respect for the utility of syllogistic reasoning."[29] Further, even Judge Jerome Frank himself (who, as has been noted, was greatly impressed with the possible role played by unconscious desires and feelings in the writing of judicial opinions) criticized Schroeder's views as extreme, pointing out (among other things) that the evidence Schroeder offered was meager and atypical[30] and as such, one might add, hardly meeting the burden of proof that one would suppose Schroeder would be prepared to meet. Indeed, Schroeder's failure in his writings on the judicial process to really begin to prove (rather than, in effect, simply to assert) his views, calls to mind the observation made by Morris R. Cohen that persons who seek to deemphasize the role of logic and reason in the law often tend to offer what really amounts to a "snap judgment unsupported by serious evidence from the realm of law."[31]

Even more to the point, however, Schroeder's view of the judicial process as essentially uninfluenced by such conscious operations of the mind as logic and reason would appear to to be demonstrably erroneous in its failure to acknowledge the indisputable effect upon the development of the law of the rationale employed by judges in the judicial decisions they render. In the words of Morris R. Cohen: "We know that the law has been constantly, if slowly, changing and that the reasons which judges and jurists have given for various legal rules have influenced the subsequent development (by the process of interpretation) of these rules. The *reasons* found in *The Federalist* or those given by John Marshall in *Marbury v. Madison* or in *McCulloch v. Maryland* have certainly been a determining factor in the subsequent development of our constitutional law."[32]   In short, whereas it may be reasonable to suppose (as have Mr. Justice Cardozo, Judge Jerome Frank and other luminaries of the bench and bar)[33] that rationalization (or something akin to it) may play *some* part in the judicial process, it hardly follows—certainly in the absence of convincing proof—that the judicial process is *completely* explicable in terms of rationalization. Whereas some lawyers and legal scholars may err by assuming *a priori* that rationalization plays no role at all in the opinions judges render,[34] it would certainly appear to be a far graver and more fundamental error for them to adopt what is, in effect, the opposite point of view and to conclude, with Schroeder, that—contrary to the beliefs of the most astute and most eminent of jurists—logic, reason and other conscious operations of the mind have little or no influence upon the decisions judges reach.

If judicial opinions may rationalize unconscious ideas and urges, so may laws passed by legislators. Before this possibility is pursued further, however, consideration must first be given to the unconscious mental mechanism psychoanalysts label "projection."

Projection—"perceiving in another person (or the outer
world in general) what is actually within
oneself." [35]

Projection is an unconscious mental mechanism or process
whereby a person attributes to another person or thing his own
thoughts or emotions. The behavior of young children reveals
many examples of projection.

It often happens that the child, when scolded for or accused of
some misdeed says that it was not he but some other child, often
an imaginary one, who really did it. As adults we are inclined
to view such as excuse as a conscious deception on the part of
the child, but child psychologists assure us that the very young
child really accepts his projection as the truth and expects his
parents or nurse to do so too. [36]

Adults also employ projection frequently. Psychoanalytic
studies have shown, for example, that anti-Semitism may be
based at times upon the projection onto Jews of urges and
traits that anti-Semites cannot bear to face up to in themselves. [37] Psychoanalytic studies have also revealed that many
of the objectionable attributes and tendencies that men ascribe
to a wartime enemy—attributes and tendencies that make
this enemy appear to be "a veritable monster of iniquity"—have
been projected by these men onto this enemy. [38] Indeed, as
J. C. Flugel has observed, men often tend to project their
most objectionable and distasteful aggressive and hostile wishes
upon just those persons (and things) that they fear the most. [39]

As has already been suggested, laws passed by legislators
(like opinions rendered by judges) may rationalize unconscious
wishes and urges. In many such instances, however, rationalization may be preceded by projection: legislators may first
project their objectionable desires onto members of the public;
and having done so, they may then formulate legislation designed to control these objectionable desires of the "public,"
failing to understand that in so doing they are, albeit unconsciously, actually seeking to control their own wishes. This is
the view of Ranyard West, who asserts in his well-known psychoanalytic study *Conscience and Society* that because a legis-

lator may project onto members of the public his own inner antisocial urgencies, this legislator is likely to be unaware that "in legislating and approving legislation to secure equitable assessments of rights and obligations, or to prevent deceit, or to arrest violence, he is legislating for the control of himself."[40]

To the extent that legislation may constitute an attempt to control objectionable urges that legislators have projected onto members of the public, however, this legislation would seem less likely to be successful in curbing the public's antisocial desires and feelings than legislation based upon an objective appraisal of the public's real desires and feelings. If, for example, as West asserts, legislators tend to project their aggressive and hostile strivings onto the public and then pass legislation designed to curb these projected strivings,[41] such legislation can hardly be expected to be as effective in dealing with the antisocial aggression of the public as legislation based upon a realistic appraisal of the actual aggressive strivings of the public. Moreover, insofar as legislation may be designed to control the inner urges and feelings of legislators that have been projected onto the public, such legislation would hardly seem likely to provide the public with standards of behavior that would begin to be as realistic and as realizable as standards based upon an objective survey of the public's actual desires and practices. Thus, if legislators project their hidden sexual desires and tendencies onto the public and then pass laws that seek to curb these projected desires and tendencies, one would expect a gap to exist, as indeed it does, between the standards of sexual conduct demanded by the law and the actual sexual practices of the public.[42] In fact, so large a gap exists today between what the law regards as proper sexual conduct and the public's actual sexual behavior that as eminent an authority on criminology as Sandford Kadish has concluded that a vast number of Americans (more, perhaps, than a majority) are made potential criminals by current legislation regarding sexual activity.[43] Further, to the extent that legislators are preoccupied (consciously or unconsciously) with the need to curb the desires and strivings that they may have projected onto the public, they would (at least to such extent) have less time and energy to devote to other, and possibly more significant, problems. For instance, if legislators project their aggressive and hostile strivings onto big business (a matter to be discussed below) and then busy themselves with seeking to control the resultant seeming dangers posed by big business, these legislators would inevitably have less time and energy to deal with other agencies and organizations (labor organizations, for example) that may actually pose a greater danger to the public than big business. In the succinct phraseology of the once very popular Herbert Spencer: "Time and human activity being limited, it necessarily follows that legislators' sins of *commission* entail corresponding sins of *omission*."[44]

This discussion of the disadvantages of projection by legislators may well appear to be abstruse and theoretical. Yet to someone who is likely to be significantly affected by certain legislation, there may be nothing abstruse or theoretical about the difference to him if this legislation deals with him not as he actually is but rather as someone upon whom legislators have projected antisocial desires and urges that require curbing. The difference involved may, for example, be the difference between staying out of jail and going to jail—and there is surely nothing abstruse or theoretical about being sent to jail. Further, it ought to be noted here that not only legislators but judges as well may project their unbearable desires and feelings onto others; and these judges may then seek to curb such projected desires and feelings by means of the judgments they render. Indeed, Jerome Frank has warned that the projection by judges of their aggressive and hostile urges onto the parties that appear before them in court may well result at times in these judges attempting to curb such projected urges with what can only be described as unduly severe judgments.[45]

Whether and to what extent the law in any field may reflect attempts by legislators and judges to control their projected desires and feelings is, admittedly, a matter of conjecture at the present time. Yet it might prove helpful to consider briefly here certain types of laws that offhand seem likely to reveal the impress of projection, for doing so may provide a number of useful starting points for programs that hopefully will be designed in the future to reduce the incidence of projection in the law.

In seeking to determine what laws are likely to reflect the impress of projection, one might find it helpful to recall that men tend to project their aggressive and hostile wishes upon the persons and things that they greatly fear.[46] Thus if, for example, as history appears to reveal, Americans have tended at times (particularly during wartime) to fear subversives greatly,[47] one might well be justified in suspecting that certain legislative and judicial attempts to cope with subversives may reflect attempts by legislators and judges to control their own aggressive and hostile strivings projected onto these subversives. In fact, if laws seeking to deal with the behavior of subversives may reflect, albeit on an unconscious level, an effort to curb the projected aggression and hostility of the legislators who designed these laws and more especially, perhaps, may reflect an effort to curb the projected aggression and hostility of the public whom these legislators presumably represent, then herein may be found one of the basic reasons why these laws have often been far more severe and far more extreme than would appear to be objectively justified. There would, for example, seem to be little doubt that the laws used by Attorney General Palmer to hunt down subversives in the post–World-War-I period and the laws passed during World War II to prevent subversion by persons of Japanese ancestry living on the West Coast were disgracefully severe and unconscionable in their effect.[48]

Just as Americans have tended to fear greatly at times the behavior of subversives, so have they tended to become greatly alarmed at times regarding the possible dangers to their well-being posed by big business. Historically, fear of big business appears to have been first aroused in the United States by the ruthless behavior of many of the leaders of industry and finance during the post–Civil-War industrialization of the North.[49] In fact, the public's alarm regarding the business and financial practices of such men as James J. Hill,

John D. Rockefeller, Andrew Carnegie and J. Pierpont Morgan became so very great that in 1890 Congress responded by passing the Sherman Anti-Trust Act (which not only sought to outlaw monopolies but also declared illegal "every contract, combination . . . or conspiracy, in restraint of trade . . . among the several states").[50] Since the passage of the Sherman Anti-Trust Act, the public's fear of possible abuses by big business has found expression in a complex of statutes and judicial decisions known as the "antitrust laws."[51] Today, two large and powerful agencies of the Federal Government—the Federal Trade Commission and the Department of Justice—are actively engaged in trying to prevent big business from violating these antitrust laws.

To the extent that big business may inspire great fear, it would (in accordance with the psychoanalytic discovery that men tend to project their aggressive and hostile wishes onto persons and things that they fear greatly) appear to be a likely target for projected aggressive and hostile wishes. If, as has been suggested, the law may help to express at times attempts by legislators and judges to curb their own projected desires and feelings—and the projected desires and feelings of the public whom these officials presumably represent—then it is certainly conceivable that the complex of statutes and judicial decisions that constitute today's antitrust laws (statutes and judicial decisions that presumably seek to prevent improper behavior by big business) may well reflect attempts on the part of the legislators and judges involved to curb aggressive and hostile urges that they, and the members of the public whom they represent, may have projected onto big business.

By no means is all this to deny that Americans have greatly admired the activities of big business at times (during a large part of the 1920's and the 1950's, for example), or that just as the public has sometimes feared big business greatly, so has the public been deeply moved at other times by feelings of admiration and respect for big business. The activities of big business are, after all, largely responsible for helping to make possible the current high standard of living in the United States (a standard of living that many economists believe would be difficult if not impossible to maintain without the advantages conferred by the methodology and capacities of big business).[52] Some members of the public, as well as the officials who represent them in legislatures and other branches of government, are indeed so admiring of big business at times and so blind to the dangers that it sometimes poses to the public's well-being that they may well have unconsciously identified themselves with big business and its leaders. If so, then (as the discussion of the unconscious mental mechanism of "identification" in the next section of this chapter will suggest) such persons are quite likely to be fervent (and possibly unreasoning) partisans of big business and to seek to advance its interests vigorously in their capacities as legislators, judges and members of the public.[53]

Further, if it may be assumed that certain legislators, judges and members of the public have unconsciously identified themselves with big business and its leaders, and as a result are strongly desirous of advancing and expanding the rights, powers and privileges of big business, and if other persons acting in similar capacities are likely to project their aggression and hostility onto big business and then try to control this projected aggression and hostility by seeking to curb and restrict the rights, powers and privileges of big business, then herein, perhaps, may be found one of the reasons why the laws that attempt to regulate the activities of big business—the anti-trust laws—are (to quote Joseph W. Burns) "a jumble of conflicting statutes and confusing court decisions."[54] In other words, the conflict and confusion which unfortunately, but indisputably, characterize the antitrust laws[55] may reflect the influence not only of such much-mooted matters as the overlapping jurisdiction of (and the consequent struggle for power between) the Department of Justice and the Federal Trade Commission in the antitrust area,[56] as well as attempts by those who enforce the antitrust laws to achieve such frequently divergent goals as promoting competition and maximizing industrial efficiency,[57] but the conflict and confusion which typify the antitrust laws may also reflect the influence of powerful but disparate unconscious processes: the influence, for example, of the unconscious process of identification—which, as observed above, may well cause members of the public to seek to extend the powers and privileges of big business—and the influence of the unconscious mental mechanism of projection—which, as has been pointed out, may well have the converse effect of causing members of the electorate to do their utmost to restrict the powers and privileges of big business. In fact, it is conceivable that if the possible effects of unconscious mental processes upon the antitrust laws were more fully understood, some headway might well be made in reworking these laws so that they would be less likely to reflect the influence of projection and other unconscious mental mechanisms and, as a result, be less conflictive and confusing than now.

More likely, perhaps, than the antitrust laws to reveal the impress of the unconscious mental mechanism of projection is the criminal law. Legislation that prohibits and punishes certain aggressive and hostile acts may, for example, reflect attempts on the part of legislators to curb aggressive and hostile strivings that these legislators have projected onto the public.[58] Ranyard West has speculated that "When Hobbes asked for laws . . . to protect himself from the aggressiveness of bad men, he was not aware that a great deal of his apprehension sprang not from the burglaries his own house had suffered, nor from the personal or group violences of which he had heard during the English Civil Wars, but from . . . his own [projected] aggressiveness."[59]

Be this as it may, there can be little doubt that the punishment of offenders by the criminal law may reflect at times the influence of projection (and other unconscious mental mechanisms) upon the law.[60] Psychoanalysts have learned, for instance, that the projection of antisocial urges onto criminals, coupled with the demand that the law punish these criminals severely, may help those who mold the law (legislators, judges, administrators and the public whom these officials represent) to deny the existence of their own antisocial urges and thus help to avoid the arousal in these persons of unbearable guilt and a concomitant need for punishment to expiate this guilt.[61] As Henry Weihofen has put it, "we cast our own sins onto the criminal. In this way we relieve our own sense of guilt without actually having to suffer the punishment."[62] In fact, some psychoanalysts believe that the projection onto criminals of the public's antisocial urgencies—coupled with the demand that the law punish these criminals severely—is so useful a device for reducing the guilt and obviating the need for expiatory punishment of the law-abiding members of the public that society may, at times, actually encourage certain persons to become criminals so that these persons might then serve as scapegoats upon whom the law abiding can project objectionable urges (and guilt and the need for punishment).[63]

To appreciate more fully why the law-abiding members of the public so frequently choose criminals as targets for the projection of antisocial desires and feelings (and in addition to appreciate the role played by guilt and the need for punishment in these and related circumstances) requires an understanding of the unconscious mental mechanism that psychoanalysts label "identification." Attention must therefore be given to this unconscious mental mechanism before the discussion of the punishment of offenders by the criminal law is continued.

> **Identification**—"When an individual, by incorporating within himself a mental picture of [somebody else] ... thinks, feels and acts as he conceives [this other person] ... to think, feel and act, the process is called identification. It is largely an unconscious process." [64]

The term "identification" (though used at times in a variety of different but related senses) is frequently employed by psychoanalysts to describe "a complex unconscious process whereby real or imagined characteristics of another person [or of an animal, or even of an inanimate object] become ... components of ... [one's own] personality."[65] So defined, identification is essentially an unconscious mental mechanism or process whereby persons attach and transfer to themselves what they conceive of as the traits, values and purposes of others. Through a sort of coalescence of personalities, the traits, values and purposes of others are regarded as one's own.[66]

As Freud points out in his seminal discussion of identification in *Group Psychology and the Analysis of the Ego*,[67] identification is made use of early in life ("identification is . . . the earliest expression of an emotional tie with another person")[68] and is frequently employed thereafter. Sometimes the effect of identification is startling: when, for example, a psychotic who has identified himself with Napoleon dons a triangular hat, places a hand beneath the fold of his jacket, and shouts orders at imaginary persons. Less dramatic, perhaps, but far more usual, are the effects of identification in an example suggested by Freud:

> Supposing, for instance, that one of the girls in a boarding school has had a letter from someone with whom she is secretly in love . . . and that she reacts to it with a fit of hysterics; then some of her friends who know about it will contract the fit, as we say, by means of mental infection. The mechanism is that of identification based upon the possibility or desire of putting oneself in the same situation. The other girls would like to have a secret love affair too. . . .[69]

Quite often a man may become intensely interested in and a partisan of those with whom he identifies himself. After all, what happens to such persons also happens, albeit in a vicarious sense, to himself as well. If, for example, a man identifies himself with certain baseball players and the teams to which they belong, then the exploits of these players and the victories of their teams become, in a vicarious sense, *his* exploits and *his* victories. In like manner, if a man identifies himself with certain well-known industrialists and the business enterprises that they own or control, then the more successful these industrialists and their business enterprises become, the more successful the man may feel. Indeed, because a man may identify himself with others (with sports figures, big businessmen or whomsoever), he may become an ardent champion of such persons and seek to advance their interests in his capacity as legislator, judge, administrator or simply as private citizen. On the other hand, a man may unconsciously identify himself with someone whom he consciously fears, dislikes or wishes to supplant[70] or (as will be seen in the discussion of the punishment of criminals to follow) with persons of whom his moral faculty or superego disapproves. If so, then the feelings of admiration and respect that are so often directed toward the persons identified with may well be replaced by far less friendly, if not by hostile, feelings. In fact, to know that a man may consciously disapprove of persons with whom he has unconsciously identified is to begin to understand why men who succeed in overcoming and taking the place of consciously hated rivals (in business, politics or personal relationships) may end up by acting just like the persons whom they replaced.

To return now to the discussion of the punishment of offenders by the criminal law, it will be recalled that infants and young children are frequently moved by powerful aggressive and hostile desires.[71] Indeed, psychoanalysts have learned that youngsters are beset at times by what can only be described as cannibalistic, incestuous and murderous urges.[72] In the words of Ernest Jones: "[S]ide by side with loving attitudes and peaceful contentment, there are always to be found [in infants and young children] mental processes reminiscent of the most primitive aspects of savage life of an intensity that is only faintly mirrored later on by the distressing aspects of our international relations, including even the tortures and other atrocities."[73] Perhaps another way of saying all this would be to observe, as has J. F. Flugel, that "we are all of us born criminals in the sense that we are extensively endowed with impulses which, if unchecked, lead to anti-social conduct."[74] Or, as Edward Glover has put it, "the perfectly normal infant . . . greedy, dirty, violent in temper, destructive in habit . . . inconsiderate, domineering and sadistic . . . [is,] judged by adult social standards [,] . . . for all practical purposes a born criminal."[75] In addition, it also ought to be stressed here that by no means are all of these antisocial or criminalistic urges dissipated or somehow worked through during infancy and early childhood. Rather, as psychoanalysts have learned, many of these infantile wishes and feelings are repressed or otherwise relegated to an unconscious level.[76] Here, cut off from motor expression and unaltered by the passage of time,[77] they are kept more or less in check by the superego.

Perhaps because of the existence of these antisocial or criminalistic urges in the unconscious of even the most law-abiding of persons, there is (as psychoanalysts have discovered) *a tendency on the part of many law-abiding persons to identify themselves unconsciously with criminals.*[78] In fact, possibly because criminals tend to act out the antisocial or criminalistic wishes (or the adult analogues of these wishes) found in the unconscious of the law-abiding, criminals may very well be a natural target for the projection of such wishes by the law-abiding. After all, by projecting antisocial or criminalistic desires onto the criminals with whom they identify themselves (and whose crimes presumably reflect these desires or their adult analogues), the law-abiding are thereby enabled, albeit in a vicarious sense, to act out these forbidden (but sometimes very powerful and insistent) infantile urgencies; and in so doing, to relieve the inner tension ordinarily created by the presence of such urgencies in the unconscious, without eliciting the terrible guilt that the superego would engender if such urgencies were actually acted out by the law-abiding, and without eliciting the consequent demand by the superego for severe punishment to expiate such guilt.

However, if and when the law-abiding unconsciously identify themselves with criminals, this alone may engender considerable guilt—if only because the superego of the law-abiding may find identification with criminals to be, in itself, morally opprobrious. Further, identification of the law-abiding with criminals may also stir up in the unconscious of the law-abiding the very antisocial or criminalistic urges that criminals act out; and as a result, the superego of the law-abiding may engender strong feelings of guilt as it seeks to try to regain control over these activated antisocial desires and feelings (which, if left without proper control, might well escape into consciousness and gain access to motility). *By demanding severe punishment of criminals, however, the law-abiding are thereby able to help their superego to control these antisocial or criminalistic urges.* This is accomplished, in the view of Franz Alexander and Hugo Staub, because "the demand that the law-breaker be punished is [in effect] . . . a demonstration against one's own inner drives, a demonstration which tends to keep these drives amenable to control . . . [P]unishment [serves] as an intimidating example . . . against one's own primitive . . . repressed instinctual drives."[79] Indeed, the demand that criminals be punished not only helps to reduce the pressure exerted against the superego by the antisocial wishes in the unconscious of the law-abiding, but this demand also helps to reduce the guilt engendered by the superego of the law-abiding because of the presence of such activated infantile impulses. As David Abrahamsen has put it: "When law-abiding citizens react mercilessly toward a criminal and his deed, it is not only because they want to see the law obeyed or because they want retribution, but also because the offender acts out anti-social impulses which so many people would like to act out but do not dare to because of fear of the consequences. Unconsciously they identify with the criminal because of their own latent anti-social tendencies and somehow vicariously demand and accept the punishment to relieve their own guilt feelings."[80]

Though this chapter's limitations preclude further consideration of the relationship between the punishment of criminals and the unconscious mental mechanisms of identification and projection, it ought to be noted that the discussion of this relationship in the preceding pages has implications that deserve far more than casual attention, particularly by persons concerned with the way in which offenders are treated by the criminal law. For example, if the discussion has been at all accurate, then there can be little doubt that (as already seen in prior chapters) the punishment of criminals may well serve a number of significant inner needs of the law-abiding.[81] If so, then those persons who (albeit quite rightly) criticize the way in which offenders are treated by the criminal law—who point out, for instance, that prisons are "warehouses of human degradation . . . breeding places of crime, violence and despair"[82]—ought to understand that the punishments employed by the criminal law are not simply a product of indifference, stupidity or wickedness. Rather, these persons ought to realize that *if there are to be meaningful reforms in the treatment of offenders by the criminal law, these reforms must take into account not only the effect upon criminals of the punishments decreed by the criminal law but also the way in which these punishments may serve the inner needs of the law-abiding as well.*[83]

Unlike the tendency of the law-abiding to identify themselves with criminals (which, as has been seen, is more or less covert), there is an openness (if not an obviousness) about what the legal philosopher Edmond Cahn has described as men's tendency to identify themselves with victims of legal oppression or injustice. Even though the core or essence of what constitutes legal oppression has, at least to date, successfully defied capture in a verbal formula,[84] there would appear to be considerable merit in Cahn's view that legal oppression or injustice tends (of course, with some exceptions) to express itself in one or more of six typical ways: (1) in the law's failure to treat persons of presumably equal merit, equally; (2) in the law's failure (within traditional and practicable limits) to reward or punish men as they deserve to be rewarded or punished; (3) in the violation of human dignity (for example, by the imposition of humiliating punishments) by the law; (4) in the disregard of normal and rational procedures by judges and other officers of the law; (5) in attempts by legal officials to extend their powers into areas traditionally free from governmental interference; and (6) in the failure of the law to fulfill what have become men's common or normal expectations regarding it.[85]

Exactly why men tend to identify themselves with victims of legal oppression or injustice is by no means certain. Cahn has suggested that at least in regard to the six instances listed above, such identification is automatic: that injustice directed towards others is automatically reacted to as an attack upon one's self—an attack to which one responds reflexively, as it were, with (to use Cahn's phraseology) "outrage, horror, shock, resentment, and anger, those affections of the viscera and abnormal secretions of the adrenals that prepare the human animal to resist attack."[86] To say that a reaction is automatic or reflexive, however, is not really to explain why this reaction occurs. Hence, it may prove useful here to adopt a somewhat different approach to the problem of why, as Cahn has observed, men tend to identify themselves with victims of legal injustice.

To begin with, it will be recalled that (as was pointed out in the discussion of unconscious symbolism), judges (and even the law itself) are frequently regarded on an unconscious level as parent substitutes or symbols.[87] Knowing that the law and some of its officials are often so regarded in the unconscious is helpful in drawing attention to the possibility that the instances of legal unfairness or injustice listed by Cahn may be equated unconsciously with instances of *parental* unfairness or injustice. For example, the first category of legal injustice cited by Cahn—the law's failure to treat persons of presumably equal merit equally—may be equated in the unconscious with the failure of a parent to treat his children equally, a form of parental behavior that (as was stressed in the discussion of the superego) children tend to consider especially unjust.[88] Similarly, the second category of legal oppression or injustice named by Cahn—the law's failure (within traditional and practicable limits) to reward or punish men as they deserve to be rewarded or punished—may be equated unconsciously with the failure of a parent to reward or punish his children as they deserve to be rewarded or punished, a parental failure particularly likely to violate a young child's sense of justice (see, for example, the discussion of the talion reaction).[89] Indeed, each of the other instances of legal unfairness or inequity listed by Cahn—the violation of human dignity by the law; the disregard of normal and rational procedures by judges and other officers of the law; attempts by legal officials to extend their powers into areas traditionally free from governmental interference; and the failure of the law to fulfill what have become men's common or normal expectations regarding it—may be equated on an unconscious level with an analogous act of parental unfairness or inequity; the humiliation of a child by his parents; the failure of parents to evaluate a child's conduct in a fair and rational manner; sudden parental interference (apparently without just cause) in an area of a child's life that had previously been ignored; and the failure, in general, of parents to behave towards their children in the ways that these children had come to expect and to rely upon.

Of course, few if any children escape being treated at times by their parents (or by parent substitutes) in one or more of these oppressive and unjust ways. It is the rare child who at some time or another has not been treated unequally, unfairly or in a humiliating manner by his parents.[90] Indeed, perhaps because of the ubiquity of these instances of parental oppression—with which the instances of legal oppression described by Cahn may be unconsciously equated—men may feel a strong kinship (albeit on an unconscious level) with the victims of legal oppression. As a result of this feeling of kinship with those who are so victimized, men may identify themselves with them, champion their causes, and do what they can to ease their plight.

Though this explanation of why men may identify themselves with victims of legal iniquity is admittedly speculative, there can be little doubt that (as Cahn has shown in his writings and as was noted at the beginning of this discussion) men do tend to so act. For example, there can be little doubt that men tend to identify themselves with persons who have been unjustly condemned or unjustly imprisoned by the law and that much of the clamor for the vindication and release of these victims of legal iniquity is a product of such identification.[91] Two cases in point that immediately come to mind (cases that are far too familiar to require further comment here) are the Sacco and Vanzetti case and the truly infamous Dreyfus case.[92]

It also ought to be observed here that lawyers particularly have long been aware (albeit intuitively) of man's tendency to identify himself with victims of legal unfairness and oppression and have frequently attempted to exploit this tendency. Clarence Darrow, for example, frequently sought to convince the juries he addressed in court that his clients were the victims of the most blatant sort of legal unfairness and oppression; and he repeatedly warned the members of these juries that someday, they might well find themselves in the very same position as his clients.[93] Thus in one celebrated case in which Darrow himself was the defendant (a case of alleged jury tampering in which Darrow was ultimately acquitted by the jury), Darrow emphasized in his charge to the jury that if he "with some influence, and some respect, and some money" could be so unjustly accused, it was even more likely that they might someday be the victims of some equally serious form of legal oppression.[94] As Darrow put it to the jury: "[W]hen you go back to your homes, you had better kiss your wives a fond goodbye, and take your little children more tenderly in your arms that ever before, because, though today it is my turn, tomorrow it may be yours."[95] In 1926 in the celebrated *Sweet* case (in which Darrow represented eleven Negroes accused of having shot and killed a white man when they sought to defend their home against a howling mob of whites determined to prevent them from living in what had hitherto been an all-white neighborhood), Darrow first stressed the indignities and injustices suffered by the Negro defendants and then asked the all-white jury before whom the case was being tried to imagine that they themselves were the Negro defendants. In Darrow's words: "Put yourselves in their place. Make yourselves colored for a little while. It won't hurt, you can wash it off . . . just make yourself black for a little while; long enough, gentlemen, to judge them."[96] Perhaps as a result of this plea by Darrow, the all-white jury acquitted the eleven Negro defendants.

Not only lawyers but many other persons concerned with the law appear to be very much aware of man's tendency to identify himself with victims of legal inequity and injustice. For example, certain dramatists and novelists who deal with instances of legal inequity or injustice in their works appear to be fully cognizant of (and particularly capable of exploiting) this tendency. Thus it would seem to be no accident that a viewer of Terence Rattigan's play *The Winslow Boy* is likely to identify himself with Ronnie Winslow and his "disgraced" family as they struggle against fierce governmental opposition to prove that Ronnie had been unjustly expelled from the Royal Naval College; and it would hardly seem a matter of chance that a reader of Herman Wouk's novel *The Caine Mutiny* is likely to identify himself with Lieutenant Stephen Maryk and his attorney Barney Greenwald as they battle to refute the false charges leveled by Lieutenant Commander Queeg in the Courts-Martial of Maryk.[97] The ability to exploit man's tendency to identify with victims of legal oppression is, of course, not limited to writers and lawyers. More than a century ago, political agitation by northern abolitionists regarding the political, legal, social and other disabilities of the slaves in the southern states may well have induced many northerners to identify themselves with the plight of these slaves and in so doing helped to pave the way for the Civil War.[98] Today, there are political agitators who by making false allegations of legal oppression (by charging, for example, that members of certain minority groups were treated improperly in the courts, when, in fact, they were treated with scrupulous fairness or by charging that the police brutalized certain demonstrators, when, in fact, the police acted with great restraint in the face of considerable provocation) seem to be attempting to prepare the ground for a new civil war in the United States. The point is, of course, that just as men's tendency to identify themselves with victims of legal injustice may lead to appropriate and desirable reforms, so may it lead (particularly when exploited by the unscrupulous) to inappropriate and undesirable consequences.

The mental mechanism of identification may find expression not only in men's tendency to identify themselves with the victims of legal oppression or injustice (and, as was seen earlier in this chapter, in the tendency of many law abiding persons to identify themselves with criminals), but this unconscious mental mechanism may also find expression in certain traditional legal doctrines or practices and in the behavior of certain persons closely associated with the law and its processes. For instance, the traditional legal doctrine or practice of failing to hold the insane criminally liable for their acts may well reflect, though admittedly in part, the failure of members of the public to identify themselves with the insane and the resultant inability of members of the public to use the punishment of the insane to help to deter themselves from committing criminal acts.[99] As a number of psychoanalytically oriented attorneys have suggested, certain sentences handed down by judges may well reflect, at times, the self-identification of these judges with their parents: Paul Reiwald has suggested, for instance, that "many harsh and over-severe judgments are traceable to the fact that the judge once identified himself with a harsh father."[100] A further example of the possible effect of the unconscious mental mechanism of identification upon legal doctrine and practice and upon persons closely associated with the law and its processes—an example now to be considered in some detail—pertains to the tendency of lawyers to identify themselves with their clients and, more especially, to the possible effects of this self-identification of lawyers with clients upon the traditional Anglo-American system of litigation: the adversary system.

As Judge Jerome Frank points out in his work *Courts On Trial*, the adversary system of litigation is based upon the belief that "the best way for a court to discover the facts in a suit is to have each side strive as hard as it can, in a keenly partisan spirit, to bring to the court's attention the evidence favorable to that side."[101] Or, in the words of Professor Edmund M. Morgan: "The theory of our adversary system of litigation is that each litigant is most interested and will be most effective in seeking, discovering, and presenting the materials which will reveal the strength of his own case and the weakness of his adversary's case so that the truth will emerge to the impartial tribunal that makes the decision."[102]

In statement, this theory may well be attractive. Yet, in practice, there can be little doubt that the adversary system of litigation has had a number of unfortunate consequences. For example, the adversary system seems to encourage lawyers to intimidate and to try to discredit honest but adverse witnesses.

> ... an experienced lawyer uses all sorts of startegems to minimize the effect on the judge or jury of testimony disadvantageous to his client, even when the lawyer has no doubt of the accuracy and honesty of that testimony. The lawyer considers it his duty to create a false impression, if he can, of any witness who gives such testimony.[103]

Also, the adversary system appears to engender in lawyers a desire to block the introduction of evidence—no matter how vital—if such evidence is in any way inimical to their client's interests.

> ... Tracy, counseling trial lawyers, in a much-praised book ... adds, "Be careful in your questions on cross-examination not to open a door that you have every reason to wish kept closed." That is, don't let in any reliable evidence, hurtful to your side, which would help the trial court to arrive at the truth.

> "In cross-examination," writes Eggleston, "the main preoccupation of counsel is to avoid introducing evidence, or giving an opening to it, which will harm his case. The most painful thing for an experienced practitioner ... is to hear a junior counsel laboriously bring out in cross-examination of a witness all the truth which the counsel who called him could not 'bring out' and which it was the junior's duty as an advocate to conceal."[104]

Further, and most unfortunately, the adversary system seems to encourage the use of outrageously partisan and often deliberately false testimony.

> We know, alas, that an immense amount of testimony is deliberately and knowingly false. Experienced lawyers say that, in large cities, scarcely a trial occurs, in which some witness does not lie. Perjured testimony often goes undetected by trial courts and therefore often wins cases. Judge Dawson of the Kansas Supreme Court found one of the "real and crying hindrances to a correct and efficient administration of justice ... the widespread prevalence of perjury practiced with impunity by litigants and witnesses. . . ." A wag has it that courts decide cases according

to the "preponderance of perjury." Some—not all—of that lying testimony results from the coaching of witnesses by dishonest lawyers.[105]

It may be that these abuses are unavoidable consequences of the adversary system and that they can be done away with completely only if the adversary system is itself abolished. But it may also be possible, without abolishing the adversary system, to minimize these abuses. Consideration of the tendency of lawyers to identify themselves with their clients may well contribute to this end.

Lawyers, like other men and women, tend to identify themselves with persons who play an important role in their lives. Psychoanalysts have learned, for example, that many a man who chooses to become a lawyer does so partly because he has identified himself with a lawyer in his family, frequently his own father.[106] Psychoanalysts have also observed, however, that lawyers tend to identify themselves with their clients and quite often with those clients accused of having committed crimes.[107]

The forces that motivate an attorney's clients are admittedly diverse. Yet, as Jerome Frank and others have pointed out, many of these clients regard litigation (consciously or unconsciously) as a fight, as a means of expressing "combat feelings."[108] That clients should so regard litigation—that they should try to use litigation as a "channel for . . . hostile and aggressive impulses"[109]—is, of course, hardly surprising, since lawsuits are historically, and even presently, substitutes for private brawls, blood-feuds and the like.[110]

If a significant number of an attorney's clients (in civil or criminal matters) are motivated by "combat feelings," then the attorney himself—assuming that he identifies himself with these clients—would presumably be influenced by such feelings as well. Like the champion at the early common law ("one of the direct ancestors of the legal profession"[111]) who risked his life fighting for his clients in trial by battle,[112] this attorney would probably be moved by powerful urges to win the "fights" for which he has been engaged. Indeed, like some of the combative clients with whom he has presumably identified himself (especially those clients accused of a serious crime), the attorney may become so emotionally aroused, so affected by strong and intense feelings, that discrediting honest witnesses, blocking the introduction of vital evidence, using outrageously partisan (and even perjured) testimony (and much more) may appear justifiable to him as a means of achieving "victory" and satisfying the aggressive urges that beset him. In short, the abuses of the adversary system detailed above may well be traceable (though, admittedly, in part) to the tendency of lawyers to identify themselves with their clients.

However, if the abuses of the adversary system described above may well be, in part, products of the self-identification of lawyers with their clients, then simply knowing this may prove of value to lawyers desirous of improving the adversary system. For one thing, simply knowing that a relationship may exist between the tendency of lawyers to identify themselves with litigants and some of the adversary system's faults may put lawyers on their guard, and to this extent, at least, may result in a reduction of the incidence and intensity of such identification and of abuses of the adversary system traceable to it. In addition, knowing of a possible relationship between the self-identification of lawyers with litigants and the faults of the adversary system may help to make lawyers more appreciative than now of the need for standards of professional conduct that try to guard against such faults. Indeed, it is in this light that certain sections of the Canons of Professional Ethics (superseded in 1970 by the Code of Professional Responsibility) gain in interest and significance. For instance, Canon 17 provides in part that "Clients, not lawyers, are the litigants. Whatever may be the ill-feeling existing between clients, it should not be allowed to influence counsel in their conduct and demeanor toward each other or toward suitors in the case." Canon 18 begins with the admonition: "A lawyer should always treat adverse witnesses and suitors with fairness and due consideration, and he should never minister to the malevolence or prejudices of a client in the trial or conduct of a cause. The client cannot be made the keeper of the lawyer's conscience in professional matters." Further, and perhaps most important, knowing that certain abuses of the adversary system may be partly traceable to the self-identification of lawyers with their clients may help to make lawyers more willing to adopt measures designed to minimize these abuses. Lawyers may, for example, reveal an increased willingness to employ the various pretrial devices (interrogatories, inspections, depositions, examinations and the like) described in the Federal Rules of Civil Procedure.[113] These pretrial devices provided for by the Federal Rules of Civil Procedure and particularly the so-called pretrial conference (described in Rule 16) at which the Court may require revelation of the facts and evidence the parties hope to adduce at the trial[114] were designed to promote the fullest possible disclosure before trial in the hope of increasing the likelihood that the trial proper will be used not for the expression of combative urges and feelings but rather for the discovery of truth and the realization of justice.[115]

PART II

PSYCHOANALYSIS AND CONSTITUTIONAL LAW

PREFATORY NOTE

CERTAIN BASIC psychoanalytic tenets were described in Part I, and an attempt was made to show, albeit in a very general way, how they might prove applicable to the law. Now, four specific, fundamental, perennial and possibly insoluble problems of constitutional law will be considered in detail, and an attempt will be made to demonstrate how they may be better understood and possibly even begin to be resolved in the light of psychoanalytic psychology.

The four questions of constitutional law to be considered here are (1) the problem of whether or not congressional legislation ought to be subject to judicial review; (2) the related problem of whether judges ought to act with self-restraint (long advocated by Mr. Justice Felix Frankfurter) or with boldness (so characteristic of Mr. Chief Justice John Marshall); (3) the problem of whether as literal as possible a reading of the Constitution's text ought to govern constitutional interpretation; and (4) the problem of securing a proper balance between the powers of the Federal Government and the powers of the states.

Before these questions are dealt with, however, certain matters require brief mention.

For one thing, to avoid asking the reader to turn back to earlier chapters and (where necessary) to re-familiarize himself with certain psychoanalytic doctrines, the chapters to follow will reintroduce (though with pertinent differences in form and content) some of the psychoanalytic material detailed in Part I. Also, to avoid sacraficing a much needed historical perspective for an elusive up-to-dateness when dealing with the basic questions of constitutional law to be considered in the text (after all, no discussion of constitutional law today can, in a sense, be as "up to date" as tomorrow's Supreme Court decisions), no attempt will be made in the pages to follow to analyze Supreme Court decisions that postdate the retirement of Mr. Chief Justice Warren.

Further, the chapters in Part II—each of which will treat in depth one of the fundamental problems of constitutional law listed above—will, perhaps inevitably, be more legalistic and technical (and require somewhat different and more extensive footnotes) than the chapters in Part I (in which, as has been seen, many possible legal applications of psychoanalytic tenets were suggested and considered briefly). Finally, it ought perhaps be noted here that considerable emphasis will be placed upon legal (and other) history in the chapters to follow—especially in Chapter X, in which the problem of securing a proper balance between the powers of the Federal Government and the powers of the states will be analyzed in the light of psychoanalytic psychology. Such an emphasis upon history is grounded in the conviction that to try to understand and possibly resolve the basic and perennial problems of constitutional law to be dealt with in Part II, a knowledge of legal (and related) history is essential. In these matters, "a page of history" (in the phraseology of Mr. Justice Holmes) may well be "worth a volume of logic."*

---

* New York Trust Co. v. Eisner, 256 U.S. 345, 349 (1921).

VII

JUDICIAL REVIEW OF LAWS ENACTED BY CONGRESS

NOWHERE IN THE CONSTITUTION is the Supreme Court (or, for that matter, is any court) expressly given the right to pass upon the validity of congressional legislation. Yet today, the right of the federal courts to determine whether such legislation is constitutional is usually taken for granted. Perhaps, as Professor T. R. Powell once suggested, this power of *judicial review*, so-called, "like Topsy ... just growed."[1] But if so, why should it have "growed"? Why should most Americans have acquiesced in its growth? After all, by building upon this right of judicial review—for which, to repeat, no express constitutional mandate exists—the Supreme Court succeeded in developing from what Alexander Hamilton regarded as "incontestably ... the weakest"[2] and by far "the least dangerous"[3] organ of government into what has been called "the most extraordinarily powerful court of law the world has ever known."[4]

Perhaps the two most usual reasons given for the development of judicial review of congressional legislation in the United States is that it was intended by the Founding Fathers and, in any event, was inevitable. "So far as the American Constitution is concerned," argues Professor Eugene V. Rostow, "there can be little real doubt that the courts were intended from the beginning to have the power they have exercised. *The Federalist Papers* are unequivocal; the Debates as clear as debates normally are. The power of judicial review was commonly exercised by the courts of the states, and the people were accustomed to judicial construction of the authority derived from colonial charters."[5]

It is true that (as Professor Rostow goes on to emphasize) Alexander Hamilton did assert in *The Federalist Papers* that the judiciary ought to have the right to rule upon the constitutionality of legislation.[6] But was it simply by chance that no explicit mention is made of this alleged right in the Constitution itself?[7] As Justice Gibson of Pennsylvania observed in his much-cited dissent in *Eakin v. Raub*,[8] had there been an intent to have the judiciary pass upon the validity of federal legislation, "the matter would surely not have been left in doubt. The judges would not have been left to stand on the insecure and ever shifting ground of public opinion as to constructive powers; they would have been placed on the impregnable ground of an express grant. They would not have been compelled to resort to the debates in the convention, or the opinion that was generally entertained at the time. . . . The grant of a power so extraordinary ought to appear so plain, that he who should run might read. . . ."

Still, the Supreme Court under John Marshall did assert very early in American history (in 1803 in *Marbury v. Madison*[9]) that it had the right to determine the constitutionality of laws enacted by Congress. This early assertion of the right of judicial review of congressional legislation would seem to lend support to Professor Rostow's contention that Americans at this time were already used to courts passing upon the validity of legislation.[10] As many eminent authorities on constitutional law (T.R. Powell, Learned Hand, and Edward S. Corwin, for example) have observed, however, the reasoning of Marshall in *Marbury v. Madison* simply does "not bear scrutiny."[11] Perhaps more important, the Court's decision in *Marbury v. Madison* was actually a strategic retreat rather than a bold exercise of judicial power. Though Marshall *asserted* in this case that the Court had the right to review the acts of Congress, what he actually decided was that the Court *lacked* the power to issue a writ of mandamus to Secretary of State Madison. In so deciding, Marshall not only avoided a potentially disastrous confrontation with President Jefferson over the Court's jurisdiction[12] but may also have avoided engendering a situation comparable to that which had occurred ten years earlier when the Court's decision in *Chisolm v. Georgia*[13] (recognizing the right of citizens of South Carolina to bring suit in the Court against the State of Georgia) provoked such determined opposition in Georgia and other states that it was, in effect, reversed by the Eleventh Amendment to the Constitution.[14]

Most significant, however, as a commentary upon Professor Rostow's view that judicial review of congressional legislation was intended and expected by our forefathers was the Supreme Court's failure after *Marbury v. Madison* to declare any law of Congress unconstitutional until the Court's decision in *Dred Scott v. Sandford* in 1857,[15] a decision that invalidated the Missouri Compromise and helped to precipitate the Civil War.[16] In fact, only after the Civil War did the Court really begin to play the role that it now plays; a role that, insofar as it is characterized by the Court's passing upon the constitutionality of laws enacted by Congress, is (as has been indicated) regarded by Professor Rostow and others as having been intended by the Founding Fathers—and as inevitable as well. Perhaps another way of describing the change in the Court's role after the Civil War would be to point out that at the time of the Constitutional Convention, and certainly until some time in the 1820's, the legislatures rather than the courts took precedence in declaring and administering the law. Only in the years following the Civil War did the courts really begin to exercise the power they now do and thereby begin to "capture popular imagination as the type and model of 'the law'."[17]

To turn now to the contention that judicial review of laws enacted by Congress was inevitable, no meaningful discussion is possible if one adopts the fatalistic view that whatever has happened was bound to happen, that because federal courts now determine the constitutionality of congressional legislation, they were bound to do so from the beginning.[18] But if this fatalistic view is set aside, then one is free to consider the inevitability of judicial review of congressional legislation in light of the practices of other nations with governments similar to our own.

In Switzerland, for example, the chief judicial institution is the Federal Tribunal, "but, unlike the Supreme Court of the United States, it is not the final authority on constitutional questions."[19] If the constitutionality of a national law is questioned, the matter may be resolved by a joint session of both houses of the legislature or by a referendum in which all citizens of the country may vote.[20] In Norway and Denmark, the government may seek the advice of the courts regarding the constitutionality of proposed laws; and in Sweden, consultation with the Law Council (composed in part of judges) regarding proposed legislation is a usual step in the law-making process.[21] But in all these Scandinavian countries, the "Supreme Courts do not appear to possess, and certainly do not exercise the power to declare laws unconstitutional."[22] In France under the Constitution of 1946, the Council (an elected but essentially advisory legislative group) had the right to pass preliminarily upon the constitutionality of legislation proposed by the Assembly. If the Council decided by majority vote that a proposed law was unconstitutional, the matter was referred for a decision to a Constitutional Committee (elected in part by the Assembly) which was set up at the beginning of each annual session of the Assembly.[23]

Further examples seem unnecessary to demonstrate that judicial review of national legislation is by no means inevitable in a constitutional democracy.[24] As observed above, there are a variety of ways in which the constitutionality of legislation may be determined. But is it not possible that special circumstances in American history or experience made judicial review of national laws inevitable in the United States?

This view finds support in the writings of Professor Edward S. Corwin, who in a landmark article The "Higher Law" Background of American Constitutional Law[25] traces the origin of the concept of judicial review to certain common law principles expressed in Coke's famous dictum in Bonham's Case[26]: "when an act of parliament is against common right and reason, or repugnant, or impossible to be performed, the common law will control it and adjudge such act to be void."[27] Corwin suggests that this idea of declaring acts of Parliament unconstitutional commended itself to Americans as a useful weapon in the agitation leading to the American Revolution.

Thus in 1765 the royal governor of Massachusetts Province wrote his government that the prevailing argument against the

Stamp Act was that it contravened "Magna Charta and the natural rights of Englishmen and therefore, according to Lord Coke," was "null and void"; and on the eve of the Declaration of Independence Judge William Cushing, later one of Washington's appointees to the original bench of the Supreme Court, charged a Massachusetts jury to ignore certain acts of Parliament as "void and inoperative," and was congratulated by John Adams for doing so.[28]

Undoubtedly, the concept of courts having the power to declare laws, and especially the acts of Parliament, invalid may well have proven attractive to Americans on the eve of the Revolutionary War. As Thayer has noted, however, this concept was voiced at such time by American judges largely as a "matter of speculation"[29]; and in no case was it enforced "where it was the single and necessary ground of the decision."[30] Further, in England—which is, after all, the home of the common law, the place where the common law sentiments that found expression in *Bonham's Case* developed—judicial review of the acts of Parliament never took root. Today in England (as, indeed, has been true since the decline of the power of the Crown), Parliament is supreme. English courts can, admittedly, delay changes decreed by Parliament by constructing parliamentary legislation "harshly." Ultimately, however, Parliament can prevail simply by passing a law that renders ineffectual a judicial decision contrary to the will of the members of Parliament.[31]

If, as the foregoing discussion has tried to suggest, the inevitability of judicial review of laws passed by Congress is questionable and if, as the preceding discussion attempted to reveal, it is also doubtful whether the Founding Fathers intended to grant to the federal courts the power to invalidate national laws—in short, if the two main reasons usually given for the existence of judicial review are (to say the least) arguable, then a basis would seem to exist to look beyond these reasons and to see whether psychoanalytic psychology can be of use in helping to explain why judicial review of congressional legislation came into existence and has persisted.[32]

As was pointed out in Part I, psychoanalytic psychology is built largely upon discoveries by Sigmund Freud and his fol-

lowers regarding the unconscious realm of the mind: for instance, upon the discovery that vestiges of the urges and ideas
of early childhood tend to remain in "the unconscious" (usually
referred to as the *id* in psychoanalytic writings) and to exert
at times a considerable influence upon behavior later in life.[33]
Pertinent here are the psychoanalytic findings, stressed in
Chapter IV, that symbolization (the use of a person, idea or
object to represent some other person, idea or object) is a prime
characteristic of unconscious mentation and that certain persons, ideas and objects are symbolized unconsciously in much
the same way by practically everybody.[34] Parents, for example,
are represented quite regularly on an unconscious level by
kings, queens and other exalted personages; and among these
other exalted personages that frequently serve as unconscious
parent symbols—and especially as unconscious father substitutes—are judges.[35]

One reason why judges may function so readily as unconscious parent symbols is that the role of the judge is akin to
that of the first "judges" a child knows: his parents. In the
words of Paul Reiwald: "The after-effect of childhood experience is particularly strong, if we encounter figures which later
in life play, in effect, a similar role to that played by the closest
early associations. Often enough the father represents the judge
to the child. So it happens that *later the judge represents the
father in man's unconscious.*"[36]

Not only the judges but the courts on which these judges
sit often serve as unconscious parent symbols. A ready example
would be the Supreme Court, which certainly "has a strong
symbolic hold over the American mind"[37] and, as Thurman
Arnold has suggested, may be "our most important symbol of
government."[38] Thus when the Supreme Court (or, for that
matter, any court or judge) declares an act of Congress to be
unconstitutional, this declaration may well be regarded unconsciously as an assertion of parental power: as a declaration
that as during childhood, the will of the parents or father takes
precedence and is supreme.[39]

Admittedly, it is difficult to imagine the hardy, self-sufficient
and often ruggedly individualistic pioneers who settled this

country as having any great need, conscious or unconscious, for such "parental" direction and control (other, perhaps, than the need fulfilled by a strongly held belief in an anthropomorphic God).[40] Indeed, herein may lie one of the reasons why from the time of the ratification of the Constitution until the Civil War—a period when America was led, first by the strong and determined generation that had successfully rebelled against England and then by their sons and grandsons who succeeded in pushing the frontier from the Appalachian Mountains to the Pacific Ocean—judicial review of the acts of Congress failed to take hold. But why then was judicial review of congressional legislation able to gain acceptance (though with some difficulty)[41] after the Civil War? Why has judicial review continued to persist since then?

To suggest that the Civil War was probably the most traumatic event in American history is hardly to advance a novel thesis. The War was, after all, one of the two major wars of the nineteenth century. ("In the size and the power of armies and in the losses sustained, the American Civil War was comparable to the Napoleonic struggles in Europe."[42]) Indisputably, the War wrought profound changes in the United States, "changes so basic that. . . .men like Henry Adams, who had lived abroad during the conflagration, were astonished—and somewhat appalled—when they returned to see the altered America that had emerged from the flames."[43] Further (and perhaps even more significant) interest in the Civil War continues to increase rather than to diminish with each passing year. As Alan Barker has observed, the Civil War is "the most popular historical subject in American history. It is the one which excites the most interest, the most acrimony and the most research. . . .No other nation except France has a subject of such abiding interest. In a sense it is true that the French Revolution of 1789 and the American Civil War are refought in every decade. . . ."[44]

Psychoanalysts have learned that terribly upsetting or traumatic events frequently stir up in the unconscious vestiges of the needs and desires of childhood. The pressure exerted by these resurrected childhood urges may be great enough to cause a significant change in behavior. In fact, these revived wishes may be so strong as to precipitate what psychoanalysts refer to as a "regression": a return or reversion to an earlier and more primitive mode of functioning.[45]

If, as psychoanalysts have discovered, traumatic events tend to stir up unconscious vestiges of the immature needs and desires of childhood; and if, as suggested above, the Civil War was the most traumatic event in American history, then the likelihood is that the Civil War aroused in many people childhood urges still extant on an unconscious level, including the very strong wish of childhood for parental guidance and control.[46] If it is now recalled that judges and courts frequently serve as unconscious parent symbols; and if it is also remembered that the striking down of congressional legislation by the judiciary may well be regarded unconsciously as an assertion of parental power, then it is conceivable that the unconscious wish for parental direction and control presumably stirred up in many people by the Civil War may have caused these people to be more willing than before to accept—indeed, to welcome—judicial review of congressional legislation.

Clearly, this admittedly speculative psychoanalytic explanation of why judicial review of the laws enacted by Congress gained acceptance after the Civil War is at best a limited or partial explanation,[47] since it fails to treat of matters that a sociologist, a political scientist, an historian, an economist, or others, might well deem highly relevant.[48] This inevitable difficulty aside, however, the problem still remains of explaining why judicial review persisted in the United States once the Civil War began to pass from memory into history: after all, once the childhood urges presumably aroused by the War began to subside, would not the need for "parental" direction and control by the Supreme Court also begin to subside?

At first sight, this would surely seem likely—and undoubtedly is to some extent true. Yet, indisputably, the Civil War had a deep and lasting effect upon many of those who witnessed or participated in it. Holmes, for example, who enlisted at twenty and served for three years in the Union Army, "continually turned back to his Civil War experience"[49] during the remainder of his ninety-four years (thirty of which were spent as an Associate Justice of the United States Supreme Court).[50] If interest in the Civil War continues to grow rather than to diminish (continuing, for example, "to provoke and inspire the most voluminous historical literature in America"),[51] then the Civil War would still seem capable of stirring considerable emotion and possibly also of arousing childhood needs and desires comparable to those it originally aroused.

More likely than memories or history, however, to stir up childhood urges capable of engendering the need for "parental" guidance by the judiciary have been the wars in which the United States has fought since the Civil War—the Spanish-American War, World War I, World War II, the Korean War and the Viet Nam War. Unhappily, the future may bring even more terrible and devastating wars: nuclear wars.

Possibly even more traumatic than the wars in which the United States has fought, have been the depressions that, especially since the rapid industrialization induced by the Civil War, have repeatedly affected the lives and fortunes of millions of Americans. Consider that "of the span between 1870 and 1910 about two-thirds of the years were years of depressions, long or short in duration: for example, 1873–1878; 1884–1887; 1893–1898."[52] He who may wonder how a depression, with its attendant misery and suffering may affect people—how, for example, it may stir up powerful demands for protection and succor by a parent substitute[53]—need only consult his memory or that of his parents regarding the Great Depression of 1929–1939.

Though the great depression began in the United States, it was accompanied by similar depressions all over the world, and within a very short time, persons in many nations seemed almost eager to exchange their freedom for the rule of an authoritarian leader or fuhrer.[54] In the United States, none of the men who offered themselves as such "leaders"—for instance, Fritz Kuhn, William Dudley Pelley and Huey Long—were able to gain national power. Yet one measure of the

very great need of Americans during the 1930's for the reas-
surance and feelings of security provided by parent symbols and
substitutes may perhaps be seen in the furious emotional reaction in 1937 to the Administration's attack upon the Supreme
Court, an attack that (as was pointed out in Chapter IV)
culminated in a plan under which Congress was asked to
authorize the appointment of an additional Supreme Court
Justice for each member of the Court who failed to retire at
seventy.[55]

Conceivably, this so-called Court packing plan was so out-
rageous that the tremendous emotional response it elicited was
fully justified. Still, the Court had (certainly during the 1930's)
"sought to engraft its own nineteenth-century laissez-faire
philosophy into the Constitution"[56] and in so doing had consciously and deliberately thwarted New Deal legislation designed to cope with the Depression.[57] For example, the Court
had stricken down such basic New Deal laws as the Railroad
Retirement Act, the Frazier-Lemke Farm Mortgage Act, the
National Industrial Recovery Act, the Agricultural Adjustment
Act and the Guffey Coal Act. Indeed, by June of 1936, the
New Deal had already lost fourteen of seventeen cases before
the Supreme Court.[58] This was, as Bernard Schwartz has put
it, "without a doubt, the apogee of the doctrine of judicial
supremacy."[59]

Despite this almost unprecedented expansion of judicial
review by the Supreme Court[60] (and despite the landslide victory that President Roosevelt had just won at the polls), the
reaction of a very large segment of the public to the Court
packing plan was so openly hostile, that the plan's defeat soon
became certain. Exactly why the public became so emotionally
aroused over the plan is a problem that clearly defies adequate
discussion in a sentence or two, whether the approach used is
psychoanalytic or otherwise. Still, once it is realized that the
Supreme Court frequently serves as an unconscious parent
symbol, mention ought to be made of the possibility (as was
done in Chapter IV) that many members of the public unconsciously interpreted the plan as an attack upon their parents

and reacted with understandable concern, alarm and, yes, panic as well.[61] In fact, once it is recalled that during the Depression, Americans (like so many other peoples) seemed to reveal an almost desperate need for "parental" guidance, then the emotionalism, hostility and panicky behavior with which many of them greeted the Administration's attempt to curb the Supreme Court seem almost to have been predictable.

The psychoanalytic explanation given in the preceding pages for the persistence of judicial review of laws enacted by Congress has been that the childhood needs presumably stirred up by the Civil War (needs which, *ex hypothesis*, engendered in part the desire for "parental" guidance by the courts) continued to have an effect for many years after the Civil War ended; and further, that comparable childhood needs (which also presumably found reflection in a desire for "parental" control by the judiciary) were aroused by the terrible wars and catastrophic depressions since the Civil War. By no means, however, does this (inevitably partial) psychoanalytic explanation exclude other pertinent reasons for the persistence of judicial review.[62]

Consider, for example, that during the 1870's and thereafter, many Americans began to exhibit a strong distrust of legislatures, a distrust that may well have resulted in a clinging to judicial review as a safeguard against legislative abuses. Indeed, the social historian Ralph Gabriel has contended that the "chief" reason for popular acceptance of judicial review by the Supreme Court was that this practice developed during a period of popular distrust of legislatures.[63]

> The Granger revolt of the 1870's had been directed against railroad control over state legislatures. The Populist crusade had as one of its objectives the purging of the Senate of the United States of millionaires and of political bosses. The initiative and referendum of the Progressive Era expressed popular discontent with the log rolling, the wire pulling, and the corruption to be found in state capitals. After 1920 the issue of the soldier's bonus dramatized the vulnerability of Congress when confronted with the demand of an insistent minority. In such a period the Supreme Court of the United States made itself the ultimate board of review not only for federal but for most of the impor-

tant state legislation. The citizens of the Republic accepted the revolution because they believed that the Court was above and beyond politics. It was a tribunal before which legislation could be discussed calmly and rationally. It was remote from the pressure politics of legislative lobbies. Its long record of impeccability put it above the suspicion of corruption.[64]

Another reason for the persistence of judicial review that deserves mention here has to do with the post–Civil-War decline of traditional religious observance in the United States (especially towards the end of the nineteenth century) and the concurrent emergence of a deeply emotional and extraordinarily reverential (perhaps even worshipful) attitude towards the Supreme Court as the leading interpreter of the Constitution.

> The Court . . . grew in importance as the social significance of religion declined. Churches do not dominate urban America as they once did the countryside and the rural village. As the religious interpretation of the fundamental law declined in prestige, the influence of the other interpreters increased. . . . The Supreme Court . . . replaced the Church as the American symbol of social stability.[65]

In the years following the Civil War, attributes normally ascribed by traditional religion to God (omniscience and omnipotence, for instance) may have been assigned by many Americans, albeit unconsciously, to the Supreme Court; and much of the reverence and veneration usually directed by these persons towards God may have been transferred by them onto the Supreme Court. If so, then it may have almost been predictable that just before the turn of the nineteenth century—the very time when the decline of traditional religion in the United States became most noticeable—judicial supremacy would reach its nineteenth century apogee.[66] It may also prove of interest to learn that from a psychoanalytic point of view, the displacement onto the Supreme Court of attributes normally associated with the god of traditional religion—in fact, the use of the Supreme Court as, in effect, a "substitute" for God—is almost to be expected at times, for the anthropomorphic god of the Judeo-Christian religions, like the Supreme Court, is frequently employed on an unconscious level as a parent substitute and as such may well be used interchangeably at times with the Supreme Court.[67]

The discussion in this chapter of the power of the federal courts (and ultimately, the Supreme Court) to pass upon the constitutionality of laws enacted by Congress began with an attempt to reveal the dubiety of the viewpoint (championed by Eugene V. Rostow) that the exercise of this power of judicial review was either inevitable or intended by the Founding Fathers. Then, the (admittedly partial) psychoanalytic explanation was advanced that judicial review gained acceptance after the Civil War because of the pressure exerted by childhood needs for parental direction and control stirred up by the War, needs which, *ex hypothesis*, engendered a desire for the "parental" direction and control implicit in judicial review. Further, it was suggested that judicial review persisted, not only because the childhood needs aroused by the War remained active for many years, but also because a succession of traumas after the War continued to stir up comparable childhood needs (which also presumably found reflection in judicial review).

During recent years, students of constitutional law have tended to assume that judicial review of the laws passed by Congress has been firmly and finally established.[68] As Professor Rostow has put it: "The debate over the legitimacy of judicial review, long-lived as it has proved to be, is settled by history."[69] If this view of judicial review is correct, then the material presented so far in this chapter would be largely of academic concern: interesting perhaps, but of little or no immediate practical value. To disagree once again with Professor Rostow, however, it is by no means certain that the debate over judicial review has been settled by history.

For one thing, if the twentieth century has proven anything, it is that very little is settled by history. Even in so "history-bound" an area as religion, this century has witnessed some remarkable changes (consider, for example, the profound changes wrought in Catholic doctrine and practice by the Ecumenical Council convened only a few years ago by Pope John XXIII). Further, judicial review may, as has frequently been contended, be inherently undemocratic.[70] To quote Alexander Bikel, "when the Supreme Court declares unconstitutional a legislative act . . . it thwarts the will of representatives of the actual people of the here and now; it exercises control, not in behalf of the prevailing majority, but against it. That, without mystic overtones, is what actually happens."[71] Thus if the future is likely to bring a greater insistence upon majority rule in the United States than now exists (and with this insistence, a corresponding diminution in the desire for counter-majoritarian safeguards), then history may ultimately prove to be not ally but an enemy of judicial review.[72]

Such speculation aside, however, it is indisputable that many attempts have been made since the Civil War to limit the Supreme Court's power to pass upon the constitutionality of congressional legislation. These attempts began with a determined attack upon the Court (and upon the presidency as well) launched by the Radical Republicans during the early years of Reconstruction, an attack that so intimidated the members of the Supreme Court that they carefully avoided passing upon the constitutionality of the restruction program.[73] Later, during the Progressive Era, a variety of attempts were made to curb the Court's power. For example, Senator William Borah proposed legislation requiring a minimum vote of seven justices to strike down a statute[74]; President Theodore Roosevelt campaigned for the right of popular recall of judges and judicial decisions[75]; and Samuel Gompers demanded a constitutional amendment giving Congress the right to revise Supreme Court decisions.[76] President Franklin D. Roosevelt's dramatic but unsuccessful Court packing fight in 1937 has already been mentioned. Often forgotten nowadays, however, is the congressional attack mounted on the Court during the late 1950's (partly because of decisions by the Court that appeared to hamper police investigations of crime and to frustrate attempts by the government to cope with communist subversion), an attack that came within a hairbreadth of limiting drastically the Court's appellate jurisdiction.[77]

If, as the preceding discussion has tried to suggest, the assumption that judicial review of congressional legislation has been firmly and finally established in the United States is questionable, then the likelihood certainly exists that debates regarding the desirability of judicial review will continue to take place in the future as they have so often in the past. Hopefully these debates will take into account the material stressed in this chapter, especially the psychoanalytic hypothesis that some of the support enjoyed by judicial review may be based upon the pressure exerted by unsatisfied childhood needs for parental direction and control. But even if this psychoanalytic view may fail to weigh heavily (if at all) in these debates, still knowing of the existence and effect of these immature wishes may aid many people in guarding against their influence. Minimizing the influence of such needs of childhood is surely desirable, if only to help make sure that so crucial a matter as whether or not the federal courts have the right to pass upon the constitutionality of congressional legislation will be decided not as a result of pressure exerted by these immature needs, but as a result of serious, informed, reflective adult thought.[78]

VIII

JUDICIAL ACTIVISM AND JUDICIAL SELF-RESTRAINT

I N 1905 in *Lochner v. New York*,[1] Mr. Justice Peckham declared for a majority on the United States Supreme Court that a New York statute forbidding the employment of bakers for more than sixty hours a week or for more than ten hours a day violated the due process clause of the Fourteenth Amendment of the Constitution and was therefore null and void. To quote from the majority opinion by Mr. Justice Peckham:

> There is no reasonable ground for interfering with the liberty of person or the right of free contract, by determining the hours of labor, in the occupation of a baker. There is no contention that bakers as a class are not equal in intelligence and capacity to men in other trades or manual occupations, or that they are not able to assert their rights and care for themselves without the protecting arm of the State, interfering with their independence of judgment and of action. . . . Statutes . . . limiting the hours in which grown and intelligent men may labor to earn their living, are mere meddlesome interferences with the rights of the individual.[2]

As Mr. Justice Holmes observed in his classic dissent, however:

> This case is decided upon an economic theory which a large part of the country does not entertain. If it were a question whether I agreed with that theory, I would desire to study it further and long before making up my mind. But I do not conceive that to be my duty, because I strongly believe that my agreement or disagreement has nothing to do with the right of a majority to embody their opinions in law. . . . I think that the word liberty in the Fourteenth Amendment is perverted when it is held to prevent the natural outcome of a dominant opinion, unless it can be said that a rational and fair man necessarily would admit that the statute proposed would infringe fundamental principles as they have been understood by the traditions of our people and our law.[3]

The position taken by Mr. Justice Peckham in *Lochner v. New York* and the views expressed by Mr. Justice Holmes in his dissent in this case mirror respectively two very different judicial attitudes that have repeatedly found reflection in American constitutional history. Peckham was a judicial activist; and like such eminent jurists of the past as Marshall, Field, Fuller and Sutherland (and like Black, until his death in 1971), he was ready and willing to step in and correct what he regarded as abuses and, if need be, to substitute his views for those of the legislature (or executive); in fact, to make of the Supreme Court at times what Harold J. Laski and others have described as "a third [legislative] chamber in the United States."[4] Conversely, Holmes believed in judicial self-restraint. His views regarding the limited role the judiciary ought to play were in the tradition of such influential justices as Taney (the *Dred Scott* decision[5] notwithstanding) and Waite and later served as a basis for the advocacy of judicial self-restraint by such renowned jurists as Brandeis, Learned Hand, and Frankfurter. Holmes insisted that courts ought (except in extraordinary circumstances) to defer to the popular will as it found expression in legislative enactments; and if Holmes had been on the United States Supreme Court in 1876, he would probably have concluded with Waite that "For protection against abuses by legislatures the people must resort to the polls, not to the courts."[6]

Paradoxically, activist judges on the Supreme Court have, in the main, been reluctant to admit to their activism.[7] In *Adkins v. Children's Hospital*,[8] for example, Mr. Justice Sutherland declared that "This Court, by an unbroken line of decisions from Chief Justice Marshall to the present day, has steadily adhered to the rule that every possible presumption is in favor of the validity of an act of Congress until overcome beyond rational doubt."[9] Yet this statement of high principle failed to deter Mr. Justice Sutherland from declaring in the majority opinion in this case that a statute fixing minimum wages for women and children was unconstitutional. Later, in *United States v. Butler*[10] (in which the Supreme Court struck down basic New

Deal legislation designed to help alleviate the terrible plight of the farmers in the United States during the catastrophic depression of the 1930's), the then activist Mr. Justice Roberts blithely stated that the Court "neither approves nor condemns any legislative policy"; rather, all that the Court does is "to lay the article of the Constitution which is invoked beside the statute which is challenged and . . . decide whether the latter squares with the former."[11] A comparatively recent and egregious example of this selfsame denial of activism by activist judges is to be found in *Miranda v. Arizona*,[12] decided by the Supreme Court in 1966. In this case, the Court promulgated rules that it held must (in the future)[13] govern the interrogation of suspects in police custody[14] and in so doing clearly made "new law and new public policy."[15] Yet even so, Mr. Chief Justice Warren (speaking for the majority on the Court) declared early in the Court's decision that "We start here . . . with the premise that our holding is not an innovation in our jurisprudence."[16]

Despite all this, it would be inaccurate to conclude that activist judges have never admitted to trying to substitute their views for those of the legislature—never admitted to adopting what T. R. Powell has described as a "judges know best" attitude. In *Nebbia v. New York*,[17] for instance, the activist Mr. Justice McReynolds contended in his dissent that when Supreme Court justices seek to determine the constitutionality of a legislative enactment, they ought to concern themselves not only with its purpose ("whether the end [sought] is legitimate, and the means [employed] appropriate") but also with the "wisdom of the enactment."[18] In Anglo-American jurisprudence, a classic example of this "judges know best" attitude is provided by Coke's celebrated conversation with King James regarding the latter's desire to expand royal powers vis-a-vis the courts and the law.

> Then the King said, that he thought the law was founded upon reason, and that he and others had reason, as well as the Judges: to which it was answered by me, that true it was that God had endowed his Majesty with excellent science, and great endow-

ments of nature; but his Majesty was not learned in the laws of his realm of England, and causes which concern the life, or inheritance, or goods, or fortunes of his subjects, are not to be decided by natural reason but by the artificial reason and judgment of law, which law is an act which requires long study and experience, before that a man can attain to the cognizance of it . . . with which the King was greatly offended, and said, that then he should be under the law, which was treason to affirm, as he said; to which I said, that Bracton saith, *quod Rex non debet esse sub homine, sed sub Deo et lege.*[19]

Unfortunately, the statements made by those few judicial activists who have been willing to admit even in part to their activism fail to provide much of a basis for generalizing meaningfully regarding the basic reasons for judicial activism. Trying to extrapolate such reasons from the cases decided by judicial activists is of little or no use, for the values these cases have protected and promoted have varied greatly over the years. Mr. Chief Justice John Marshall and Mr. Chief Justice Earl Warren, for example, both deserve the name "judicial activist"; yet John Marshall's activism was devoted largely to defining and strengthening federal powers and to ensuring the inviolability of property rights, whereas Earl Warren's activism was devoted in large measure to protecting the civil rights of minorities presumably unable to protect themselves. Again, in the post–Civil-War era, judicial activist Mr. Justice Stephen J. Field was almost obsessive in his preoccupation with protecting capital and business from what he feared would be "a war of the poor against the rich"[20]; and in recent years, a similar intenseness was discernible in the statements of activist Mr. Justice Hugo L. Black—with reference in this later era, however, to the need to prevent any infringement of the freedoms (of religion, speech, press, assembly, and petition) guaranteed by the First Amendment to the Constitution, freedoms which Black insisted were "absolutes."[21]

As Mr. Chief Justice Stone once intimated in a much mooted footnote in *United States v. Carolene Products Co.,*[22] judicial activism may well become appropriate (in fact, may well be a necessary adjunct of the democratic process) when legislation "restricts those political processes which can ordinarily be expected to bring about a repeal of undesirable legislation"[23] (when, for example, the legislature so manipulates the election laws as to prevent an electoral majority from designating a legislative majority). Yet, in the main, is not the thrust of judicial activism essentially counter majoritarian? Does not judicial activism ordinarily imply rule by one or a few rather than rule by the legislative representatives of the many? Is there not something inherently oligarchic and undemocratic in the conduct of judges who (acting as though they have been granted legislative powers) attempt to resolve problems that have traditionally been considered within the province of the legislature and, where need be, substitute their views for those of duly elected legislators who presumably seek to carry out the wishes of the electorate?

By no means does it follow, however, that oligarchic or undemocratic practices are necessarily undesirable or un-American. The electoral college, the indirect election of senators and the President's right to veto legislation are but three of a variety of nondemocratic devices that the Founding Fathers deliberately inserted into the Constitution. In so doing, the Founding Fathers may have conceivably revealed an overacute awareness of the danger of unrestrained rule by a majority degenerating into mob rule.[24] Still, as Thucydides pointed out more than two thousand years ago, when a people in the name of democracy commit the conduct of government to the unrestrained "whims of the multitude" (as apparently was done in ancient Athens during the Peloponnesian War),[25] disintegration and self-destruction become all too likely.

The contention that judicial activism is essentially undemocratic is one of the arguments advanced by those jurists who favor a policy of judicial self-restraint (and who, it might be added, seem far more willing to admit to their self-restraint than judicial activists have been willing to admit to their own activism). In addition, however, certain other contentions by proponents of judicial self-restraint deserve mention here.

For one thing, advocates of judicial self restraint often point out that judicial activism almost inevitably tends to involve courts in the political conflicts of the age, with the resulting danger that partisan emotions aroused by these conflicts will be directed towards the courts and seriously diminish their prestige. This happened after the *Dred Scott* decision, for instance, and during the 1930's when the Supreme Court began to strike down New Deal legislation.

Those who favor judicial self-restraint also frequently contend that judicial activism tends to debilitate popular government: such activism, it is asserted, "deflects responsibility from those on whom in a democracy it ultimately rests—the people."[26] Or, to quote a blunter statement of this theme: "a people must make their own salvation and not expect it to be served up to them by the judges."[27]

Another reason advanced by proponents of judicial self-restraint for eschewing judicial activism is that judges frequently lack the breadth of view needed to make policy in some areas and the expertise needed to make policy in other areas. "Judges," it is contended, "because of the highly specialized and concentrated education in law and the training in professional practice that they have undergone, are. . .manifestly not the best equipped persons for translating community values into constitutional policies, and the concept of judicial notice . . .is hardly an adequate tool for the fact-finding necessary to an informed policy choice."[28] Indeed, the frequently seen tendency to appoint men to the Supreme Court with broad experience in public life or expertise in certain nonlegal areas may reflect in part the view that "informed policy-making requires intellectual qualities transcending the boundaries of strict professional competence."[29]

Perhaps the most persuasive of the objections to judicial activism raised by advocates of judicial self-restraint has to do with attempts by activist judges to use lawsuits as a vehicle for policy-making in areas of traditional legislative concern. The bringing and prosecution of lawsuits is, after all, largely dependent on the whims of litigants; and the decisions rendered in these lawsuits frequently turn upon arbitrary, and sometimes highly unusual fact patterns. As Mr. Justice Frankfurter has stressed: "Courts are not equipped to pursue the paths for discovering wise policy. A court is confined within the bounds of a particular record, and it cannot even shape the record. Only fragments of a social problem are seen through the narrow windows of a litigation. Had we innate or acquired understanding of a social problem in its entirety, we would not have at our disposal adequate means for constructive solution."[30]   In short, it can be argued that the inherent limitations of a lawsuit provide judges with very good reasons indeed for eschewing the role of legislators and for following a policy of judicial self-restraint.

But (and there is always a "but" when contrasting the relative merits of judicial activism and judicial self-restraint), despite the arguments in favor of judicial self-restraint described above, activist judges have, indisputably, played a significant role in the transformation of the United States from a loose aggregate of poor and weak colonies into the world's strongest and wealthiest nation. The decisions of such great activist judges as Mr. Justice Joseph Story and Mr. Chief Justice John Marshall, for example, were of crucial importance in the development of a strong and effective Federal Government in the United States, a government that was able to emerge victorious and more powerful than ever from the bloody struggle with the champions of state's rights during the Civil War. Further, it was such activist pro-business judges as Mr. Justice Stephen J. Field and Mr. Justice Rufus W. Peckham who helped to make possible the phenomenal growth of American industry, and in so doing, helped to pave the way for America to serve as the "arsenal of democracy," first during World War I and later during the climactic struggle with Fascism and Nazism during World War II. Finally, in such leading cases as *Brown v. Board of Education of Topeka*,[31] *Baker v. Carr*[32] and *Miranda v. Arizona*,[33] the judicial activists of the past decade or so (most certainly Mr. Chief Justice Earl Warren and Mr. Justice Hugo L. Black) led the way in dealing with problems that legislators had previously seemed unwilling or unable to face up to: the problem of racial segregation in the schools, the disproportionate rural representation in state legislatures, and the protection of the civil rights of persons accused of crimes.

Admittedly, these arguments are by no means unanswerable: counter arguments can readily be formulated (as indeed, can replies to such counter arguments). Still, as perhaps can be seen from the material presented so far, the arguments that have been formulated regarding judicial activism and judicial self-restraint seem unlikely, by themselves, to provide a definitive basis for choosing between this activism and this self-restraint. Hence, instead of continuing to try to construct similar arguments, it might prove more useful here to introduce certain psychoanalytic concepts (as was done in the disscussion in the preceding chapter regarding the power of the federal courts to pass upon the constitutionality of congressional legislation), in an effort to determine whether such psychoanalytic material can help to provide a basis for choosing between judicial activism and judicial self-restraint.

Psychoanalysts place considerable emphasis upon the goal of psychic independence—upon man's need to free himself from emotional dependence upon his parents. As Erich Fromm has put it: "To cut through the navel string, not in the physical but in the psychological sense, is the great challenge to human development and also its most difficult task."[34] Or in the words of Sigmund Freud: "From the time of puberty onward the human individual must devote himself to the great task of freeing himself from the parents; and only after this detachment is accomplished can he cease to be a child and so become a member of the social community."[35] In addition, however, psychoanalysts stress that parents must help children to gain the courage and strength needed to exist separately. The mother, according to Erich Fromm, "must not only tolerate, she must wish and support the child's separation."[36]

These concepts have found ready application in psychoanalytically oriented studies of politics, especially in conjunction with the psychoanalytic discovery that nations and their leaders are often regarded unconsciously as parent symbols or substitutes and as such frequently serve as legatees of parent-oriented desires and feelings.[37] Psychoanalysts have noted, for example, that when a State is unduly supportive, its citizens tend "to transfer to the State that attitude of dependence which...[was] originally adopted in relation to...[the] parents, failing to extent to attain that...full development of individual power, initiative and self-reliance which can only be obtained by a high degree of emancipation from the primitive attitude of dependence on the parents."[38] Similarly, psychoanalysts have noted that in totalitarian States—those nations in which the leaders say, in effect: "Leave everything to me. I will take care of you. You are not to think. Just obey my commands."[39] —the very real danger exists that the citizenry will fail to become responsible, mature and self-reliant but will instead tend to become increasingly "dependant emotionally on the father-image provided by the dictator or the state apparatus."[40]

Clearly the relationship between a State and its citizens differs from that between judges and legislators (and the people these legislators represent). Once it is recalled, however (as was pointed out in the discussion of the right of federal judges to pass upon the constitutionality of laws enacted by Congress), that judges are frequently regarded unconsciously as parent-substitutes, then one cannot help wondering whether the activist judge who refuses to defer to the popular will as it finds expression in legislative enactments, and who seeks instead to substitute his views for those of the legislature, may arouse in legislators (and ultimately in the electorate) parent-oriented dependent needs and feelings akin to the needs and feelings engendered in the citizenry by the leaders of unduly supportive or dictatorial regimes. In fact, some such possibility may have been sensed by Thayer at the turn of the century when he noted that judicial activism tends to induce the electorate to "become careless as to whom they send to the legislature; too often they cheerfully vote for men whom they would not trust with an important private affair, and when these unfit persons are found to pass foolish and bad laws, and the courts step in and disregard them, the people are glad that these few wiser gentlemen on the bench are so ready to protect them against their more immediate representatives."[41]

Unlike the judicial activist, the judge who exercises judicial self-restraint (who seeks not to maximize but to minimize his role in the legislative process) almost inevitably tends to underscore the need for emotionally mature and self-reliant legislators (and, in turn, the need for an informed and responsible electorate). On an unconscious level, such a judge would presumably be regarded more like the parent who desires and supports his child's independence than the parent who seeks to keep his children psychically dependent upon him. If so, then rather than arousing the parent-oriented dependent feelings that, as pointed out above, may well be engendered by the judicial activist, the judge who practices judicial self-restraint may help to foster the growth of self-reliance and emotional independence—not only in legislators but in the electorate as well.

By no means, however, ought it to be concluded from the preceding discussion that psychoanalysis necessarily favors judicial self-restraint as opposed to judicial activism. For one thing, no attention has yet been given to the relevence of psychoanalytic tenets regarding passivity and activity.

For the psychoanalyst as well as for such renowned thinkers of the past as Aristotle and Goethe, activity is, in most instances, preferable to passivity.[42] In fact, psychoanalysts believe that one of the soundest measures of a person's emotional health is the extent to which he actively seeks to master life's inevitable challenges rather than passively sitting by and letting these challenges overcome him.[43] Bernard Baruch may well have caught the essence of this psychoanalytic attitude when he declared "That old 'nothing can be done' philosophy never did appeal to me. I have never believed that man had to lie down dumbly before anything, whether flood, fire, famine, disease, drought, earthquake. . .or. . .war."[44]

The psychoanalytic preference for activity rather than passivity is based in part upon psychoanalytic studies which reveal that one of the more useful measures of healthy emotional development during early childhood is the willingness, speed and completeness with which a child outgrows the so-called passive-receptive stage of childhood (a time when the child tends to rely almost exclusively upon influencing his parents or parent substitutes to get what he wants) and then goes on to try to do things and get things for himself.[45] Further, psychoanalysts have learned in their daily work with patients that passivity is in very many instances a regressive reaction to a failure of activity—"a regression to the more primitive passive-receptive type of mastery of the outer world following. . .failure to succeed in an active way."[46] In addition, passivity may prove to be dangerous, in that it tends to find expression in "a helpless state of expectation which makes the individual susceptible to shocks. . . ."[47] Indeed, the more passive a person is, the more likely he is to succumb to the onslaught of the ultimate in mental illness—psychosis.[48]

To continue now by aligning activity with judicial activism and passivity with judicial self-restraint may seem at first sight to be unduly facile—especially if the conclusion is then drawn that insofar as psychoanalysis favors activity, so must it favor judicial activism; and insofar as psychoanalysis deprecates passivity, so must it deprecate judicial self-restraint. After all, judicial activism may camouflage (as compulsive activity sometimes does) deep-rooted passive desires[49]; and judicial self-restraint may conceivably reflect a sophisticated activism that permits legislators to accomplish its objectives for it. In most instances, however, when a judicial activist on the Supreme Court votes to grant *certiorari* so as to be able to pass upon the constitutionality of legislation and then after examining the legislation votes to strike it down as repugnant to the Constitution (as judicial activists on the Supreme Court did so often during the New Deal era) ; or when a judicial activist finds it impossible to sit by and wait for legislators to remedy social abuses that seem to him to cry out for correction and instead boldly sets out to remedy these abuses by enunciating new law (as the Supreme Court surely did in *Brown v. Board of Education of Topeka, Baker v. Carr* and *Miranda v. Arizona*) ; the judicial activist is being far more active than passive and in this sense is behaving in a manner approved of by psychoanalysis. Conversely, when a judge who believes in judicial self-restraint declares that if social abuses are to be corrected, it is the duty of the legislature, and not of the courts, to remedy these abuses and that if the legislature fails to remedy these abuses, "the people must resort to the polls, not to the courts"[50]; or when a judge who advocates judicial self-restraint refuses to pass upon or to strike down legislation, contending that (within certain limits) it is his duty to permit a dominant opinion to find expression in the law (as Holmes, Frankfurter and other believers in judicial self-restraint have so frequently contended); the likelihood is that the judge is being more passive than active and in this sense is adopting a course of conduct that psychoanalysis would disapprove.

Thus, as indicated above, the psychoanalytic preference for activity and the concomitant psychoanalytic rejection of passivity would seem to favor judicial activism rather than judicial self-restraint. Yet, as was seen in the preceding discussion of the psychoanalytic goal of psychic independence, psychoanalytic tenets regarding man's need to free himself from emotional dependence upon his parents would appear to support judicial self-restraint instead of judicial activism. This seeming impasse may be resolved, however, once attention is given to what for the lawyer is a most significant body of psychoanalytic knowledge: psychoanalytic discoveries concerning the "court" or "judge" that rules man from within: man's superego.

The superego (one of three major and related mental agencies identified in psychoanalytic writings and already described in some detail in Chapter III)[51] is frequently referred to by psychoanalysts as the "judicial branch of the personality."[52] As such, the superego (which, though largely unconscious, includes what is ordinarily meant by the term "conscience" and in a sense is comparable to what psychologists used to label man's "moral faculty") performs certain functions, including "(1) the approval or disapproval of actions and wishes on the grounds of rectitude, (2) critical self-observation, (3) self-punishment, (4) the demand for reparation or repentance of wrongdoing, and (5) self-praise or self-love as a reward for virtuous or desirable thoughts and actions."[53]

As was pointed out in Chapter III, man's moral faculty or superego does not exist at birth. Rather, it develops slowly and tentatively during the first few years of life. In fact, only when a child reaches the age of six years or so—the time when the child unconsciously internalizes ("introjects") the image he has formed of his parents—does the superego proper come into existence. From then on, the superego—as the successor and representative of the child's parents—rules the child from within, as his parents once ruled him from without.[54]

Though originally a sort of internalized (and largely unconscious) parent image, the superego (if at all healthy) fails to remain simply as such. Rather, as was noted in Chapter III, it generally develops and changes, most usually by having new authorities (teachers and political leaders, for example) replace (though only in part) the internalized parent image. Further, the parent-like vigilance and imperiousness of the superego's strictures tend to diminish to some extent. In the emotionally mature, however (and unfortunately, all too few persons deserve to be so described), there seem to be further superego changes as well: the superego becomes not so much an advocate of the values and goals of parents and other authority figures as of the person's own values and goals—in short, not so much "other-directed" as "self-directed."[55]

To go on now to suggest that the superego's role vis-a-vis man is, in a sense, akin to the role of a judge vis-a-vis legislators whose laws he passes upon may seem, at least at first sight, to be farfetched. Yet if, as indicated above, the superego, like the judge, often functions (though in a somewhat different way) as an unconscious parent substitute; and if, as can be seen from the list of superego activities detailed above (particularly the basic superego activity of indicating "approval or disapproval of actions and wishes on the grounds of rectitude"), the superego and the judge frequently act in similar ways; and if, as even a cursory examination of judicial decisions soon reveals (for example, decisions of the Supreme Court during the 1930's overturning New Deal legislation, or decisions by the Court during the past decade or so striking down legislative attempts to circumvent the judicial ban on school segregation set forth in *Brown v. Board of Education of Topeka*), judges often behave as though they were the censors or conscience of society itself;[56] there would then seem to be some basis for comparing the role of the superego vis-a-vis man to that of a judge vis-a-vis legislators whose laws he passes upon.

When, therefore, judges who believe in and practice judicial self-restraint (be these judges "self-directed" or "other-directed," emotionally mature or emotionally immature) try not to be "the Supreme Censor(s) of all legislation"[57], but instead permit the dominant opinions of legislators (which presumably reflect the dominant opinions of the public) to find reasonably free legislative expression, it can be argued that these judges are acting in a manner similar to that of the superego of the emotionally mature person which seeks not to try to impose upon him what are really the values and goals of others, but rather to allow his own values and goals to express themselves. Conversely, when activist judges (who may be "self-directed" or "other-directed," emotionally mature or immature) intervene in the legislative process by striking down legislation that reflects views contrary to their own,[58] or enunciate what as in *Brown v. Board of Education of Topeka, Baker v. Carr, and Miranda v. Arizona* clearly amounted to new judge-made law, it can be argued that their behavior is akin to that of the immature superego which seeks to force upon a person what are in reality the values and goals of others, instead of permitting his own intrinsic values and goals to develop and ultimately find expression. In short, psychoanalytic discoveries regarding the superego would seem, at least on the preceding basis, to favor judicial self-restraint rather than judicial activism.

As psychoanalysts have learned, however, the emotionally mature "self-directed" man is, comparatively speaking, a rarity. So far as psychoanalysts have been able to ascertain, most men are (albeit in varying degrees) governed by a less than mature, "other-directed" superego; and to this extent, at least, have a need for authoritarian or "parental" direction and control.[59]

Thus insofar as legislators truly reflect their constituents, these legislators would also presumably be governed to a considerable extent by an "other-directed" parent-oriented superego; and like their constituents would also presumably have a need for "parental" guidance and control—especially by such authority figures as judges, who frequently serve as unconscious parent symbols.[60] If so, it can then be argued that judges who believe in and practice judicial self-restraint may well fail to provide the direction and control legislators require. Conversely, judicial activists who, in effect, intervene in the legislative process and try to impress upon the law their own solutions to unresolved social problems may well be responding to a very real need of legislators for authoritative leadership regarding these problems.[61]

From this point of view then, psychoanalytic discoveries concerning the superego would appear to favor judicial activism rather than judicial self-restraint. But isn't such a finding contrary to the conclusion advanced previously that psychoanalytic discoveries regarding the superego seem (albeit on a somewhat different basis) to lend support to judicial self-restraint? In addition, doesn't this finding compound the seeming confusion resulting from psychoanalytic doctrines concerning psychic independence appearing to favor judicial self-restraint, whereas psychoanalytic doctrines pertaining to passivity and activity seem to favor judicial activism?

Implicit in these questions is the view that psychoanalysis (or at least psychoanalytic tenets concerning a particular topic) if at all relevant to judicial activism and judicial self-restraint ought to point to one or the other. Yet is it not possible that psychoanalytic tenets, especially in the aggregate, point to a need for *both* judicial activism and judicial self-restraint; and that rather than providing a means for helping to choose between judicial activism and judicial self-restraint, psychoanalysis may instead lend support to the view that *both* judicial activism and judicial self-restraint are useful and desirable?

If so, then knowing this may prove of considerable value, if for no other reason than it may help to produce a greater open-mindedness than now exists among the proponents of judicial activism and among the champions of judicial self-restraint. It may, for example, cause the proponents of judicial activism to be less certain than before that the arguments supporting their position are irrefutable and, by the same token, induce such persons to be more willing than before to appraise with patience and respect the contentions advanced by advocates of judicial self-restraint. Further, knowing that psychoanalysis appears to lend support to both judicial activism and judicial self-restraint may help to induce the champions of these respective positions (and persons who are presumably "uncommitted" as yet) to face up to the indisputably vital role that *both* judicial activism and judicial self-restraint have played in the constitutional history of the United States. Indeed, one of the great (but, as yet, seemingly insufficiently understood) lessons of American constitutional experience may well be that the United States needs *both* its judicial activists and its practitioners of judicial self-restraint: both its John Marshalls and its Felix Frankfurters.

IX

THE LITERAL APPROACH TO CONSTITUTIONAL INTERPRETATION

DESPITE THE POPULARITY of the view (certainly prior to the advent of the Warren Court) expressed in Mr. Dooley's celebrated remark that "th' supreme coort follows th' iliction returns,"[1] and despite the indisputable element of truth in the more reverent and seemingly contrary view expressed in the observation noted by John Chipman Gray that "whoever hath an *absolute authority* to *interpret* any written or spoken laws, it is he who is truly the Law-giver,"[2] few if any responsible students of constitutional law would seriously contend that the text of the Constitution ought to be considered irrelevant when the Supreme Court interprets the Constitution. However, the converse view that constitutional interpretation ought, so far as is possible, to turn upon a close reading of the text of the Constitution has found many responsible advocates from the Constitution's inception to very recent times.[3]

Perhaps the most dramatic modern expression of the viewpoint that the mainspring of Constitution interpretation ought to be as literal as possible a reading of its words was the late Mr. Justice Black's insistence that the Bill of Rights (especially the First Amendment) contained "absolute" prohibitions. Specifically, Mr. Justice Black contended that the language of the First Amendment—"Congress shall make no law . . . abridging the freedom of speech, or of the press"—meant not that a "balancing of interests"[4] or other similar standard of constitutional interpretation was to be used to determine the validity of congressional legislation restricting freedom of speech or of the press, but rather that no congressional laws abridging freedom of speech or of the press—none whatsoever—were to be tolerated.[5] "I read 'no law . . . abridging' to mean no law abridging," Black insisted.[6]

Far more consistent and thoroughgoing than Black in demanding a literal interpretation of the Constitution, however, was Mr. Justice Sutherland, who served on the Supreme Court from 1922 to 1938. In *West Coast Hotel v. Parrish*,[7] for example, Sutherland insisted that "the meaning of the Constitution does not change with the ebb and flow of economic events" and that those who contend that "the words of the Constitution mean today what they did not mean when written . . . rob that instrument of the essential element which continues it in force."[8] Again, in *Home Building and Loan Association v. Blaisdell*,[9] Sutherland (quoting Taney) declared that insofar as "the Constitution remains unaltered [by amendments] it must be construed now as it was understood at the time of its adoption . . . it is not only the same in words but the same in meaning."[10] In reply to those who would require judges who pass upon the constitutionality of laws to take into account society's ever-changing desires and needs, Sutherland not only stressed that constitutional interpretation "cannot be aided by counting heads"[11] but went on to assert that "If the provisions of the Constitution be not upheld when they pinch as well as when they comfort, they may as well be abandoned."[12]

Despite Sutherland's belief that the decisions he rendered turned upon the exact phraseology of the Constitution, students of constitutional law have contended that many of his decisions striking down remedial social legislation reflected not so much the words of the Constitution as *laissez-faire* economic theories that Sutherland and other like-minded judges seemed to be trying to read into the Constitution.[13] Of course, *the* classic example in American constitutional history of a judicial opinion purportedly rendered in strict accordance with the words of the Constitution, but which actually went far beyond these words, is Mr. Chief Justice Taney's opinion in *Dred Scott v. Sandford*.[14] Taney, it will be recalled, insisted in this opinion that the Constitution "speaks not only in the same words but with the same meaning and intent with which it spoke when it came from the hands of its framers"; and hence, it "must be construed . . . as it was understood at the time of its adoption."[15] Yet despite these professed sentiments, Taney's decision that Dred Scott, being a Negro, could not be a citizen of the United States and that Congress was prohibited from regulating slavery in the territories of the United States clearly went far beyond a literal reading of the words of the Constitution.[16] Inded, this very divergence between the professions and practices of some Supreme Court justices may have prompted T. R. Powell to remark (in unduly caustic fashion, perhaps): "some Supreme Court justices . . . seek to impress upon us in effect that it is not they that speak but the Constitution that speaketh in them. Somehow this reminds me of the biographer who wrote of Gladstone that his conscience was not his guide but only his accomplice."[17]

Assuming, however, that a judge not only declares that the Constitution means no more or less today than what it meant in 1787 (with the exception of the amendments), *but in addition, he reveals in the decisions he renders an intent to so interpret the Constitution,* how is he to discover exactly what the Constitution meant when it was first adopted?

One seemingly obvious way to learn what the Constitution meant at first would be to examine the intentions of its framers (as, for example, one might examine the intentions of legislators to determine the meaning of legislation they had voted for). Unfortunately, however, it is by no means an easy task to ascertain the legislative intentions of the Constitution's framers.

For one thing, it is not at all clear who the framers of the Constitution actually were. Is it to be assumed, for example, that they were the maximum of fifty-five delegates who attended the Constitution Convention or only the thirty-nine delegates who finally signed the Constitution? This question admits of no easy answer, for a number of the thirty-nine signers of the Constitution said little or nothing during the meetings of the Convention and were present for only relatively short periods of time, whereas four of the Convention's most active and hardworking delegates (Elbridge Gerry, Luther

Martin, George Mason and Edmund Randolph) refused to sign the Constitution when it was finally completed.[18]

But even if it were possible to agree as to who the framers of the Constitution really were, determining their legislative intentions would still present a formidable problem since the Convention's sessions were held in secret and the records that have survived are "mainly unofficial and decidedly incomplete."[19] It is known, for example, that Gouverneur Morris was an active member of the Convention and one of the Constitution's main final stylists; yet the records available of the views and intentions of Gouverneur Morris are, to say the least, "disappointingly incomplete."[20] The beliefs of such other members of the Convention as Alexander Hamilton are well-documented. Yet Hamilton was but one among a number of the signers of the Constitution who, partly because of aristocratic leanings, had grave doubts about the wisdom of some of its clauses. In fact, the greatest service of the then 81-year-old Benjamin Franklin to his country may have been his ability to induce his fellow delegates to sign the Constitution, even though there was much in it that was contrary to their individual wishes.[21] In short, it is difficult to avoid the conclusion that "there was no single 'intention of the framers' as to the Constitution as a whole, beyond perhaps the generalities of the Preamble and the intention to submit the Constitution to the people for adoption as a measure that might result in more effective government."[22]

Perhaps it also ought to be noted here that if the meaning of the Constitution is to be determined by looking to the intentions of its framers, then not only their intentions but the legislative intentions of the framers of its twenty-odd amendments would have to be examined as well. He who would seek to undertake this task had better keep in mind that there is considerable disagreement regarding the legislative intentions of the framers of some of the amendments. For instance, what the "framers of the 14th Amendment intended has become a subject for debate almost as keen as the debate over the intentions of the original framers."[23]

If, then, the legislative intentions of the Constitution's framers are, to say the least, far too debatable and unclear so as to provide sufficient guidance to the judge who insists that the Constitution means today what it meant in 1787 and that he intends to so interpret it, perhaps he can determine what the Constitution meant when it was first adopted by seeking not to ascertain these apparently elusive legislative intentions but rather by simply *seeking to determine what the words used in the Constitution actually meant in 1787.*

By far the most ambitious and best known of the attempts to ascertain the original meaning of the words used in the Constitution is Professor William W. Crosskey's two-volume work published in 1953: *Politics and the Constitution in the History of the United States.* In these volumes, Professor Crosskey makes a prodigious effort to provide his readers with what he describes as "a specialized dictionary of the eighteenth-century word-usages, and political and legal ideas, which [he asserts] are needed for a true understanding of the Constitution."[24] Unfortunately, however, Professor Crosskey fails to dispel the generally held view that the original meaning of the words used in the Constitution is "as difficult to establish as the intention of the Framers."[25]

Professor Crosskey's failure to lay bare the original meaning of the Constitution is traceable in part to such causes as his insistence that from the beginning, the Supreme Court constantly misinterpreted the Constitution[26]; his championing of the dubious thesis that the Constitution's framers intended to establish "a unitary national system of government with no regard for states' rights"[27]; and his straining of the evidence to document these theories.[28] Requiring separate attention here, however, is Professor Crosskey's methodological assumption that thorough enough research will reveal a consensus among the delegates to the Constitutional Convention regarding the meaning of all of the words of the Constitution—including the meaning of what have proven to be its most mooted clauses.[29]

Unfortunately for Professor Crosskey's theories, it is doubtful (especially in regard to many of the Constitution's more controversial clauses) that such a semantic consensus ever existed. As John P. Roche has put it: "The Convention was not a seminar in analytic philosophy or linguistic analysis. . . . The delegates were in a hurry to get a new government established; when definitional arguments arose, they characteristically took refuge in ambiguity."[30]   Such well-known phrases of the Constitution as "necessary and proper," "the general welfare," "obligation of contracts" and "commerce . . . among the several states," for instance, are believed by many authorities on constitutional law to have been purposely ambiguous[31]; and in so being, to reflect what has been termed the Founding Fathers' "genius for studied imprecision or calculated ambiguity."[32] Thus if the Constitution contains phrases designed to be less than clear (or, if you will, "designed to have . . . the chameleon's capacity to change . . . color with changing moods and circumstances")[33]—then those who like Professor Crosskey seek to establish the "true" meaning of the Constitution by searching for the original meaning of all of its words, search in vain.

Even more significant for purposes of constitutional interpretation than the Constitution's ambiguities are the many matters that the Constitution simply passes over in silence. For example, although the Constitution provides in article III for the establishment of a Supreme Court, no explicit statement is made in the Constitution delineating the Court's powers (stating, for instance, whether or not the Court has the right to pass upon the constitutionality of congressional legislation—a matter which, as observed in an earlier chapter, has caused what would seem to be endless controversy). Or, to use an example cited by Mr. Justice Jackson: although Congress is granted power under the Constitution to regulate commerce among the states, the Constitution fails to "say what the states may or may not do in the absence of congressional action . . . [or] how to draw the line between what is and what is not commerce among the states."[34]

Some of these so-called "great silences"[35] of the Constitution are believed to have been the result of the Founding Fathers' desire to avoid raising matters that might have jeopardized the Constitution's ratification by the states.[36] But in addition, it may well be contended that the very nature of a constitution tends to preclude too great specificity. Mr. Chief Justice John Marshall so believed; and in 1819 in the celebrated case of *McCulloch v. Maryland*[37]—in which the Supreme Court ruled that despite the Constitution's complete silence regarding the establishment of a national bank, Congress had the right to create it (and the states lacked the power to tax it)—Marshall declared

> A constitution to contain an accurate detail of all the subdivisions of which its great powers will admit, and of all the means by which they may be carried into execution, would partake of a prolixity of a legal code, and could scarcely be embraced by the human mind. It would probably never be understood by the public. Its nature, therefore, requires, that only its great outlines should be marked, its important objects designated, and the minor ingredients which compose those objects be deduced from the nature of the objects themselves. That this idea was entertained by the framers of the American constitution, is not only to be inferred from the nature of the instrument, but from the language . . . . we must never forget that it is a *constitution* we are expounding.[38]

Whether or not jurists who seek to interpret the Constitution literally find these views expressed by Marshall to be acceptable, the fact is that the Constitution has proven to be either extremely vague or completely silent regarding most of the great problems that the Supreme Court has been called upon to resolve. Indeed, Professor Leonard L. Levy has contended that the Constitution offers no more help than "the comic strips . . . on how to decide most of the great cases that involve national public policy, whether the question relates to legislative apportionment, racial segragation, the regulation of utility rates, subversive activities, the curtailment of crop production, or the seizure of steel mills."[39] In short, the many silences of the Constitution—be they "great" or small—would appear to reduce the literal approach to constitutional interpretation (except in a limited number of clear-cut cases) largely to an exercise in futility.

Perhaps *the* fundamental difficulty inherent in attempts to interpret the Constitution literally has to do with the assumption implicit in such attempts that the Constitution is essentially static: that (except for the amendments) it neither grows nor changes and hence (with the exception of the amendments) means today exactly what it meant in 1787.

One method of trying to disprove this assumption that the Constitution means no more now than it did in 1787 would be to point out, as have many authorities on constitutional law, that the Founding Fathers may have deliberately written the Constitution in such a way that (without resort to the formal amending procedures described in article V) constitutional development could take place. Mr. Justice Frankfurter, for example, believed that the Constitution was "designed . . . with purposeful vagueness," so as to make possible—in fact, so as to invite—constitutional growth and change.[40] Similarly, Professor Alexander M. Bickel has asserted that the Constitution's framers deliberately wrote what only amounted to "chapter headings," thereby leaving it to future generations "to write the text."[41] Professor Robert G. McCloskey has contended that "The framers . . . said in effect: with respect to certain questions, some of them very momentous, the Constitution means whatever the circumstances of the future will allow it to mean."[42]

Admittedly, these views concerning the actions of the Founding Fathers may well be speculative. Nevertheless, it is indisputable that the Constitution now has a gloss of almost two hundred years of judicial interpretation. Though a judge called upon to interpret the Constitution would presumably have sworn in his oath of office to support and defend the Constitution itself (and not the gloss put upon it by his predecessors), he would surely be seriously remiss if he failed to take this gloss into account when interpreting the Constitution. A court asked to interpret the contract clause of the Constitution,[43] for instance, would certainly be expected to take into consideration relevant judicial decisions of the past concerning this clause—judicial decisions which, beginning with Chief Justice Marshall's seminal opinion in *Fletcher v. Peck*[44] and his even more powerful opinion in *Trustees of Dartmouth College v. Woodward*[45] have clearly gone far beyond the original meaning of the contract clause.[46] Similarly, a court required to interpret the commerce clause of the Constitution[47] would hardly ignore the relevant judicial history of this much-construed clause—judicial history which, given direction in 1824 by Marshall's far-reaching decision in *Gibbons v. Ogden*,[48] has witnessed the stretching of the meaning of the words of this clause beyond recognition.[49]

By no means is all this to suggest that the Supreme Court is necessarily bound by the judicial history of the Constitution. There have been many cases in which the Supreme Court has chosen, as Mr. Justice Douglas has put it, "to re-examine its own doctrine."[50] In 1954 in *Brown v. Board of Education of Topeka*,[51] for example, the Supreme Court, in effect, overruled its 1896 decision in *Plessy v. Ferguson*[52] and in so doing rendered unconstitutional a practice of at least fifty-eight years in many southern states of providing "separate but equal" facilities for Negroes. Similarly, in *Erie R.R. Co. v. Tompkins*,[53] decided in 1938 (a case which, from the point of view both of the practicing lawyer and the legal theoretician, is surely one of the most significant judicial decisions of this century), the Supreme Court overruled *Swift v. Tyson*,[54] decided by it back in 1842, and thereby discarded, in effect, ninety-six years of "general law" developed in the federal courts.

The overturning of precedents of such long standing by the Supreme Court and especially its actions in such leading cases as *Pollock v. Farmers Loan and Trust Co.* (in which, in 1894, it first divided four to four on the constitutionality of the income tax[55] and later the same year, declared the income tax to be unconstitutional[56]) and *Knox v. Lee*[57] (in which, in 1871, it repudiated its invalidation of the Legal Tender Acts fifteen months before in *Hepburn v. Griswold*[58]) have cast doubt upon the view (championed especially by Mr. Justice Holmes and

Mr. Justice Brandeis) that the Constitution is "a living organism",[59] and that as such, the meaning of its provisions "is to be gathered . . . by considering their origin and the line of their growth."[60] That is, although looking upon the Constitution as "a living organism" may appear to be plausible when the Supreme Court follows and reasons from its prior decisions and in so doing tends to stretch gradually the meaning of the Constitution; the contrary appears to be true when the Supreme Court openly and repeatedly overturns precedents—especially precedents of short duration that could not as yet have possibly been "outgrown."

This very repudiation by the Supreme Court of its own decisions, however, reveals as dramatically as perhaps anything could that the Supreme Court has interpreted the Constitution quite differently at different times. Indeed, a number of scholars aware of the diverse ways in which the Supreme Court has interpreted the Constitution's clauses have suggested that the work of the Supreme Court might well be compared to that of a "continuous constitutional convention" which continually modifies the Constitution in accordance with society's ever-changing needs.[61] Thus *despite the assumption* (noted earlier) *implicit in attempts to interpret the Constitution literally that the Constitution is essentially static and means today exactly what it meant in 1787* (with the exception of the amendments), *the fact is that the Supreme Court has failed to treat it as such.* Rather, the Supreme Court has, in the main, tended to act in accordance with the precepts of Mr. Justice Holmes, who declared that the words of the Constitution "must be considered in the light of our whole experience, and not merely in that of what was said a hundred years ago."[62] In fact, many Supreme Court justices have simply taken it for granted that the Constitution's meaning changes with changing times and conditions, believing with Mr. Chief Justice Hughes that "If by the statement that what the Constitution meant at the time of its adoption it means today, it is intended to say that the great clauses of the Constitution must be confined to the interpretation which the framers, with the conditions and outlook of their time, would have placed upon them, the statement carries its own refutation."[63]

Such a taking for granted of the Constitution's mutability by many Supreme Court justices might conceivably be the product of unthinking judicial aggrandizement. Yet the assumption that the Constitution has changed and will probably continue to change may also be based upon the realization that the Constitution's very survival may well depend upon its adaptability in the face of changing times and circumstances. If the Constitution had been interpreted in a rigidly literal fashion from the beginning and if as a result, the Constitution had proven incapable of helping Americans to cope successfully with the new and difficult problems that changing times and circumstances inevitably brought, it might soon have been discarded as a useless relic of the dead past. To quote Bernard Schwartz: "It is true . . . of a Constitution that 'The letter killeth': it can hardly serve as a living instrument of government if read in a purely literal vacuum."[64] However, the Supreme Court has mainly aided the development of the Constitution as a useful and useable instrument of government. Instead of permitting what has been described as an "antiquarian historicism"[65] to govern constitutional interpretation, most Supreme Court justices have played a part in helping to stretch and, in effect, to alter boldly at times the Constitution's clauses. In so doing, these justices have enabled the Constitution to continue to be relevant to society's ever-changing needs and thus to continue to endure as "the fundamental law of an ever-developing people."[66]

The possibility that the rejection of the literal approach to constitutional interpretation by most Supreme Court justices may well have enabled the Constitution to survive as a useful and useable instrument of government would seem to be reason enough to view with hesitation and suspicion, if not with alarm, attempts to have constitutional interpretation turn upon a close reading of the Constitution's text. Yet as the discussion in the preceding pages has sought to reveal, there are many other persuasive reasons why the literal approach to constitutional interpretation appears to be deserving of rejection. For one thing, the basic assumption implicit in the literal approach that the Constitution is essentially static and means today exactly what it meant in 1787 is, as has been seen, erroneous. Also, as Mr. Chief Justice John Marshall observed in *McCulloch v. Maryland*,[67] a constitution (as compared with a detailed legal code) is to be expected to be general and incomplete; and hence, it is hardly surprising that the many "great" and small silences of the Constitution have tended to defeat attempts to interpret the Constitution in a literal manner. Similarly, as was observed in the discussion of Professor Crosskey's unsuccessful efforts to determine the original meaning of the words of the Constitution, the probability that the Founding Fathers failed to reach a semantic consensus regarding some of the Constitution's more controversial clauses (revealed especially by the ambiguous words and phrases that appear throughout the Constitution) has also helped to reduce attempts to interpret the Constitution literally to exercises in futility. Further, those who hope to interpret the Constitution literally can gain comparatively little help from efforts to study the legislative intentions of the Constitution's framers, for the records available of these intentions are, at best, incomplete and unclear, and it is difficult to determine exactly who the Constitution's framers actually were. Finally, mention ought to be made once again of the failure of jurists who declare that they have interpreted the Constitution literally to succeed in actually doing so (a failure that appears to have caused T. R. Powell to doubt "the capacity or the candor" of such jurists).[68]

If the preceding reasons for rejecting attempts to have constitutional interpretation turn upon a close reading of the Constitution's text are truly persuasive, why then have some jurists persisted in making such attempts? One possible way of answering this question would be to suggest that efforts to interpret the Constitution literally reflect the view that such is the surest way to achieve stability and certainty in the law.[69] Another possible approach to this question would be to take into account what has been variously termed "constitutional fetishism," "the cult of the Constitution" or simply "Constitution worship" and to suggest that efforts to interpret the Constitution literally may reflect the belief of "Constitution worshippers" that it is a sacred document, the meaning of which must be sought in a close reading of its text.[70] The approach to be used here, however, will be the same as that employed in earlier chapters regarding judicial review of congressional legislation and judicial activism *versus* judicial self-restraint; that is, an attempt will be made to determine whether psychoanalytic tools and insights can help to explain why a number of jurists have persisted in believing—some (Mr. Justice Black, for example) almost to this very day—that a literal reading of the words of the Constitution ought to be the mainspring of constitutional interpretation. However, as before, it will be kept in mind that any psychoanalytic explanation adduced is likely to be a *partial* explanation, which must be supplemented by explanations based upon the data of such other disciplines as history, sociology, economics and political science.[71]

Psychoanalysts, following the lead of Sandor Ferenczi (one of Sigmund Freud's most influential disciples), have identified a number of stages in the cognitive development of children.[72] For example, psychoanalysts have noted the existence of a so-called animistic period, during which the one- or two-year-old appears to believe that things as well as people are alive, feel and react.[73] More important for present purposes, however, psychoanalysts have identified a later period of cognitive development—the stage of the "omnipotence of words"—during which the two- or three-year-old seems to overestimate greatly the power of words. As Gerald S. Blum has put it: "There arises [in the child] a magical belief that one can master what one can name . . . . The child's earliest speech is a charm directed toward forcing the external world to do those things which have been conjured up in words."[74] Indeed, the child appears to believe at times that words can, in a physical sense, create or destroy: that words are somehow equivalent to acts.

. . . words frequently become, for the child, a substitute for action. He obtains from them a hallucinatory satisfaction: When he cannot get what he wants by acting, he often turns to words as a method for obtaining what he desires. With words he creates his own reality. . . . The child . . . is a wishful thinker and . . . finds that words are an invaluable aid for creating a desired picture of events. . . .[75]

In short, the period of the omnipotence of words is a time when words seem capable of accomplishing extraordinary things—a time of word magic.[76]

It may be theoretically possible for a child to pass so very successfully through the stage of the omnipotence of words that no unconscious traces of his "magical" treatment of words remain in his mind.[77] It is far more likely, however, that some unconscious vestiges of this stage will survive in his mind; and like remnants of other periods and aspects of early childhood, they will play a significant role during adulthood.[78] The fact that traces of the stage of the omnipotence of words may be found in the strange and seemingly senseless verbalizations of severely regressed schizophrenics is, for instance, well established—as, indeed, is the connection between this stage and obsessional neurotic disturbances in which a person repeatedly feels compelled to utter (or not to utter) certain word patterns, in the hope of thereby warding off fantasied dangers.[79] But more important here, the influence of the magical ideas of childhood regarding words is also to be seen in the behavior of many normal persons—in the oaths they pronounce, in the poetry they write, in the obscenities they utter, in the blesses and curses they voice and in the ritualistic mumbo jumbo they often employ when, for example, they induct members into secret organizations.[80]

Whether and to what extent these selfsame vestiges of the childhood stage of the omnipotence of words may find reflection in the insistence by some jurists that a literal reading of the words of the Constitution ought to govern constitutional interpretation can hardly be ascertained definitively in the absence of a thoroughgoing psychoanalytic investigation of these jurists and of the judicial opinions they have rendered.[81] Nevertheless, persuasive reasons do exist for believing that the insistence of such jurists that constitutional interpretation ought to turn upon the closest possible reading of the Constitution's text reflects the influence of traces of the magical ideas of childhood regarding words.

For one thing, there is a similarity between the attitude towards words of the judge who seeks to interpret the Constitution literally and the attitude towards words exhibited by the child during the period of the omnipotence of words. The judge who seeks to resolve today's most difficult social problems by searching the Constitution for a word or two that might be considered relevant (in spite of the fact that it is unrealistic for him to believe that the Constitution's text resolves or even refers to many of these problems) would appear to be acting like the child who thinks that if he can only discover the name for something he can thereby master it. Indeed, even if the Constitution actually did refer (whether in a word, in a phrase or even in a sentence or two) to many or most of the difficult problems of modern-day life, such a reference could hardly be expected to provide a sufficiently clear or complete blueprint for the solution of the vast majority of these problems. To believe otherwise is, in a sense, to react like the child who (equating words with deeds) thinks that if he is able to utter a few words or phrases somehow relevant to a desired event, he will thereby be able to cause this event to occur. In short, the judge who advocates the closest possible reading of the words of the Constitution as the mainspring of constitutional interpretation would, like the child during the stage of the omnipotence of words, appear to have an unrealistic and irrational confidence in the power of words: to be a believer in word magic.

To suggest that unconscious vestiges of the childhood period of the omnipotence of words may find reflection in the insistence of some jurists upon a literal interpretation of the Constitution is, of course, to assume that the behavior of these jurists (like the behavior of their fellowmen) is to some extent influenced by unconscious traces of the ideas and feelings of early childhood.[82] Admittedly, some scholars still appear to believe that they themselves and the work they do are somehow immune to unconscious influences.[83] Edwin W. Patterson, for example, declared in the 1953 edition of his text on jurisprudence that he was "not impressed by an appeal to an 'unconscious' . . . to explain human conduct"; and he went on to contend that even though the unconscious "may be something with which . . . all judges and lawyers are tainted along with other men . . . it has not been shown to have any distinctive bearing on law or its administration."[84] Nevertheless, as was pointed out in Chapter II, some of America's most famous jurists—Mr. Justices Holmes, Cardozo and Frankfurter, for instance—observed many years ago that unconscious forces may influence significantly the work of lawyers and judges.[85] In fact, in an article praising Mr. Justice Holmes and his work, Mr. Justice Frankfurter declared that the unconscious may play "an enormous role in the exercise of the judicial process."[86] Further, a number of psychoanalytic studies ranging from Freud's landmark case histories to reports by modern psychoanalysts reveal that the behavior of lawyers and judges, like that of other human beings, is almost inevitably affected by unconscious traces of the thoughts and urges of early childhood.[87] In the words of Ranyard West: "Underneath the mind that tries always to remember that it is the mind of a lawyer . . . is the mind of the child, self-seeking, apprehensive of fraternal rivalry, and, more deeply still, seeking the satisfaction of infantile desires and the soothing of infantile fears."[88]

Unconscious vestiges of such infantile feelings and ideas may, as Jerome Frank has suggested, be aroused more frequently in lawyers and judges than, for example, in chemists and physicists—if for no other reason than the law, as contrasted with chemistry and physics, deals regularly with very personal and highly emotion-laden matters, akin to those with which a young child is sometimes greatly concerned.[89] In fact, Jerome Frank devotes a considerable portion of his well-known work *Law and the Modern Mind* to these and related considerations, pointing out, among other things, that the magical ideas of childhood regarding words (and particularly the tendency to exaggerate the influence and the power of words) would appear to play a large role in the thinking of a number of lawyers and judges.[90] If Frank is right, then it is certainly conceivable that unconscious remnants of the childhood stage of the omnipotence of words may well have a significant effect upon the briefs these lawyers write and the opinions these judges render.

As pointed out in prior chapters, however, it hardly follows from this that the opinions a judge renders are nothing but "a justification of the personal impulses of the judge"[91] or that these opinions are "little more than a special plea made in defense of impulses which are largely unconscious."[92] Unconscious urges may, to some extent, help to mold judicial opinions; but so do logic, reason, precedent and myriad social, political, economic and personal considerations.[93] For example, as Morris R. Cohen observed in his work *Reason and Law*, it is indisputable that the reasons given by judges in many leading cases (and certainly in such outstanding decisions as *Marbury v. Madison* and *McCulloch v. Maryland*) have had a profound impact upon the subsequent development of the law.[94] Nevertheless, if unconscious traces of the magical ideas of childhood regarding words may well have a significant effect upon the opinions some judges write, then herein may be found some support for the view that the similarities pointed out earlier in this discussion between such magical notions and the literal approach to constitutional interpretation are not simply coincidental but rather that the literal approach to constitutional interpretation may actually *reflect the influence* of unconscious vestiges of these magical ideas of childhood concerning words.

Not only are there similarities between the child's attitude towards words during the period of the omnipotence of words and the attitude towards words of jurists who demand a literal interpretation of the Constitution, but comparable similarities appear to exist between these magical ideas of childhood and many other aspects of the law.[95]

Real property law, for instance, provides many examples that call to mind the tendency of the child during the period of the omnipotence of words to overestimate greatly the power of words—in fact, to believe that words can actually create or destroy. Consider that at the common law, a successful *inter vivos* transfer of a fee simple in Blackacre from A (its owner in fee simple) to B required use of the words "to B and his heirs." If, for example, A used the words "to B in fee simple," or even "to B forever," all that B got was a life estate.[96] Thus the phrase "to B and his heirs" was infused with a sort of magic: *only if this phrase was used could A successfully convey a fee simple in Blackacre to B.*[97] Of course, by far the best-known and most feared "magical" formula of the law of real property is the Rule Against Perpetuities: the rule (unless modified by statute) that, with certain exceptions, a future interest in real property must vest, if at all, within "lives in being and twenty-one years".[98] It is a fortunate lawyer indeed whose career has not witnessed the "amending" by a court of a document drawn by him disposing of real property because he failed to consider a highly remote but theoretically possible chance that some contingent future interest in the property might vest beyond "lives in being and twenty-one years."[99] Thus, like the child during the stage of the omnipotence of words, the law of real property, in effect, invests certain phrases with great potency—in fact, with such potency that, in a legal sense, these phrases can (as the child believes that words actually can) create or destroy.

An even more glaring example of the law's tendency (akin to that of the child during the period of the omnipotence of words) to treat words as though they can create or destroy is to be found in the situation which arises when an attorney asks a trial judge to strike from the record certain words that a witness has just uttered and to instruct the jury to disregard these words. The assumption seems to be that the judge's instructions to the jury will somehow destroy whatever effect the striken testimony may have had upon the jury. But is this assumption, if made, really tenable? To quote the psychoanalyst Lawrence Kubie: "It is unrealistic to assume that the officially 'stricken-out' words do not influence feelings and thoughts because no one talks about something . . . to which an objection has been raised and sustained. This is as naive as is the parent's idea that what the child does not talk about is not affecting profoundly the child's feelings and actions."[100] As Robert Keeton points out in his book on trial tactics, requiring a trial judge to instruct the jury to disregard certain testimony may result not in the testimony being disregarded by the jury but rather in the jury giving it greater attention and thought.[101]

Other illustrations of the law's tendency to exaggerate the power of words can be found in common law rules concerning the word formulas known as the "forms of action": in the rule, for example, that the cause of action proven at the trial must match exactly the form of action chosen by the plaintiff at the beginning of the case.[102] Thus, at the common law, a plaintiff who proved a valid cause of action in *trespass* would be non-suited if he had begun the suit under the form of action known as *trespass on the case*; or if he proved at the trial a cause of action in *assumptsit*, he would be nonsuited if he had brought the suit under the form of action called *debt*.[103] Admittedly, the law has become far less strict regarding matters of form than it was at the common law or even than it was several generations ago, when convictions were reversed on such absurdly technical grounds as a written verdict reading "guily" rather than "guilty," or reading "murder in the *fist* degree" instead of the "first" degree, or because the word "the" was omitted from the constitutionally prescribed formula in the original indictment.[104] Yet even today this selfsame demand for phraseological "correctness" finds reflection in reversals on appeal; for example, in reversals on appeal because in a judge's charge to a jury "a phrase, or a sentence, meaningless to the jury . . . [was] included in or omitted from the charge."[105] The words "meaningless to the jury" deserve emphasis here, for it is notorious that jurymen all too often fail to understand completely or properly a judge's charge, especially if (as is usual) the charge contains legal words of art that have "acquired their meaning as the result of hundreds of years of professional disputation in the courts."[106]

Little perspicacity is needed to point to additional illustrations of the treatment of words by the law that call to mind the extraordinary emphasis that the child places upon words (as well as his misapprehensions as to what words can actually accomplish) during the period of the omnipotence of words—to point, for instance, to the word magic inherent in the so-called judicial oath taken by witnesses before they testify at trials.[107] It is believed, however, that a sufficient number of examples have been given so as to reveal that striking similarities exist between the magical ideas of childhood regarding words and the attitude towards words to be found in a number of diverse areas of the law. Indeed, the existence of these similarities suggests that the comparable likenesses described earlier between the child's attitude towards words and that of judges who seek to interpret the Constitution literally may (as was suggested in the discussion of the influence of unconscious traces of the stage of the omnipotence of words upon the opinions rendered by judges) be more than coincidental—and may, in fact, be part of a larger pattern in which unconscious remnants of the childhood period of the omnipotence of words play a part in molding not only the literal approach to constitutional interpretation but other aspects of the law as well.

Admittedly, it is one thing to know that unconscious vestiges of the childhood stage of the omnipotence of words may play a causal role in attempts by jurists to interpret the Constitution literally (as well as have other effects upon the law) and quite another thing to prevent these vestiges of childhood from so influencing the judicial process. As psychoanalysts learned many years ago, simply explaining to a patient the unconscious dynamics of why he acts as he does—why, for example, he has fear of heights or of crowds, or why he feels compelled to count the letters in signs he sees on the streets or in the words he utters—usually fails to prevent him from so acting again.[108] Nevertheless, insofar as men are free to guide their behavior by logic and reason (and contrary to the general, and erroneous, impression that psychoanalysis denies the view inherent in the law that man is endowed with free will),[109] knowing that the demand for a literal interpretation of the Constitution is not only intellectually indefensible but also reflect the magical ideas of childhood concerning words may well result in judges emphasizing far less frequently than in the past the desirability of constitutional interpretation turning upon a close reading of the words of the Constitution. Hopefully, the legal and psychoanalytic material presented in the preceding pages will help to contribute to this end.

X

BALANCING FEDERAL AND
STATE GOVERNMENTAL POWERS

DURING THE PAST two decades, the Supreme Court (acting ostensibly under the Fourteenth Amendment to the Constitution) has extended the authority of the Federal Government and limited the hegemony of the states in regard to such matters as legislative apportionment, the civil rights of Negroes and the treatment of persons accused of having committed a crime.[1] Typical, in a sense, is the leading case of *Mapp v. Ohio*[2] decided in 1961, in which the Supreme Court held that it was reversible error for evidentiary matter obtained in an unreasonable search and seizure to be introduced into evidence in a state criminal prosecution. In so deciding, the Supreme Court—reversing its own ruling of only twelve years before in *Wolf v. Colorado*[3]—imposed upon state courts the same judicially created rule of evidence that (not in response to a specific congressional or constitutional mandate but rather in the exercise of the Court's supervisory powers over the federal judiciary) it had previously imposed upon the federal courts.[4] "The *Mapp* case," to quote Professor Francis A. Allen, "subjects the state officer to a constitutional standard of performance no lower or different from that governing federal law enforcement." As such, the *Mapp* case "intrudes farther into areas of local policy and self-determination than earlier decisions of the Court affecting state criminal procedures" and in so doing almost inevitably requires "more frequent and extensive assertion of federal power" in these areas than in the past.[5]

The Supreme Court's readiness during the past number of years (revealed so unambiguously in the *Mapp* case) not only to increase federal power in certain areas at the expense of the powers of the states but to do so by freely overruling precedents has evoked considerable opposition. This opposition has expressed itself in part in a barrage of charges leveled at the Court. For example, the Court has been accused of usurping the legislative function[6] and of adopting "the role of policy maker without proper judicial restraint."[7] Also, the Court's frequent overturning of precedents (and the seeming disregard of the knowledge and wisdom of the past implicit in these reversals) has led to charges of intellectual arrogance—indeed, to the charge that the Court's behavior has made a mockery of the "American boast that we have a government of laws and not of men."[8] In addition, the Court has been accused of so limiting the powers of the states as to make it difficult for useful social experiments to be undertaken (as in the past) within the insulated areas of the separate states. Conversely, the Court has been accused of so extending the powers of the Federal Government as to raise the specter, not only of a wearying and deadening uniformity among the states but also of totalitarian control by an unduly powerful central government.[9]

What is significant about these charges for present purposes is not so much their validity or invalidity, but rather that similar if not identical charges have been made in the past when (as has happened repeatedly for more than 175 years) attempts have been made to alter the balance of federal and state powers. Since it is the perenniality of these efforts to find a satisfactory balance between the powers of the Federal Government and those of the states (and the extremely strong emotional reactions that such efforts have so often produced in the past) that are of central concern here, some of the highlights of the long and dramatic history of efforts to balance federal and state governmental powers in the United States will now be considered.

The thirteen American colonies that declared their independence from England in 1776 considered themselves to be thirteen independent and sovereign states, each with the right to conduct its own affairs as it saw fit. Largely because of the exigencies of the Revolutionary War, however, these colonies soon banded together and ratified what is often referred to as the first American constitution—the *Articles of Confedera-tion*.[10] Though under the Articles of Confederation each state retained its "sovereignty, freedom and independence," author-ity was delegated to a central government—a single legislative body known as the Congress of the Confederation—to perform such vital governmental functions as signing treaties, borrow-ing money and raising armies.[11] Unfortunately, however, the Congress of the Confederation found itself unable to perform these governmental functions in a satisfactory manner. To quote from Professor Andrew C. McLaughlin's celebrated study of the Articles of Confederation: "the Congress of the Confederation . . . could ask for money but not compel pay-ment; it could enter into treaties but not enforce their stipula-tions; it could provide for raising of armies but not fill the ranks; it could borrow money but take no proper measures for repayment; it could advise and recommend but not com-mand. In other words, with some of the outward seemings of a government, and with many of its responsibilities, it was not a government."[12] Yet despite these indisputable weaknesses, the Articles of Confederation *did* constitute a useful experi-ment in government; at the very least it provided what Pro-fessor Morris D. Forkosch has termed "a start towards fed-eralism,"[13] in that it attempted to divide powers between two "sovereign" governments operating in the same territory, an arrangement that was soon to find more permanent form in the Constitution of the United States.

In 1787, the Congress of the Confederation passed a reso-lution calling for a convention to be held in Philadelphia "for the sole and express purpose of revising the Articles of Con-federation."[14] This call for a convention stemmed in large measure from a meeting held in Annapolis the year before, where the persons who had attended had stressed the need to find ways of overcoming the trade barriers that had been erected among the states during the years that the Articles of Confederation had been in force.

> . . . some of the states, which having no convenient ports for foreign commerce, were subject to be taxed by their neighbors

through whose ports, their commerce was carried on. New Jersey, placed between Philadelphia and New York, was likened to a cask tapped at both ends: and North Carolina, between Virginia and South Carolina, to a patient bleeding at both arms.[15]

Fortunately for the future of the United States, however, most of the delegates to the Convention (who met in Philadelphia in the late spring and summer of 1787) soon revealed a willingness to disregard their instructions: rather than simply trying to patch up the Articles of Confederation, they proceeded instead to write a new document—the Constitution of the United States—and in so doing, brought into being a far more powerful central government than had previously existed.

Under the new Constitution, the Federal Government was to consist not only of a legislative branch but also of an executive branch and a judicial branch. The legislative branch (now bicameral rather than unicameral) was to have a number of new powers, including two that, under the old Articles of Confederation, had been conspicuous by their absence: the power "To lay and collect Taxes, Duties, Imposts and Excises" and the power "To regulate Commerce with foreign Nations, and among the several States, and with the Indian Tribes."[16] Indeed, as was pointed out earlier in Chapter IX, Professor William W. Crosskey has advanced the thesis that the powers granted to the Federal Government under the Constitution revealed a desire by the delegates who attended the Philadelphia convention to create a centralized unitary nation with little or no regard for states' rights.[17] However, such a thesis is, to say the least, dubious: the evidence available of the debates at the Convention (and certainly the political realities of the time) indicates that the very most the delegates could realistically expect to have ratified by the states (such ratification being essential for the Constitution to take effect) was a more equitable balance of powers than had previously existed between the central government and the state governments, a balance that would hopefully enable the new national government created by the Constitution to survive the challenges that were almost certain to arise during the post-Convention years.[18]

One of the earliest and most dangerous challenges to the Constitution and the balance it tried to establish between the powers of the Federal Government and those of the state governments had to do with the amenability of the states to direction and control by the federal judiciary. Article III of the Constitution provided for the existence of a federal judiciary and listed certain situations in which this judiciary had the power to act. For example, article III specified that the judicial power of the Federal Government "shall extend to all . . . Controversies . . . between a State and Citizens of another State . . . and between a State . . . and foreign States, Citizens or Subjects; and, in addition, article III provided that in all such controversies, suit was to be brought directly in the Supreme Court. In 1792 in the case of *Chisholm v. Georgia*,[19] two citizens of South Carolina, acting as executors of an English creditor, sued the State of Georgia in the Supreme Court (under the preceding constitutional provisions) for property Georgia had confiscated. Though a number of months before, Georgia had itself brought suit in the Supreme Court in *Georgia v. Brailsford*[20] to prevent the transfer to English creditors of property Georgia had confiscated, Georgia now refused to appear in the *Chisholm* case. When a judgment was entered by the Supreme Court against Georgia in the *Chisholm* case,[21] not only did the Georgia authorities fail to comply with the judgment but the Georgia House of Representatives passed a bill making any attempt to carry out the Court's judgment a capital offense.[22] Indeed, shortly after the Supreme Court decided *Chisholm v. Georgia*, a constitutional amendment was proposed in Congress that would deprive the federal courts of jurisdiction in such a case. This constitutional amendment (which, when ratified in 1798, became the Eleventh Amendment to the Constitution) provided that "The Judicial power of the United States shall not be construed to extend to any suit in law or

equity, commenced or prosecuted against one of the United
States by Citizens of another State, or by Citizens or Subjects
of any Foreign State."

Fortunately for the future of the Constitution, there were
other early and significant challenges by the states to the jurisdiction of the federal judiciary that ended quite differently.
Under section 25 of the Judiciary Act of 1789, Congress had
granted to the Supreme Court the right to review on appeal
decisions of the highest court of a state where the validity of
a treaty or law of the United States had been questioned and
the state court had declared the treaty or law to be invalid
and where the validity of a state statute had been questioned
as being contrary to a treaty or law or the Constitution of the
United States and the state court had upheld the statute.[23]
The constitutionality of these provisions for review by the
Supreme Court of decisions by the highest courts of the states
was challenged in 1816 in *Martin v. Hunter's Lessee*,[24] a case
that under the name of *Fairfax's Devisee v. Hunter's Lessee*[25]
had first reached the Supreme Court in 1813 on appeal from a
decision by the highest court of Virginia upholding a state
statute that appeared to violate federal treaties.[26] The Supreme Court met the challenge head on in the *Martin* case,
insisting (in the words of Mr. Justice Story) "that the appellate power of the United States does extend to cases pending
in the state courts and that the 25th section of the judiciary
act, which authorizes the exercise of this jurisdiction in the
specified cases . . . is supported by the letter and spirit of the
constitution."[27] Similarly, in the leading case of *Cohen's v.
Virginia*[28] (decided a few years later in 1821), Mr. Chief Justice Marshall not only reiterated Story's insistence that the
Supreme Court had the power to review certain state court decisions[29] but went on to limit the effect of the Eleventh Amendment by declaring that the amendment failed to prevent the
Supreme Court from reviewing a state court decision when
(as in the *Cohen* case) the state itself had originally brought
the action in the state court.[30]

Another group of early and significant Supreme Court decisions that helped to establish the hegemony of the Federal Government and the Constitution vis-à-vis the states had to do with the Supreme Court's interpretation of the contract clause of the Constitution, the clause which provided that "No State shall . . . pass any . . . Law impairing the Obligation of Contracts. . . ."[31] In 1810 in *Fletcher v. Peck*,[32] for example (the first case in which the Supreme Court held a state law to be unconstitutional), Mr. Chief Justice Marshall declared that a law passed by the Georgia legislature rescinding an earlier sale by it of a tract of land was unconstitutional, in that such a law, among other things, impaired the obligation of contracts in violation of the contract clause of the Constitution.[33] Again, in *Trustees of Dartmouth College v. Woodward*[34] (a leading case decided by the Supreme Court in 1819), Mr. Chief Justice Marshall held that the charter granted by King George III to Dartmouth College in 1769 was "plainly a contract . . . within the letter of the constitution" and that an unconstitutional impairment of the obligations of this "contract" occurred when the New Hampshire legislature passed a law in 1816 attempting to amend the college's charter.[35]

Other contract clause suits of the period (*Sturges v. Crowninshield*,[36] for instance, in which Mr. Chief Justice Marshall ruled that a New York bankruptcy act constituted an unconstitutional impairment of the obligation of contracts, at least in regard to contracts entered into before the act was passed) might also be cited here as illustrating the Supreme Court's use of the contract clause to help establish the hegemony of the Federal Government vis-à-vis the states. What was probably the most significant Supreme Court decision of the period pertaining to federal and state powers, however (and what was surely one of the greatest judicial opinions Marshall ever penned), was the decision handed down by the Supreme Court in 1819 in the case of *McCulloch v. Maryland*.[37]

The case began in Baltimore, Maryland, when an action was brought against one John McCulloch, a cashier in the

Baltimore branch of the federal bank chartered by Congress—the Second Bank of the United States—for failing to pay a tax that Maryland had imposed upon notes issued by the Bank. The dispute ultimately reached the Supreme Court on an agreed set of facts, and the Supreme Court found itself called upon to determine (1) whether a state could legally tax an instrumentality of the national government such as the United States Bank and (2) whether Congress had the right to charter the Bank in the first place. As to the right of Maryland (or any other state) to tax a federal bank, Mr. Chief Justice Marshall, reasoning from the seemingly indisputable premise that "the power to tax involves the power to destroy,"[38] contended that "if the right of the states to tax the means employed by the general government be conceded, the declaration [in article VI of the Constitution] that the constitution, and the laws made in pursuance thereof, shall be the supreme law of the land, is empty and unmeaning declamation."[39] Thus if the Constitution were to survive as written, concluded Marshall, the Court had no choice but to declare that "the law passed by the legislature of Maryland, imposing a tax on the Bank of the United States, is unconstitutional and void."[40] As to the question of whether Congress had the power under the Constitution to create a federal bank in the first place, Marshall had to admit that no such power was specifically given to Congress in the Constitution. Marshall noted, however, that certain powers regarding the fiscal affairs of the national government (the power to borrow money and the power to lay and collect taxes, for example) were specifically enumerated and granted to Congress under article I, section eight of the Constitution. Marshall also observed that in the final paragraph of this article and section of the Constitution, Congress was given the right to "make all Laws which shall be necessary and proper for carrying into Execution the foregoing Powers." This grant to Congress of the right to pass all laws that are "necessary and proper" for the carrying out of its specifically listed powers, Marshall reasoned, gave to Congress (when it sought to exercise its other specifically enumerated powers regarding the fiscal affairs of the national government) the authority to charter a federal bank. In Marshall's celebrated phraseology: "Let the end be legitimate, let it be within the scope of the constitution, and all means which are appropriate, which are plainly adapted to that end, which are not prohibited, but consistent with the letter and spirit of the constitution, are constitutional."[41]

To summarize: Marshall accomplished two basic objectives in *McCulloch v. Maryland*. On the one hand, he successfully restricted the power of the states by ruling that they lacked the right to tax the United States Bank or other instrumentality of the Federal Government. On the other hand, by using the "necessary and proper" clause of the Constitution to validate the chartering of a national bank by Congress, Marshall showed how Congress could begin to expand its specifically enumerated powers. In achieving these two seemingly disparate but actually complementary objectives, Marshall helped to set in motion and give direction to a basic process of American Constitutional Law—a sometimes hurried but usually gradual process under which the powers of the states have been restricted and the powers of the Federal Government expanded—a process which, with some temporary retrogressions, has continued from the time of *McCulloch v. Maryland* to this very day.[42]

The group of Supreme Court decisions that illustrates particularly well the expansion of federal powers and the more or less concomitant restriction of state powers that has taken place since the time of *McCulloch v. Maryland* are those decisions based upon the commerce clause of the Constitution, the clause which provides that "[The Congress shall have Power . . .] To regulate Commerce with foreign Nations, and among the several States, and with the Indian Tribes."

The commerce clause was first interpreted by the Supreme Court in 1824 in the celebrated case of *Gibbons v. Ogden*.[43] In this case, Aaron Ogden (a licensee of a monopoly originally granted to Robert R. Livingston and Robert Fulton by the Legislature of the State of New York to navigate steamboats in the various waterways of New York) sought to enjoin Thomas Gibbons from operating steamboats between points in the state of New York and points in the state of New Jersey. Gibbons defended on the grounds that he was operating in New York waterways under a "coasting license" issued by the Federal Government under the authority of an Act of Congress regulating the coastwise trade. Mr. Chief Justice Marshall attempted to resolve the controversy by interpreting the commerce clause in such a manner as to make it relevant to the controversy. For one thing, he pointed out that the power to regulate commerce given to Congress under the commerce clause included "the power . . . to prescribe the rule by which commerce is to be governed."[44] Further, he asserted that the word "among" in the phrase *among the several states* in the commerce clause extended the reach of congressional power over commerce into the interior of the various states. As he put it: "A thing which is among others, is intermingled with them. Commerce among the States cannot stop at the external boundary line of each State, but may be introduced into the interior."[45] Moreover, instead of limiting the meaning of the word "commerce" in the commerce clause "to traffic, to buying and selling, or the interchange of commodities,"[46] Marshall insisted that commerce had a broader meaning which included navigation. To employ his much quoted phraseology: "Commerce, undoubtedly, is traffic, but it is something more— it is intercourse. It describes the commercial intercourse between nations, and parts of nations. . . . All America understands, and has uniformly understood, the word 'commerce' to comprehend navigation."[47] Having thus interpreted the commerce clause so as to leave little doubt of its relevance to the controversy between Gibbons and Ogden, Marshall went on to point out that in regard to both foreign and interstate commerce, congressional power is supreme. In Marshall's words, "the sovereignty of Congress, though limited to specified objects, is plenary as to those objects."[48] Hence when Marshall—using what Felix Frankfurther termed "esoteric statutory construction"[49]—then found what he conceived to be a conflict between the federal statute under which Gibbons claimed he operated his steamboats and the monopolistic grant from the legislature of the State of New York under which Ogden had brought the present action, Marshall insisted that maintaining congressional supremacy vis-à-vis the states regarding interstate commerce required him to strike down the New York monopoly and to dismiss the suit Ogden had brought under it against Gibbons.[50]

Three years later in *Brown v. Maryland*,[51] Marshall employed the commerce clause once again to restrict state powers, this time striking down a Maryland statute taxing imports on the ground that it conflicted with a federal tariff statute that implicitly[52] forbade local taxation of imports in their original packages in the hands of the original importers. In 1829 in *Willson v. Black Bird Creek Marsh Company*,[53] however, Marshall revealed that by no means had the commerce clause actually deprived the states of the ability to exercise some of their long-standing rights regarding commerce. He did this by upholding the validity of a Delaware statute authorizing the construction of a dam across a tidal creek in Delaware, even though the dam would obstruct completely navigation of the creek by vessels (including vessels licensed under a federal coasting statute) which might seek to use the creek on voyages to and from such salt water bodies as the Delaware River and the Atlantic Ocean. Though Marshall presumably regarded the Delaware statute to be (at least in theory) not a state law attempting to regulate commerce but rather (upon the assumption that no conflicting federal law existed) to be what in *Gibbons v. Ogden* and again in *Brown v. Maryland* he had described as the valid exercise of a state's inherent "police power,"[54] the practical result of his decision in *Willson v. Black Bird Creek Marsh Company* was to serve notice that at least for the time being, the Supreme Court (in the absence of conflicting federal legislation) would not use the commerce clause to strike down state legislation designed to regulate the very great number of matters that in 1829 were still considered to be of essentially local concern.[55]

Certainly comparable in significance to the *Brown* and *Willson* decisions (and possibly even to Marshall's opinion in *Gibbons v. Ogden*) was the Supreme Court's decision in 1851 in *Cooley v. Board of Port Wardens.*[56] The Supreme Court's specific holding in the *Cooley* case was that a Pennsylvania statute requiring the masters of vessels entering or leaving Philadelphia either to take on a local pilot or to pay half pilotage fees towards maintaining the needy among local pilots was a valid exercise of state powers. What has proven to have been of major significance in the case, however, was the distinction Mr. Justice Curtis sought to draw in the majority opinion between what he concluded were two basic categories of subjects that Congress had the power to regulate under the commerce clause: those subjects that required a single uniform national rule and those other subjects of the commerce power that could best be regulated by a number of diverse local rules.

> Now the power to regulate commerce embraces a vast field, containing not only many, but exceedingly various subjects, quite unlike in their nature; some imperatively demanding a single uniform rule, operating equally on the commerce of the United States in every port; and some, like the subject now in question, as imperatively demanding that diversity, which alone can meet the local necessities of navigation.[57]

As to those subjects of the commerce power best governed by diversity of regulation, Mr. Justice Curtis declared that the states had the right to pass laws concerning them—provided, however, that Congress had failed to do so and also that the laws passed by the states in no way conflicted with existing federal legislation. But as to those subjects of the commerce power requiring a single uniform rule, the states were *not* to act, even though no federal legislation existed regarding these matters. Thus the distinction Mr. Justice Curtis drew between subjects of the commerce power needing diverse rules and subjects of the commerce power requiring a single national rule—a distinction that is still much used by the courts[58]—had the effect of continuing the process (begun in *Gibbons v. Ogden*) of constricting the powers of the states vis-à-vis commerce. Not only was the right of the states to act in regard to those subjects of the commerce power best regulated by diverse laws to exist only on sufferance (the right would be automatically lost if Congress acted concerning these subjects), but the states were also absolutely forbidden to pass laws regarding those subjects of the commerce power needing a single uniform rule, *even though Congress might actually never pass laws regulating these subjects.*[59]

After the Civil War, the Supreme Court still concerned itself to some extent with the need to guard against state legislation that impinged upon federal powers regarding commerce. (In *Wabash, St. Louis and Pacific Railway Company v. Illinois,*[60] for example, decided in 1886, the Court held that the states lacked the power to regulate the rates charged by railroads engaged in interstate transportation, even though Congress had as yet failed to act in regard to these rates.[61]) Of greater and ever-growing concern to the Court, however, was the need to find a way of exercising control over (or at least, of coming to terms with) the tendency of Congress, acting under the aegis of the commerce clause, to expand the reach of federal regulation to fields that had traditionally been regulated by the states or, indeed, had never been regulated at all.

One of the more immediate results of the Supreme Court's decision in the *Wabash* case mentioned above was the passage of the Interstate Commerce Act in 1887, which sought to regulate the rates charged by railroads engaged in interstate transportation and which set up the first great "modern" federal regulatory agency—the Interstate Commerce Commission—to ensure compliance with the Act by the railroads.[62] This legislation was followed three years later by the Sherman Anti-Trust Act, in which Congress—acting under the authority of the commerce clause—declared that "every contract, combination in the form of trust or otherwise, or conspiracy, in restraint of trade or commerce among the several states, or with foreign nations, is hereby declared to be illegal."

The first great judicial test of the Sherman Anti-Trust Act came in 1895 in *United States v. E. C. Knight Co.,*[63] in which the Supreme Court ruled that the business activities of the so-called Sugar Trust (which, concededly, had succeeded in monopolizing the manufacture of more than 95 percent of the refined sugar used in the United States) in no way violated the Act. In reaching this decision, the Court drew a sharp distinction between manufacturing and commerce, insisting that the control of manufacturing, unlike the control of commerce, belonged solely to the states.

Commerce succeeds to manufacture, and is not a part of it. . . . The fact that an article is manufactured for export to another State does not of itself make it an article of interstate commerce, and the intent of the manufacturer does not determine the time when the article or product passes from the control of the State and belongs to commerce.[64]

Three years after the Supreme Court decided the *Knight* case, Congress (ostensibly exercising its powers under the commerce clause) passed a law prohibiting railway workers from signing so-called yellow dog contracts (agreements under which workers, as a condition of their employment, renounced the right to remain in labor unions). The Court invalidated this law in 1908 in *Adair v. United States*,[65] declaring that no connection existed between commerce and membership in labor unions and that the statute had unconstitutionally interfered with liberty of contract "under the guise of regulating interstate commerce."[66]

Possibly the most crucial commerce clause decision of the era was the Supreme Court's opinion in *Hammer v. Dagenhart*,[67] decided in 1918. In this case, the Court held that the Keating-Owen Child Labor Act passed by Congress in 1916 (which prohibited the "transportation in interstate commerce" of goods made at factories employing children under the age of fourteen) interfered unconstitutionally with the reserved powers of the states. Speaking for a majority on the Court, Mr. Justice Day insisted that the statute really sought not to regulate interstate transportation but rather to deny to manufacturers in the states the right to employ child labor, a power which was for the states alone to exercise.

(T)he thing intended to be accomplished by this statute is the denial of the facilities of interstate commerce to those manufacturers in the States who employ children within the prohibited ages. The act in its effect does not regulate transportation among the States, but aims to standardize the ages at which children may be employed in . . . manufacturing within the States. . . .[68]

In a powerful dissent, Mr. Justice Holmes excoriated the practice of child labor.

(I)f there is any matter upon which civilized countries have agreed—far more unanimously than they have with regard to intoxicants and some other matters over which this country is now emotionally aroused—it is the evil of premature and excessive child labor.[69]

He then went on to insist that regulating child labor was by no means exclusively within the powers of the states. "They [the states]," he declared, "may regulate their internal affairs and their domestic commerce as they like. But when they seek to send their products across the state line they are no longer within their rights."[70] Here, according to Holmes, Congress has the right (and sometimes the duty) to intervene and carry out what it conceives to be the public policy of the United States.

The climax of the Supreme Court's attempts to prevent Congress from employing the commerce clause to extend federal control to fields that had traditionally been regulated by the states or had gone unregulated was reached in 1935 in *Schechter Poultry Corp. v. United States.*[71] In this case, the Court examined the National Industrial Recovery Act of 1933 (a highly complex and extraordinarily comprehensive attempt by Congress, presumably acting under the authority of the commerce clause, to regulate American industry), which sought—by providing for the drawing up of so-called codes of fair competition for each industry—to accomplish such objectives as eliminating child labor, reducing unemployment, conserving natural resources, stimulating the growth of business and ordering labor relations (for example, by specifying minimum wages and maximum working hours). As perhaps Congress and President

Roosevelt ought to have foreseen, the Supreme Court held (and, here, unanimously) that this legislation clearly exceeded the permissible limits of congressional action under the commerce clause. In so ruling, the Supreme Court—speaking through Mr. Chief Justice Hughes—rejected the contention of the government that Congress could exceed its normal constitutional powers in an emergency (and on this basis, pass the National Industrial Recovery Act, which was clearly intended to help meet the extremely grave economic crisis that was then threatening the government's very existence). In the words of Mr. Chief Justice Hughes: "Undoubtedly, the conditions to which power is addressed are always to be considered when the exercise of power is challenged. Extraordinary conditions may call for extraordinary remedies. But the argument necessarily stops short of an attempt to justify action which lies outside the sphere of constitutional authority. Extraordinary conditions do not create or enlarge constitutional power."[72]

The opinion of Hughes in the *Schechter* case, coupled with the Court's finding in 1936 in *United States v. Butler*[73] that the Administration's attempt to aid the country's impoverished farmers—the Agricultural Adjustment Act of 1933—was unconstitutional, helped to precipitate the so-called Court packing fight of 1937, in which President Roosevelt sought to add six additional judges to the Supreme Court. Although President Roosevelt lost the fight in the sense that Congress refused to give to him the right to appoint these additional (and presumably pro New Deal) members to the Court, a dramatic change occurred during the fight in the Court's interpretation of the commerce clause and in its reaction to New Deal legislation (the so-called "switch in time that saved nine"), a change that revealed a new willingness by the Court to interpret federal powers broadly under the commerce clause and to validate congressional legislation that it and previous Courts had stricken down.

Signaling this change in the Court's attitude was the decision of the Court in *National Labor Relations Board v. Jones*

& Laughlin Steel Corp.[74] aannounced in April of 1937 during the height of the Court packing fight.[75] In this case, the Court held that the National Labor Relations Act of 1935 was constitutional, even though this legislation (a comprehensive attempt by Congress to regulate labor-management relations in manufacturing and other industries) was based upon the collective bargaining provision (Section 7a) of the National Industrial Recovery Act of 1933, an Act that only two years before had been declared unconstitutional in the *Schechter* case as exceeding the permissible limits of congressional power under the commerce clause. As in the *Schechter* case, it was Mr. Chief Justice Hughes who delivered the opinion of the Court. Yet now in *National Labor Relations Board v. Jones & Laughlin Steel Corp.*, Hughes chose to stress the point that if activities "have such a close and substantial relation to interstate commerce that their control is essential or appropriate to protect that commerce from burdens and obstructions, Congress cannot be denied the power to excerise that control."[76] On this basis, Hughes found (contrary to views expressed by the Court back in 1895 in *United States v. E. C. Knight Co.*) that manufacturing and commerce were by no means necessarily separate and distinct, and that when a close and intimate relationship exists between manufacturing and interstate commerce, Congress has the right under the commerce clause to so regulate manufacturing as to protect interstate commerce. Further, Hughes went on to insist (despite such precedents as the 1908 case of *Adair v. United States*, in which the Court had refused to admit that a connection might exist between membership in a labor union and commerce) that when "industries organize themselves on a national scale, making their relation to interstate commerce the dominant factor in their activities," it was inconceivable "that their industrial labor relations constitute a forbidden field into which Congress may not enter when it is necessary to protect interstate commerce from the paralyzing consequences of industrial war."[77] Thus in *National Labor Relations Board v. Jones & Laughlin Steel Corp.*, the Court struck off the shackles of what appeared to be outworn

precedents and began to extend the reach of federal law under the commerce clause to matters that had traditionally been regulated (if at all) by the states.

The Supreme Court's decision in the *Jones & Laughlin Steel* case was followed by other decisions of the Court that encouraged the expansion of congressional powers under the commerce clause. In *United States v. Darby Lumber Co.*[78] decided in 1941, for example, not only did the Supreme Court declare that Congress had the right under the commerce clause to prohibit the interstate shipment of goods produced under what Congress regarded as substandard labor conditions, but the Court also specifically overruled *Hammer v. Dagenhart*, in which the Court had held—despite a powerful dissent by Holmes—that Congress lacked the power to prohibit the interstate shipment of goods produced by child labor. "The conclusion is inescapable," declared Mr. Justice Stone in the *Darby* case, "that *Hammer v. Dagenhart*, was a departure from the principles which have prevailed in the interpretation of the Commerce Clause... [S]uch vitality, as a precedent, as it then had, has long since been exhausted. It should be and now is overruled."[79]

A final commerce clause decision by the Supreme Court to be considered here—one that illustrates graphically the permissive attitude adopted by the Court since the *Jones & Laughlin* case towards attempts to extend congressional powers under the commerce clause—is *Wickard v. Filburn*,[80] decided in 1942. In this case, the Court upheld as a proper exercise of congressional power under the commerce clause the Agricultural Adjustment Act of 1938 (as amended in 1941), which authorized the Secretary of Agriculture to limit the production of farm products by assigning quotas for these commodities to the country's farmers and by imposing penalties for production in excess of the assigned quotas. Specifically, the Court upheld the imposition of a penalty under this Act against a farmer named Filburn who produced more than his allotted quota of wheat *but who intended to use the wheat produced in excess of his quota solely on the farm where it had been grown (to feed livestock, etcetera) rather than offering it for sale in interstate commerce.* In seeking to explain why Congress had the right under the commerce clause to control the production of such home-consumed wheat, the Court pointed out that although the extra wheat produced for consumption on Filburn's farm might never enter the stream of commerce, this wheat still supplied a need that Filburn would have otherwise had to meet by making purchases on the open market. In this sense, the home-consumed wheat produced on Filburn's farm—coupled with the home-consumed wheat produced on other farms— would, so the Court contended, inevitably have a substantial effect upon interstate commerce and would therefore be regulable by Congress under the commerce clause.[81]

The implications of the Court's decision in *Wickard v. Filburn* have, to say the least, hardly gone unnoticed.

> With the Court's decision in *Wickard v. Filburn,* a climax is reached in the recent broadening of the Congressional commerce power. Under the doctrine of that case, federal authority may be exerted over purely local transactions, though they themselves are not commercial in character. Even so, under the Court's reasoning, they have sufficient effect upon commerce to furnish the occasion for the exercise of Congressional power.[82]

Indeed, some students of constitutional law believe that as a result of *Wickard v. Filburn* and subsequent cases, meaningful constitutional limitations on the Federal Government's power over commerce no longer exist. To quote Leonard W. Levy: "Congress may do as it wishes; policy is politically determined, without constitutional restraints. There is now only a constitutional law of the commerce clause as a source of limitations upon state authority."[83] Be this as it may, there can be little doubt that the powers exercised by the Federal Government are greater today than they have ever been; and indisputably, they are immeasurably greater than they were when what is usually referred to as America's first constitution—the Articles of Confederation—was adopted in 1781. In fact, the balance of federal and state powers has, in a sense, been completely reversed since such early days in American history. Today, contrary to the time when America was still young, it is the states that are dependent and subordinate and the Federal Government that has become extraordinarily powerful and is clearly supreme.

The perennial problem of constitutional law considered in the preceding number of pages—the problem of trying to find a proper balance between the powers of the Federal Government and those of the states—has never lent itself to easy or to completely peaceful resolution. In fact, as will now be seen, this search for a satisfactory accommodation between federal and state powers—a search that began at the time of the writing of the Articles of Confederation and that has continued to this very day—has from the beginning frequently aroused powerful emotions and has all too readily led to threatened, and sometimes actual, violence.

Back in 1793, for instance, the decision in *Chisholm v. Georgia*[84] that a suit could be brought and a judgment obtained in the Supreme Court against the State of Georgia by citizens of another state (and the holding implicit in the case that Georgia was, at least to this extent, subject to direction and control by the federal judiciary) caused great shock and generated considerable alarm.[85] The Court's ruling was, for example, attacked in newspaper articles as involving "more danger to the liberties of America than the claims of the British Parliament."[86] In fact, so outraged was public opinion in Georgia regarding the case, that the House of Representatives of Georgia passed a bill providing that any person who attempted to enforce the judgment handed down by the Court would be declared "guilty of felony and shall suffer death, without benefit of clergy, by being hanged."[87] Though this bill never actually became law in Georgia, it seems to have had the desired effect, in that no attempt was made by federal authorities to try to compel Georgia to comply with the Court's decision.

Another early and emotion-packed controversy pertaining to the power of the Federal Government vis-à-vis the states arose a few years later in 1798 when Congress passed the

notorious Alien and Sedition Laws.[88] By far the most controversial of these laws was the Sedition Act, which provided
for the criminal prosecution of anybody who uttered, wrote or
printed "any false, scandalous and malicious" statement against
"the government of the United States, or either house of the
Congress of the United States, or the President of the United
States."[89] Attempts by President Adams and the Federalists
(the political party in power at the time) to institute prosecutions under the Sedition Act[90], and especially the vigorous enforcement of the Act in the Federal Circuit Court in Philadelphia by Mr. Justice Samuel Chase, resulted in a furious
controversy with the Democratic-Republicans (the opposition
political party) and led within a few months to the drafting
of the celebrated Virginia and Kentucky Resolutions by James
Madison and Thomas Jefferson respectively. The Virginia Resolutions (fathered by James Madison and adopted by the
Virginia legislature) opined that the states had the right to
"interpose" their authority to prevent the Federal Government
from exercising unconstitutional powers; and the Kentucky
Resolutions (written by Thomas Jefferson and passed by the
Kentucky legislature) appeared to declare that the states had
the right to nullify acts of Congress which they believed to be
unconstitutional.[91] The intense feelings that had originally been
aroused by the Alien and Sedition Laws and that had led to
the drafting of the Virginia and Kentucky Resolutions began
to recede when the Democratic-Republicans came to power
in 1800. Nevertheless, anger and resentment concerning the
prosecutions conducted under the Sedition Act still simmered
and appear to have played a major role in the attempt by the
Democratic-Republicans in 1804 to curb the power of the federal judiciary by trying to impeach Mr. Justice Chase.[92]

During the next decade or so, certain Supreme Court decisions that emphasized and extended the hegemony of the
Federal Government vis-à-vis the states produced emotional
reactions of considerable intensity. The Supreme Court's ruling
in 1810 in *Fletcher v. Peck*,[93] for example, invalidating an attempt by Georgia to rescind fraudulent land sales by a corrupt

Georgia legislature—the first ruling by the Court declaring a state law to be unconstitutional—provoked a widespread emotional storm. "Not only Georgia, but most of the rest of the nation as well, was deeply aroused by the Court's action."[94] In Congress, the Court's decision was bitterly attacked as one "which the mind of every man attached to Republican principles must revolt at."[95] Indeed, George M. Troup (who represented Georgia in the House of Representatives) declared that if "the arch-fiend had in his hatred to mankind resolved the destruction of republican government on earth, he would have issued a decree like that of the judges."[96]

Similarly intense and quite widespread as well was the reaction to the decision handed down by the Supreme Court in 1819 in *McCulloch v. Maryland*.[97] The Court's dual ruling in this case—that (1) Congress had the right under the "necessary and proper" clause of the Constitution to create a national bank and that (2) the states lacked the power under the Constitution to tax such an instrumentality of the Federal Government—aroused passionate opposition, especially in the western and southern states. In Kentucky, for instance, it was charged that the principles of the Court's decision "must raise an alarm . . . [in that they] strike at the roots of State-Rights and State Sovereignty."[98] In Mississippi, a newspaper asserted that the Court's ruling obliterated the "last vestige of the sovereignty and independence of the individual States."[99] To quote from the writings of Thomas Ritchie (a correspondent and ally of Thomas Jefferson)`: "If such a spirit as breathes in . . . [McCulloch v. Maryland] is forever to preside over the Judiciary, then . . . it is high time for the States to tremble."[100] Perhaps the most determined opposition to the Court's decision occurred in Ohio, where state officials simply refused to recognize its validity. Thus, when the persons who ran the federal bank in Ohio refused to pay a tax levied upon the bank by the Ohio legislature (a tax that under the Court's ruling in *McCulloch v. Maryland* was clearly unconstitutional), the Ohio tax collector simply entered the bank's vaults and removed $120,475.[101] Indeed, for almost five years thereafter, Ohio carried on what one writer has termed "guerilla warfare" against the Court's decision.[102]

Though very much aware of the bitter opposition aroused by the Court's decision in *McCulloch v. Maryland*, Chief Justice Marshall (apparently undaunted)[103] provoked another emotional storm two years later by holding in 1821 in *Cohen's v. Virginia*[104] that the Eleventh Amendment to the Constitution failed to bar the Supreme Court from reviewing a decision involving a federal question handed down by a state court in a case originally instituted by the state itself.[105] Opposition to this ruling by Marshall in *Cohen's v. Virginia* was, as perhaps might have been expected, particularly intense in Virginia (the representatives of Virginia walked out on the Supreme Court after contending that the Court had no right to hear the case), finding expression, among other ways, in bitter and vitriolic denunciations of the case by such eminent Virginians as Spencer Roane (Chief Justice of the Virginia Court of Appeals)[106] and Thomas Jefferson. For example, Roane described the Court's decision as "monstrous and unexampled"; and he declared that it could be understood only as a reflection of "that love of power which all history informs us infects and corrupts."[107] Thomas Jefferson went even further, referring to the case as "an act of venality . . . [which] makes me ashamed that I was ever a lawyer"[108] and declaring with reference to Marshall that "the battle of Bunker Hill was not fought to set up a Pope."[109] Perhaps it also ought to be mentioned here that the Supreme Court's decision in *Cohen's v. Virginia* alarmed many non-Virginians as well: Senator Johnson of Kentucky, for example, proposed to "cure" the Court's ruling by having appellate federal jurisdiction in certain cases in which a state was a party lie not in the Supreme Court but rather in the Senate.[110]

Another (and certainly one of the most ominous) of the pre–Civil-War crises pertaining to the relative powers of the Federal Government and the state governments arose in 1832, when the legislature of South Carolina called for the election of delegates to a state convention that was to determine whether the federal tariff acts passed by Congress in 1828 and 1832 ought to be "nullified" by South Carolina. In so acting, the South Carolina legislature was putting into practice the views advanced in 1828 in *The South Carolina Exposition and Protest* by John C. Calhoun (who served as vice-president of the United States from 1825 until late in 1832).[111] In essence, Calhoun had contended that the Constitution was a "compact" among sovereign states and that if the Federal Government (the "agent" of these states) appeared to act in such a way as to exceed the powers delegated to it by the states, any one of these states could then ask its citizens to elect delegates to a convention to be held in the state to consider the matter. If the convention then found that the Federal Government had indeed acted unconstitutionally, the convention would have the right to "nullify" the federal act and declare it to be un-enforceable within the boundaries of the state.[112]

When President Jackson learned of South Carolina's call for a convention to nullify the tariffs imposed by Congress in 1828 and 1832, he despatched General Scott to Charleston to survey and report upon the military situation there. When the convention met and "nullified" the federal tariffs, Jackson rushed five thousand stand of muskets to Castle Pinckney and ordered a sloop of war and a number of smaller vessels to Charleston harbor.[113] In addition, he threatened to hang Calhoun, issued a proclamation warning South Carolina that upon it would "inevitably fall all the evils" of the "mad project of disunion," and sought to rally patriotic support by declaring that nullification was "incompatible with the existence of the union, contradicted expressly by the letter of the Constitution, unauthorized by its spirit, inconsistent with every principle on which it was founded, and destructive of the great object for which it was formed."[114]

South Carolina remained defiant, however. Its legislature declared that Jackson's views regarding nullification were "erroneous and dangerous" and that the state would "repel force by force ... and maintain its liberty at all hazards."[115] Further, officials in South Carolina began to call for volunteers to help fight any federal attempt to enforce the "nullified" tariffs.

The eloquent Preston, addressing a mass meeting in Charleston, declared that "there are 16,000 black countrymen with arms in their hands and cockades in their hats, ready to march to our city at a moment's warning to defend us. . . . I will pour down a torrent of volunteers that will sweep the myrmidons of the tyrant from the soil of Carolina."[116]

In short, an armed clash between South Carolina and the Federal Government appeared imminent.

Fortunately, passions were quieted at this juncture by a compromise worked out in Congress between Henry Clay and Calhoun, under which federal tariff rates were lowered and South Carolina withdrew its nullification of the federal tariffs of 1828 and 1832. Thus the crisis had seemingly passed—but not really. The strong feelings aroused by the crisis (especially in South Carolina and other parts of the South) never subsided completely; and when the South began during the 1840's and 1850's to feel apprehensive once again about federal legislation inimical to its interests,[117] talk in South Carolina and other Southern States turned not simply to nullification but to the more drastic remedy of secession. With ever-increasing frequency, southerners advanced the argument that if the Constitution was, as Calhoun had contended, a compact among sovereign states, then, as Calhoun had also contended, "a State, as a party to the constitutional compact, has the right to secede."[118] Perhaps not surprisingly, it was South Carolina that, after President Lincoln's election in 1860, led the secession of the southern states from the Union.

The four Civil War years that followed (the years beginning with the firing on Fort Sumter by the Confederates on April 12, 1861 and ending with the surrender of Robert E. Lee to Ulysses S. Grant at Appomattox on April 9, 1865) were probably the most traumatic and surely the bloodiest years in American history. As was pointed out in Chapter VI, the Civil War was one of the two major wars of the nineteenth century: in the size of armies raised (approximately four million men were brought under arms) and in the casualties sustained (nearly six hundred thousand deaths were attributable to the conflict), the Civil War was comparable to the Napoleonic struggles in

Europe.[119] In fact, the Civil War was, in a sense, a fiercer conflagration than the Napoleonic struggles, in that it "concentrated into four years an amout of destruction and anguish which in the Old World was extended over more than a decade and a half."[120]

The causes of the Civil War were many and varied[121]; and it would be both misleading and inaccurate to try to describe them simply in terms of a deep-rooted conflict over the right of the southern states to secede from the Union or solely in terms of deeply felt differences regarding the more general problem of determining the proper relationship between the state governments and the Federal Government. There can be no question, however, that one of the basic results of the passion and bloodshed of the Civil War was the denial of the right of the southern states (or, indeed, of the right of any of the states) to secede from the Union ("The Constitution, in all its provisions, looks to an indestructible Union, composed of indestructible states"—so declared the Supreme Court in 1869 in its Civil War postmortem *Texas v. White*).[122] Another fundamental result of the Civil War was the establishment of an extremely strong national government, one clearly superior in prerogatives and powers to the various state governments. It is true, of course, that (as before the War) the need to achieve an accommodation between national and state powers continued to exist after the War—as it has to this very day ("The war did not of course obliterate the nation-state issue, for that issue is interminable in a federal republic."[123]). Since the War, however, there has been little doubt that in any federal-state conflict, the Federal Government could, if it wished, forcibly impose its will.[124]

From the end of the era of Reconstruction that followed the Civil War until the conclusion of the Court packing fight of 1937, emotional outbursts frequently greeted attempts by the courts to find a proper balance between federal and state powers in cases involving economic legislation. When, for example, the Supreme Court decided in 1876 in *Munn v. Illinois*,[125] despite a most vigorous dissent by Mr. Justice Field, that an Illinois law setting maximum storage rates for grain (most of which came from midwest farming areas and was stored in Chicago before moving to eastern markets) failed to impinge upon the power of Congress to regulate interstate commerce,[126] a furious controversy ensued. Words such as "thievery" and "brigandage" peppered articles and editorials in eastern newspapers attacking the decision.[127] On the other hand, the Court's decision was supported vigorously by farmers in the Midwest—especially by those who had banded together into organizations known as "granges"—who declared that the Illinois legislation upheld by the Court was an understandable (if not inevitable) reaction to extortionate charges by grain warehouses in Chicago.[128] Further heat was added to the controversy by leaders of the Bar (imbued, perhaps, with what Robert G. McCloskey has referred to as "the conservative bias that has always characterized the American legal fraternity"[129]) who excoriated the Court's decision. Thus John Norton Pomeroy (one of the luminaries of the legal profession of the time) declared in 1883 that the decision in *Munn v. Illinois* was a "menace to business and material interests of all kinds. No other decision," he averred, "has ever been made in the course of our judicial history—not even excepting the notorious Dred Scott Case—which threatens such disastrous consequences . . . [The decision] strikes . . . at rights which lie at the very foundation of modern society and civilization." In fact, Pomeroy went on to charge that the decision was being relied upon by "demagogues . . . to sustain . . . yet more communistic and destructive legislation which they demand."[130] Apparently influenced by such charges, the Supreme Court soon began to back away from its ruling in *Munn v. Illinois*; and by the 1890's, it had, in effect, reversed it.[131] In so doing, the Court leaned more and more towards the views expressed in the dissent in the *Munn* case by Mr. Justice Field, who had warned that by holding the Illinois statute fixing maximum storage rates for grain to be a valid exercise of state power, the Court had, in a sense, laid the groundwork for "all property and all business in the State . . . [to be] held at the mercy of a majority of its Legislature."[132]

Like the Court's ruling in the *Munn* case, its decision in

1905 in *Lochner v. New York*[133] (in which, it will be recalled, the Court—in spite of a powerful dissent by Mr. Justice Holmes—struck down a New York statute setting maximum working hours for bakers) evoked a powerful emotional reaction. The decision was immediately attacked by labor leaders (decidedly unimpressed by Mr. Justice Peckham's reasoning in the majority opinion concerning the need to prevent a state from extending its regulatory powers under the guise of exercising its so-called police powers)[134] who threatened to call a national bakers strike, and who declared that they would continue to fight for limitations on working hours "in defiance of the Supreme Court."[135] More effective, however, were attacks upon the Court's decision by the social reformers of the early 1900's—the "Progressives," who (as a means of dramatizing the need for judicial reform) constantly cited the *Lochner* decision as a prime example of how the Court functioned as an obstacle to what was termed "social justice legislation."[136] Largely because of agitation by these Progressives, the Court retreated from the position it had taken in the *Lochner* case; and in 1908 in *Muller v. Oregon*,[137] and more especially in 1917 in *Bunting v. Oregon*,[138] it upheld state legislation comparable to that which it had stricken down in the *Lochner* case.

Though the reactions evoked by the *Lochner* case were surely deeply felt, they were relatively mild when compared with the excitement and fury aroused when the Supreme Court began to strike down New Deal legislation designed to help meet the challenge of the Great Depression that had begun in 1929. From October, 1933 to the middle of 1936, the Supreme Court declared twelve acts of Congress to be unconstitutional (usually on the ground that the act in question unduly stretched the powers of the Federal Government); and in so doing, the Court (in the view of Robert H. Jackson, then the Attorney General of the United States) "all but nullified the New Deal."[139] The outrage provoked by the Court's determined opposition to the New Deal found extremely vivid and blunt expression in Congress. Senator Guffey of Pennsylvania, for example, demanded of his colleagues: "How much longer will we let the Supreme Court sanctify the sweatshop and pervert democratic processes?"[140] Representative Cross of Texas labeled the Supreme Court the "country's Nemesis" and declared that Congress would "dethrone this judicial oligarchy and issue another proclamation of emancipation that will wipe out this 'no man's land' of sweatshop slavery."[141] Perhaps even more revealing were the comments of Mr. (later Chief) Justice Stone. He accused his colleagues of adopting a "tortured construction of the Constitution,"[142] reminded them that the "Courts are not the only agency of government that must be assumed to have the capacity to govern,"[143] and declared that the term of the Court completed in June, 1936 was "one of the most disastrous in its history."[144]

Buoyed by this intense and extremely vocal opposition to the rulings of the Supreme Court as well as by a landslide victory at the polls in 1936, President Roosevelt proposed his so-called Court packing plan on February 5, 1937, under which he asked Congress for authority to appoint additional justices to the Court (one for each member of the Court who failed to retire at seventy, but in no event more than six). To Roosevelt's consternation and surprise, however, his proposed bill generated even greater opposition than had been aroused by the Court's anti–New Deal stance.

> Bar associations met and condemned the bill furiously. The churches . . . showed signs of acute uneasiness. The senates or assemblies in several states . . . prepared to pass resolutions against the court bill. No day passed without a statement from some more or less eminent citizen . . . denouncing . . . [Roosevelt's] court plan.[145]

Especially significant was the congressional opposition to Roosevelt's proposal, opposition which was both immediate and unrelenting. Thus at the very moment that the proposal was being read to Congress, Vice-President Garner left the rostrum and expressed his opposition "by holding his nose with one hand and energetically making the Roman gesture of the arena, thumbs down, with the other."[146] This opposition (so crudely expressed by Garner) continued unabated until the Senate Judiciary Committee finally rejected the bill on the grounds that (among other things) it would "undetermine the independence of the courts . . . [violate] all precedents in the history of our Government . . . permit alteration of the Constitution without the people's consent or approval . . . and . . . make this Government one of men rather than of law."[147]

Whether President Roosevelt ultimately won the Court packing fight is a question upon which it is all too easy to disagree.[148] Yet there can be no doubt that (as was pointed out earlier) the Supreme Court stopped invalidating New Deal legislation at the height of the fight; and that since 1937, the Court has interpreted the commerce clause so as to enable the Federal Government to expand greatly its powers concerning economic matters.[149] Admittedly, attempts by the Supreme Court to balance federal and state powers have continued to arouse passions and provoke emotional outbursts since 1937; but these post-1937 emotional storms have tended to occur not so much when the Court has dealt with economic problems, as when it has tried to cope with political and, more especially, with social problems.

The leading post-1937 case that immediately comes to mind here is *Brown v. Board of Education of Topeka*,[150] decided by the Supreme Court in 1954. In this landmark decision, the Court served notice upon the states (notice that was supplemented by later decisions of the Court and by congressional legislation) that the Federal Government would no longer continue to practice what (with some minor exceptions)[151] had amounted to a "hands off" policy regarding the regulation of education by the states, a policy that had allowed the states to determine for themselves whether or not their elementary schools and high schools were to be segrated.[152] Specifically, the Court struck down a practice of very long standing in many southern states—a practice that had presumably been sanctioned by the Court more than fifty years earlier in *Plessy v. Ferguson*[153]—of providing Negroes with what purported to be "separate but equal" educational facilities.[154] To quote from the

Court's decision in *Brown v. Board of Education of Topeka*: "[I]n the field of public education the doctrine of 'separate but equal' has no place. Separate educational facilities are inherently unequal.[155] Therefore, we hold that the plaintiffs . . . by reason of the segregation complained of . . . [have been] deprived of the equal protection of the laws guaranteed by the Fourteenth Amendment."[156] Then, in a subsequent segment of the decision, the Court ordered the offending states to integrate their schools with "all deliberate speed."[157]

Since the tumult and fury aroused by the Court's ruling in *Brown v. Board of Education of Topeka* are still within memory, they need hardly be recounted here in detail. Nevertheless, it is of interest to recall that the initial southern reaction to the Court's ruling was comparatively mild: though many southern leaders expressed their shock regarding the outcome of the *Brown* case and some of them uttered vaguely defiant threats, most of these officials appeared willing (at least at first) to abide peaceably with the Court's decision.[158] Senator Russell Long of Louisiana, for example, after expressing his chagrin concerning the decision, declared: "My oath requires me to accept it as law . . . ."[159] What seemed to galvanize and radicalize Southern opposition to the Court's ruling, however, was a manifesto issued on March 11, 1956 by ninety-six southern congressmen, a manifesto which (among other things) decried "encroachments [by the Court] on rights reserved to the states. . .contrary to established law," and pledged the use of "all lawful means" to bring about a reversal of the holding in the *Brown* case—a holding that the ninety-six congressmen declared to be, indisputably, "contrary to the Constitution."[160]

It was now that angry passions began to erupt, that excited mobs began to encircle school buildings and that many young Negroes who sought to enter formerly segregated schools feared for their very lives. Though many high public officials (President Eisenhower, for example) tried to quiet passions and prevent violence, other public officials failed to so act. Governor Orval Faubus of Arkansas, for instance, aroused considerable excitement when he signed a proclamation on September 2, 1957 calling upon the Arkansas State Militia to help prevent ten Negroes from entering the previously all white Central High School of Little Rock. Though the militia was finally withdrawn by Governor Faubus, a howling mob took its place and President Eisenhower ultimately felt impelled to call out Army troops and enforce integration at Central High School at bayonet point. A similar (but eventually more violent) integration crisis occured five years later when Governor Ross Barnett of Mississippi refused to permit a Negro named James Meredith to enroll at the University of Mississippi. Before the Federal Government finally succeeded (after three unsuccessful attempts) in forcing Governor Barnett to yield and permit Meredith to register at the University, mobs had formed, violence had erupted and men had died.

When Congress passed the Civil Rights Act of 1964, the upheaval sparked ten years earlier by the Supreme Court's decision in the *Brown* case appeared to be finally passing into history. But soon a new and ominous development occurred: some of the Negroes who had migrated from the rural South to the slums of the northern cities during the ten years from 1954 to 1964 began to listen to the exhortations of extremists who urged them to riot, burn and loot. The so-called Negro "ghettos" of such cities as Los Angeles, Detroit, Newark and Washington, D.C. became the scenes of bloody riots and widespread devastation. To psychoanalysts familiar with man's tendency to identify unconsciously with persons whom he fears (termed by psychoanalysts "identification with the aggressor")[161] or to sociologists familiar with the unrest and disorder that appear when man's expectations and the opportunities to fulfill these expectations are in disequilibrium (a state-of-affairs called "anomie" by the great French sociologist Emile Durkheim),[162] the violent behavior of some of the new Negro inhabitants of the northern slums may well have been both understandable and predictable. The general public, however, was shocked by the disturbances; and by the time of the presidential election campaign of 1968, the problem of maintaining "law and order" seemed to have become a major preoccupation—if not *the* major preoccupation—of the American people.

The unrest and disorder described in the preceding pages that presumably arose as a consequence of the Supreme Court's decision in the *Brown* case have, unfortunately, been exacerbated by powerful emotional reactions to other rulings of the Court restricting the powers of the states and enlarging the powers of the Federal Government. For example, the Court's precedent-shattering decision in 1962 in *Baker v. Carr*[163]—signaling the abandonment of the Federal Government's traditional policy of non-interference regarding the apportionment of representation in state legislatures—provoked a furious controversy that almost led to the adoption of a constitutional amendment reversing both the decision and later cases based upon it.[164] Similarly, the revolution in the treatment of persons accused of having broken the criminal law that the Court sought to effect by insisting that the states adopt federal procedures[165] or totally new procedures[166] when dealing with such persons produced a roar of public disapproval; and this disapproval found expression (among other ways) in the charge that the Supreme Court was responsible for the constantly increasing crime rate,[167] in the passage by Congress of the Omnibus Safety Crime Control Act of 1968 rescinding some of the Court's decisions concerning criminal procedure, and in the demand that Mr. Chief Justice Warren be impeached. Surely, however, no further examples need be given to demonstrate that during the past number of years (as, indeed, during all of American history from the time of the adoption of the Articles of Confederation until the present) attempts to adjust the balance of federal and state powers have produced extremely strong emotional reactions. In fact, some of these emotional reactions have been so intense, that they literally threatened (certainly until the end of the Civil War) to tear the United States apart.

So far, the discussion of the problem of achieving a proper balance between the powers of the Federal Government and the powers of the states has highlighted certain basic findings: (1) Attempts to balance federal and state powers have been made continually from the time of the drafting of the Articles of Confederation to this very day. (2) Though the state governments were originally more powerful than the Federal Government, this situation gradually reversed itself and today, there can be little doubt that the Federal Government is supreme. (3) Throughout the history of the United States, the balancing of federal and state powers—and certainly the gradual (and sometimes not so gradual) increase in federal powers at the expense of state powers—has tended to provoke strong emotional reactions.

Many political scientists believe that when, as in the United States, two "sovereigns"—the Federal Government and the states—operate in the same territory in a nonstatic society, accommodations and adjustments between the powers of these sovereigns must occur at times if the society is to survive.[168] If so, then so long as the United States retains the dual or federal system of government provided for in the Constitution, the likelihood is that, as in the past, the balancing of the powers of the Federal Government with those of the states will continue in the future. Similarly, the likelihood is that (unless the champions of states' rights prove far more influential and convincing than they have so far)[169] American constitutional history will continue to be characterized by a trend towards increasing the powers of the Federal Government and diminishing the powers of the states, at least in the foreseeable future. Indeed, as a number of students of constitutional law have pointed out, the accretions in federal powers and the diminutions in the powers of the states that have occurred during the course of American history, and especially since the Civil War, have been the result not so much of such matters as political calculations, fortuitous Supreme Court decisions or ideological commitments (or conspiracies and the like) by certain individuals or groups, but rather of "the inexorable pressures of wars, depressions, new means of communication, urbanization, industrialization, technology, and all the other factors which have shrunk the size of our world and created problems so large and urgent that of necessity they are pushed up to the national level for handling."[170]

If, then, the future is likely to bring not only further efforts to find ever new accommodations between federal and state powers but also a further expansion of federal powers largely at the expense of the powers of the states, does it follow that these processes will continue to be accompanied by emotional outbursts as in the past?

Not necessarily. For one thing, the emotional upsets and stresses that have so often accompanied the balancing of federal and state powers (and especially the shift in these powers in favor of the Federal Government) have frequently been in part (in fact, sometimes in large part) the product of ideas and feelings having little or nothing to do with the problem of achieving a proper federal-state division of powers. Thus, even though *Brown v. Board of Education of Topeka* was followed by a spate of "learned" articles and books attacking the Supreme Court's ruling in this case as a flagrant and unprecedented extension of federal power to an area (elementary and high school education) that had traditionally been within the exclusive control of the states,[171] there can be no doubt that much of the passionate opposition to the decision was the result of powerful feelings regarding the mixing of the Negro and Caucasian races in the schools. Similarly, even though a good deal of the opposition to *Baker v. Carr* and to subsequent apportionment decisions by the Supreme Court was expressed in terms of the alleged violation of states' rights by the rulings in these cases, few persons would doubt that the threat implicit in these cases of a reduction in the political strength of overrepresented rural counties in state legislatures played a decisive role in arousing strong emotions and in causing certain politicians to seek the reversal of *Baker v. Carr* and the subsequent cases based upon it, if need be by constitutional amendment.

Of greater interest for present purposes, however, is the possibility that the outrage and fury aroused by certain decisions of the Supreme Court balancing federal and state powers (particularly those decisions in which the Court attempted to stretch the powers of the Federal Government at the expense of the powers of the states) have reflected not only the influence of conscious ideas and feelings (be they the "respectable" ones expressed in traditional states' rights arguments[172] or the not so respectable ones that, as intimated above regarding the *Baker* and *Brown* cases, are less likely to find public expression), but have also reflected the influence of unconscious material—of vestiges of urges and ideas of early childhood that have remained in "the unconscious" and that frequently affect behavior significantly during adulthood.[173] Indeed, it is this possibility that unconscious forces may have been in part responsible for the emotional storms that have been aroused so often by the balancing of federal and state powers that will now be explored with the aid of psychoanalytic tools and insights (as, in earlier chapters, psychoanalytic discoveries were employed to gain a greater understanding of such matters as judicial review of congressional legislation, judicial activism and judicial self-restraint, and the literal approach to constitutional interpretation). Hopefully, the proper employment here of psychoanalytic tools and insights will result in a better understanding of these emotional storms than now exists and may possibly even lead to a reduction in their frequency and intensity. But, as in earlier efforts in this book to apply psychoanalytic knowledge to legal phenomena, no attempt will be made to disguise the fact that psychoanalytic explanations of the law are at best partial explanations; and that for completeness, they must be supplemented by social, economic, historical and other explanations.

As has been stressed in a number of chapters in this book (and especially in Chapter V), psychoanalytic studies contradict the view that infancy is a period of simple blissful contentment. Rather, these studies show that infancy is a time when loving attitudes and peaceful contentment exist side by side with "darker" urges and feelings—with what Ernest Jones has described as "the weakened derivatives of a very sinister inheritance we bring to the world and which somehow has to be worked through and chastened in the painful conflicts and emotions of infancy."[174]

The fact that infants sometimes exhibit anger and hostility (by yelling, biting, scratching, hitting and kicking) is, of course, well known. In fact, it can be argued that the absence of anger and hostility during the first few years of life would be surprising if, as Freud believed, "aggression is an innate, independent, instinctual disposition in man."[175] What may come as somewhat of a shock to persons unfamiliar with psychoanalytic studies of early childhood, however, is the psychoanalytic discovery that infants are moved at times by what can only be described as the most primitive and savage of desires and emotions.[176] Indeed, psychoanalysts actually speak of both a "cannibalistic" period and an "anal-sadistic" period when describing the urges and feelings that beset infants.[177]

Some of the "dark" feelings of early childhood seem to arise spontaneously and to affect the behavior of youngsters even if they are reared benignly. Thus even children raised with considerable love, understanding and care tend at about the age of two or so to want something to hurt and destroy simply for the sake or "joy" of hurting and destroying.[178] On the other hand, the rage and fury exhibited by an infant may sometimes be the product of little more than ill-timed and undue environmental pressures—of attempts, for example, to wean the youngster too early or to force him to conform too early to a feeding schedule.

Psychoanalysts have discovered, however, that some of the stormiest emotions of early childhood tend to reflect the influence of what might be best described as a combination of innate and more or less unavoidable environmental causes. For example, psychoanalysts have noted that the appearance of a new brother or sister seems to arouse in a young child an almost instinctual reaction of unhappiness and hostility. Indeed, the new sibling is all too often greeted by the unhappy older child with what can only be described as obvious jealousy and, at times, outright hatred.[179]

> One mother told me how her little son, usually a very docile child, was found by her one day, when he was two, preparing to smite his little sister on the head in her cot with a large piece of firewood. Another child, a little girl of three and a half, locked her baby brother into a drawer and threw the key out of the window. A little boy just under three expressed his disgust with his new-born brother in the following pregnant phrase:

'No teeth, red, and stinks.' . . . Such instances are endlessly available. The cause of the jealousy and rage is, naturally, the fact that the earlier favourite must now share the parents' love with the new arrival. In certain families, where a strict upbringing prevents the child from open expression of such 'wicked' feelings, one may often observe a radical transformation in its behavior. From being docile and obedient it may become difficult and rebellious. Many children, formerly gay, turn quiet and sad after the arrival of another baby in the family and one often observes in them, temporarily at any rate, the signs of neurotic disturbance: waking in fright at night, anxieties, nervous vomiting, loss of appetite, and so on.[180]

More profound and often fiercer than the feelings of sibling rivalry described above are the emotions that beset young children in the throes of what Freud described as the "Oedipus complex."[181] Specifically, Freud noted that at about the age of three and a half, youngsters begin to direct strong erotic feelings toward the parent of the opposite sex and to experience at times powerful jealous and hostile feelings regarding the parent of the same sex. Freud labeled this concatenation of emotions (and the ideas associated with them) the "Oedipus complex," deriving the phrase from Sophocles' classic tragic drama *Oedipus Rex*, in which Oedipus kills his father Laius and marries his mother Jocasta. In Freud's words

If the *Oedipus Rex* is capable of moving a modern reader or play-goer no less powerfully than it would the contemporary Greeks, the only possible explanation is that the effect of the Greek tragedy does not depend upon the conflict between fate and human will, but upon the peculiar nature of the material by which this conflict is revealed. There must be a voice within us which is prepared to acknowledge the compelling power of fate in the Oedipus. . . . And there actually is a motive in the story of King Oedipus which explains the verdict of this inner voice. His fate moves us because it might have been our own, because the oracle laid upon us before our birth the very curse which rested upon him. It may be that we were all destined to direct our first sexual impulses towards our mothers and the first impulses of hatred and violence towards our fathers; our dreams convince us that we were. King Oepidus, who slew his father Laius and wedded his mother Jocasta, is nothing more or less than a wish-fulfillment—the fulfillment of the wish of our childhood. But we, more fortunate than he, insofar as we have not become psychoneurotics, have since our childhood suc- ceeded in withdrawing our sexual impulses from our mothers and in forgetting our jealousy of our fathers. We recoil from the person for whom this primitive wish of childhood has been fulfilled with all the force of the repression which these wishes have undergone in our minds since childhood. As the poet brings the guilt of Oedipus to light by his investigation, he forces us to become aware of our own inner selves, in which the same impulses are still extant. . . .[182]

When a little boy of three or four declares that he wants to marry his mother or when a little girl of four or five states that she wishes her mother would go away so that she might have her daddy all to herself,[183] adults tend to smile indulgently at this "cute" behavior, usually concluding that the child is simply playing at being grown up. Yet in so doing, adults may fail to perceive the meaning and intensity of the feelings that fre- quently lie hidden behind these seemingly "cute" declarations by children—a meaning and intensity that have been described by such phrases as "passionate love" and "wild jealousy and hate."[184] The French philosopher and encyclopedist Denis Diderot may have caught the essence of the Oedipal desires and emotions of children when he declared in his celebrated dialogue Le Neveu de Rameau (written more than one hundred years before Freud announced the existence of the Oedipus com- plex): "If we [as youngsters] were left to ourselves and if our bodily strength only came up to that of our phantasy we would wring our fathers' necks and sleep with our mothers."[185]

Despite the intensity of a child's Oedipal urges, they are presumably destined to remain unfulfilled.[186] Unlike King Oedipus of the celebrated Sophoclean drama, children of four and five years are hardly likely (to say the least) to kill one parent and then espouse the other. Rather, as a child's sense of reality develops, he soon comes to realize that in a conflict between his wishes and those of his parents (and there are many such conflicts), it is his wishes that must usually give way. The child soon learns that his parents are so much more powerful than he, that he must ordinarily obey when they command and follow when they lead—whether he likes it or not (and there are times when he does not like it at all). Indeed, this great disparity between the powers of parents and those of their young children tends to require these children (despite strong feelings that may beset them) to do and be what their parents want them to do and be—which normally means that the children are required to behave (within limits imposed by age differences) more or less like their parents. In fact, children of about five and a half to six years of age usually begin to make a virtue of necessity by identifying themselves with the parent of the same sex.[187] Thus a little girl of this age may smudge lipstick and rouge on her face in an effort to imitate her mother's appearance or may suddenly take an interest in her mother's household duties and become her mother's "little helper." Similarly, a little boy of five or six may start to act very much like his father, apeing his movements, mannerisms, habits and so on. Psychoanalysts believe that as a result of this self-identification of the boy with his father and the girl with her mother, the Oedipal desires of these children may gain some measure of vicarious satisfaction. That is, insofar as boys are able to "become" their father, they also become their mother's husband; and insofar as girls are able to identify themselves with their mother, they also identify themselves with her as their father's wife.[188] Psychoanalysts have, indeed, pointed out that the tendency of children about six years of age to identify themselves with the parent of the same sex is one of several major psychic events at this time of life (the appearance of the superego proper is another such event)[189] that help to reduce the intensity of Oedipal wishes and emotions and contribute to the disappearance of these wishes and emotions from consciousness.[190]

Not only do Oedipal desires and feelings tend to disappear from consciousness at about the time that a child reaches the age of six, but they—and many of the other "dark" wishes and urges of the first few years of life (the cannibalistic and sadistic wishes of early childhood, the angry and hostile urges

associated with sibling rivalry, and so on)—seem to disappear
at this time from memory as well. In fact, all that most adults
appear to be able to remember of the first five or six years of
life are what has been described as "a few incomprehensible
memory fragments."[191] This inability of most adults to remember more than a few fragments of a period of life when "we
have vividly reacted to impressions . . . have manifested human
pain and pleasure. . .have expressed love, jealousy and other
passions. . .[and] are told that we have uttered remarks which
proved to grownups that we possessed understanding and a
budding power of judgment"[192]—this "infantile amnesia"—was
in Freud's view caused by the progressive suppression or "repression"[193] of the sexual feelings of early childhood.[194] Ernest
G. Schachtel, on the other hand, has suggested in a well-known
psychoanalytic study that the mind of an adult is so structured
that it lacks the categories or schemata for the inclusion of childhood memories.[195] Infantile amnesia, in Schachtel's view, "may
be due to a formation of the memory functions which makes
them unsuitable to accommodate childhood experience, rather
than exclusively to. . .repressing objectionable material which,
without such repression, could and would be remembered."[196]
Whether or not this is so, there can be no doubt that remnants
of the ideas and feelings of early childhood often continue to
exist throughout life on an unconscious level; that these vestiges
are capable of being aroused by persons, situations or events
actually or *symbolically* reminiscent of the persons, situations
or events of early childhood; and that such unconscious vestiges
may exert, especially when aroused, a most profound effect
upon behavior during adulthood.[197]

To try to relate the psychoanalytic insights and discoveries
outlined in the preceding pages to the specific problem of constitutional law considered in this chapter—the problem of
securing a proper balance between federal and state governmental powers—is, of course, this chapter's ultimate goal. In an
effort to find a basis for achieving this goal, it might prove
helpful to recall here that many examples have been cited in
the preceding chapters regarding the possible influence exerted

by unconscious vestiges of the ideas and feelings of early child-hood upon the law and those who affect and are affected by the law. For instance, it has been suggested that the dis-graceful squabbles that occur so frequently between attorneys in court may reflect at times the influence of remnants of the anger and hostility aroused during childhood by siblings.[198] As has been pointed out in a variety of contexts, the criminal law (and particularly the punishment of criminals) may help to ventilate a number of urges and emotions of infancy, including those that are most primitive and savage.[199]

By no means, however, can these and the many other sug-gestions advanced in the preceding chapters be considered to provide more than the sketchiest sort of introduction to the myriad ways in which unconscious vestiges of the desires and feelings of early childhood may affect the law and those who influence and are influenced by it. For instance, in the dis-cussion of labor relations and labor law in Chapter IV, it was pointed out that unconscious parent-oriented ideas and urgen-cies may well be displaced from employees onto employers; and it was suggested that insofar as these ideas and urgencies may affect labor relations (particularly when a strike occurs) they ought to be taken into account by the law. No attempt was made, however, to consider the possibility (if not the likeli-hood) raised by Joel Morris and George Soule that these parent-oriented wishes and feelings are to a considerable extent Oedipal[200] and as such may well have a profound effect upon labor relations and ultimately upon labor law.[201] Indeed, the preceding chapters failed to consider specifically any of a large number of possible ways in which the Oedipal desires and emotions of childhood may affect the law. To cite a few ex-amples, Oedipal desires and emotions may well play a part in family law and particularly in the law of divorce.

> . . . a divorce signifies a permanent separation of spouses—a separation that would, in effect, fulfill the Oedipal wish of child-hood for the elimination of the main rival for the affection of the Oedipally-loved parent. Hence the idea of divorce may well stir up vestiges of the Oedipal desires of childhood. And these

vestiges may prove powerful enough to mold thought and belief concerning divorce . . . to the extent of finding expression in
legislation regarding divorce.[202]

Also, Oedipal ideas and feelings may play a role in the imposition by the law of restrictions upon the powers of such parent
surrogates as judges. It is conceivable, for instance, that hostile
father-oriented Oedipal urgencies may be responsible, in part,
for some of the "limitations on judicial powers implicit in the
use of accusatorial (rather than inquisitorial) criminal proceedings in the United States and perhaps even partly responsible for the persistence of the jury system in the United
States."[203] It is possible that the once widely held and clearly
erroneous belief that judges only find but do not make law may
also have reflected the influence of jealous and hostile Oedipal
feelings vis-à-vis the father of childhood.[204]

To return, however, to the problem of securing a proper
balance between the powers of the Federal Government and
those of the states, it will be recalled that symbolization (the
use of a person, idea or object to represent some other person,
idea or object) is a salient characteristic of unconscious mentation.[205] It will also be recalled that nations and their leaders
often serve as unconscious parent symbols and as such tend to
have parent-oriented desires and feelings displaced onto them.[206]
Indeed, psychoanalysts believe that the relationship between
a nation (or its leaders) and its citizens is frequently equated
unconsciously with the relationship between parents and their
children; and psychoanalysts believe that as a result, the attitudes, emotions and behavior of a people are likely to reflect
the influence of this unconscious identification of the nation-
citizen relationship with the parent-child relationship.[207]

These facts bring to mind the possibility that, like the
relationship between a nation and its citizens, the relationship
in the United States between the Federal Government and the
various state governments may be unconsciously regarded at
times as though it were a parent-child relationship.[208] If so,
then attempts to find a proper balance between federal and

state powers may symbolize on an unconscious level attempts
to find a proper balance between the powers of parents and
their children. Consequently, adjustments of the federal-state
power balance, especially if accomplished at the expense of the
states, may well stir up in the unconscious vestiges of the intense feelings of childhood regarding the relative powers of
parents and children. For example, decisions of the Supreme
Court limiting the freedom of action of the states by forcing
them to conform to certain federal standards (as in *Mapp v.
Ohio*)[209] may be unconsciously equated with demands during
childhood that children renounce their freedom regarding certain matters and, instead, obey parental rules of conduct. As a
result, such decisions by the Court may stir up in the unconscious vestiges of the outraged feelings and accompanying rage
and fury that parents so frequently engender in a child when
they try to train him too early or, indeed, when they may
simply restrict his freedom and demand (often quite rightly)
that he obey the rules they formulate. In like manner, decisions
of the Supreme Court enlarging federal powers in certain areas
and effecting a reduction of the powers of the states in these
areas (as in *Brown v. Board of Education of Topeka*)[210] may
well be unconsciously interpreted as an expansion of parental
powers at the expense of the powers of their children. If so,
then unconscious remnants of the great parent-child power
struggle of early childhood—the Oedipal conflict—may be revived, including remnants of the intense wishes and powerful
emotions that originally accompanied this struggle. The old
anger, hostility and rage of childhood may be aroused once
again as the enlargement of federal powers and the corresponding reduction of state powers is unconsciously reacted
to as though it were a replay of the Oedipal struggle in which
the child was ultimately forced (in large measure because of
overwhelming parental power) to renounce his fervently desired Oedipal goals.[211]

It will be recalled, however, that children tend to identify
themselves with a parent—in a sense, to "become" this parent
unconsciously[212]; and as a result, children may unconsciously

tend to regard accretions in parental power as accretions in their own power. If so, then an expansion in the powers of the Federal Government may (as indicated above) not only be equated unconsciously with an expansion of parental powers but may also be unconsciously interpreted, especially by a person who had identified himself strongly with a parent during childhood, as an expansion of the person's own powers. Indeed, herein may be found a major unconscious reason why a man may not only fail to oppose but may actually champion increases in federal powers—as, for example, John Marshall championed increases in federal powers during his thirty-five years as Chief Justice of the Supreme Court of the United States.[213]

To the extent that a man (because of a strong self-identification with a parent or for some other reason) unconsciously equates the enlargement of the powers of the Federal Government with the enlargement of his own powers, he would probably fail to such extent to regard unconsciously any increase in the powers of the states as an increase in his own powers. Nevertheless, insofar as the relationship between the Federal Government and the various state governments continues to symbolize for him on an unconscious level the relationship between parents and their children, he would presumably still tend unconsciously to interpret any emphasis upon or addition to the rights and powers of the states as an emphasis upon or an addition to the rights and powers of the other children in the family of childhood—his brothers and sisters, especially. Hence, situations in which the Supreme Court emphasizes or expands the rights and privileges of the states (as in *Erie R. R. Co. v. Tompkins*)[214] may be identified unconsciously with childhood situations in which parents emphasized or expanded the rights and privileges of siblings. Consequently, Supreme Court rulings stressing the rights and privileges of the states may stir up unconscious vestiges of the furious jealousy, hostility and rage that parental stress upon the rights and privileges of siblings once evoked—vestiges that, when aroused, are all too capable of producing intense emotional storms.

To suggest further ways in which the balancing of federal and state powers may stir up unconscious remnants of the ideas and emotions of early childhood requires little perspicacity, for unconscious reactions to adjustments in the federal-state power balance are, certainly in an individual sense, at least as numerous as there are people who react unconsciously to these adjustments. Detailing such further possible unconscious reactions to the balancing of federal and state powers would appear to be unnecessary, however, to reveal that *insofar as the federal-state relationship is unconsciously equated with the parent-child relationship, attempts to balance federal and state powers are likely to stir up vestiges of the desires and feelings of early childhood regarding the relative powers of parents and children—vestiges of desires and feelings so primitive, irrational and emotion-laden that their arousal would seem almost inevitably to lead to emotional outbursts of great intensity.*

Admittedly, this psychoanalytic explanation of why adjustments in the federal-state power balance tend to produce emotional reactions of great intensity is (like the other psychoanalytic explanations presented in earlier chapters of this book) a partial explanation that must, for completeness, be supplemented by political, social, economic, historical and other relevant explanations. Yet even so, this psychoanalytic explanation deserves attention and may prove to be significant, for if the balancing of federal and state powers is capable of stirring up unconscious vestiges of the urges and feelings of early childhood—which, in turn, produce very powerful (and sometimes prolonged) emotional storms—then the likelihood is that these urges and feelings will influence to some extent the result of this balancing. After all, wishes and feelings able to engender an intense (and lengthy) emotional reaction concerning a matter would certainly seem capable of influencing decisions regarding the matter—especially if such wishes and feelings operate on an unconscious level beyond the reach of conscious knowledge, evaluation and control.[215]

The likelihood that the urges and emotions of early childhood play a role in the task of helping to secure a proper federal-state power balance can, however, hardly be considered desirable. So vital and perennial a constitutional problem as balancing the powers of the Federal Government with those of the states would, one would hope, be affected not by infantile urges and emotions but rather would be governed as much as possible by conscious, mature, informed, reflective adult thought.

Still, it is helpful to know that unconscious traces of the ideas and feelings of early childhood may well influence attempts to adjust the federal-state power balance. Not that such knowledge will somehow magically eradicate the effect of these infantile ideas and feelings, however: as psychoanalysts have learned, merely familiarizing one's self with unconscious forces is hardly enough to prevent these forces from affecting one's behavior.[216] Nevertheless, knowing that activated vestiges of the desires, urges and feelings of early childhood are probably in part responsible for the emotional outbursts that so frequently greet the balancing of federal and state powers may well prove helpful in tempering these emotional outbursts (much, for example, as knowing that obesity is frequently a sign of serious emotional difficulties has helped to shame many persons into controlling their weight). Hopefully, such a tempering of these emotional storms will not only reduce the influence of the infantile ideas and feelings that have presumably played a part in their appearance but will also enable more appropriate ideas and feelings regarding the need to achieve a proper federal-state power balance to find expression. After all, as indicated above, it is surely desirable that the periodic resolutions of the fundamental and perennial constitutional problem of balancing the powers of the Federal Government with those of the states be, as much as possible, the product of conscious, informed, reflective and mature considerations: the product of the best thought that Americans are capable of devoting to the problem.

XI

CONCLUSION

IN THE HOPE OF gaining new and meaningful insights regarding the law (and thereby facilitating improvements in it and the resolution of some of its basic problems) this book has sought to stimulate an interest in synthesizing psychoanalytic psychology and the law. Thus in Part I, certain fundamental psychoanalytic tenets were presented and then applied in a general way to the law. In Part II, four specific, basic and perennial problems of constitutional law were detailed and then examined in the light of psychoanalytic doctrines.

The syntheses of psychoanalysis and law offered in the preceding chapters were, as has been seen, many, varied and quite detailed at times; and presenting a summary of them now in brief and general terms would hardly seem likely to increase their ability to convince. Yet, certain related matters (some of them implicit in the discussions in the preceding chapters) ought to be mentioned here.

For one thing, it ought to be noted that a complete psychoanalytic explanation—be it of a neurotic symptom or of some aspect of the law—is likely to draw upon a *number* of psychoanalytic discoveries. For example, a reasonably complete psychoanalytic explanation of the punishment of criminals must draw upon psychoanalytic insights pertaining to such matters as aggression, unconscious symbolism, the supergo, unconscious motivation and the mental mechanisms of projection and identification. Relevant here is the psychoanalytic principle of "over-determination"—the principle that almost all behavioral events have more than one determinant; or as Ruth L. Munroe has put it: "several different trends, conscious or unconscious, typically operate *simultaneously* to determine a given psychic event."[1]

Further, it ought to be observed that this book has given considerable emphasis to some parts of the law—to procedure, for instance, and particularly to the criminal law—while slighting such areas of the law as sales, corporations, negotiable instruments and the like. Perhaps it would be possible to defend this apparent disproportionate treatment of the law by pointing out that this book constitutes only a first effort to synthesize psychoanalysis and the law, and by expressing the hope that future books on the subject will redress any apparent imbalance. Yet if the research done for this book is any criterion, it would appear to indicate that psychoanalytic psychology is likely to shed very little light, now or in the future, upon those technical parts of the law (for example, many—if not most—segments of the law pertaining to commercial transactions) in which justice often seems less important than definiteness and certainty—parts of the law in which, in a sense, it is "not so important that a law be 'just' . . . as that it be settled."[2] Rather, psychoanalytic psychology seems likely to contribute most to those areas of the law that reflect the play of strong emotions and in which justice is of paramount importance.

Another observation that ought perhaps to be made here is that, certainly at this time, it would appear to be practically impossible to write a definitive psychoanalytic study of the law. Not only is the law constantly changing, but psychoanalytic psychology itself (like any ongoing and presumably open-ended psychological system) is also subject to modification and change, no matter how well-settled its basic tenets may appear to be.[3] Moreover (as one soon learns when trying to apply psychoanalysis to the law), there would seem to be an almost unlimited number of possible connections between psychoanalytic psychology and the law. As a result, one is hard put to do more than examine what is hopefully a representative sampling of the ways in which psychoanalytic psychology may prove applicable to the law.

Perhaps all this is another way of saying that although this book's paramount objective of seeking, through a synthesis of psychoanalysis and law, to obtain a better understanding than hitherto of the law and the related objective of helping to resolve some of the law's problems by finding ways of improving it may have been fulfilled in the preceding chapters, only a beginning has been made in this book in the task of demonstrating how psychoanalysis may be applied to the law and how it may help to point the way to desirable changes, particularly in those areas greatly in need of reform. For instance, the preceding chapters have offered at most a brief comment or two concerning the law of evidence; yet there can be little doubt that the law of evidence is in great need of improvement and that psychoanalytic insights are likely to be of immediate value in helping to suggest needed reforms in this part of the law.[4] Judge Bazelon has pointed out, for example, that psychoanalytic discoveries concerning guilt cast strong doubt upon the traditional evidentiary assumptions "(1) that one who flees shortly after a criminal act is committed or when he is accused of committing it does so because he feels some guilt concerning that act and (2) that one who feels some guilt concerning an act has committed that act."[5] Further, it is surely arguable that the hearsay exception which permits the introduction into evidence of "declarations against interest," though clearly hearsay—an exception based upon the view that no person will knowingly make a false statement to his own pecuniary or proprietary detriment, nor intentionally manufacture false evidence against himself[6]—is untenable in the light of psychoanalytic discoveries regarding masochism.[7] As scholars have begun to point out, evidentiary rules concerning the credibility of witnesses and techniques for testing the credibility of witnesses would certainly benefit from an examination in the light of psychoanalytic tenets.[8]

A final matter that ought to be mentioned is that psychoanalytic theories have almost traditionally aroused considerable opposition.[9] In fact, incredible as it may now seem, Freud was regarded in pre–World-War-I days as a dangerous psychopath and his theories (much the same theories outlined in this book) were considered a grave threat to civilized, communal life.

> In those days Freud and his followers were regarded not only as sexual perverts but as either obsessional or paranoic psychopaths as well, and the combination was felt to be a real danger

to the community. Freud's theories were interpreted as direct incitements to surrendering all restraint, to reverting to a state of primitive license and savagery. No less than civilization itself was at stake. As happens in such circumstances, the panic aroused led in itself to the loss of that very restraint the opponents believed they were defending. All ideas of good manners, of tolerance and even a sense of decency—let alone any thought of objective discussion or investigation—simply went by the board.[10]

This attitude towards psychoanalysis is hard to conceive of today, especially since Freud seems to have become something of a folk or culture hero here in the United States.

> In America today, Freud's intellectual influence is greater than that of any other modern thinker. He presides over the mass media, the college classroom, the chatter at parties, the playgrounds of the middle classes where child-rearing is a prominent and somewhat anxious topic of conversation . . . . he is being treated as a culture hero.[11]

Nevertheless, opposition to psychoanalysis certainly continues to persist, though usually finding expression nowadays in a somewhat subdued (and often subtle) fashion. In *Uses and Abuses of Psychology*, for example, H. J. Eysenck praises Freud as an innovator and genius but states (ever so sadly) that until psychoanalysis becomes more scientific and its practitioners employ "traditional methods of scientific inference and experimentation" (which, of course, neither patients nor society itself would long tolerate), psychoanalytic tenets simply cannot (alas) be given any credence.[12]

Though legal scholarship has, in the main, ignored psychoanalytic discoveries (incidentally, a most effective form of opposition), a number of legal scholars have openly indicated a disrelish for these discoveries—especially for applying them to the law. Typical perhaps are the views of Professor Edwin W. Patterson, who has rejected any and all explanations of human behavior that rely upon the existence of unconscious motives and who (as was pointed out in Chapter IX) has contended that even if lawyers and judges do indeed have an unconscious, it has not been shown to have a distinctive or significant influence upon the law or its enforcement.[13] On the other hand, an as yet very small but increasing number of lawyers are beginning to take an active interest in the applicability of psychoanalytic psychology to the law.[14] If the attitude and enthusiasm of this group are valid harbingers, there is reason to believe that a reasonably large number of their fellow lawyers will ultimately accept this book's invitation; and in an effort to increase their understanding of and to help improve and resolve the problems of the law, they will familiarize themselves with psychoanalytic discoveries and will attempt to apply them to the law.

As Mr. Justice Story stated when inaugurated as Dane Professor of Law in Harvard University in 1829: "The perfect lawyer, like the perfect orator, must accomplish himself for his duties by familiarity with every study. It may be truly said, that to him nothing, that concerns human nature or human art, is indifferent or useless."[15]

REFERENCE NOTES

CHAPTER I

1. Brenner, An Elementary Textbook of Psychoanalysis 136–38 (Doubleday Anchor Books ed. 1957); Weihofen, The Urge to Punish 28–29 (1956).
2. "Dean Roscoe Pound long ago said: 'Historically, our substantive criminal law is based on a theory of punishing the vicious will. It postulates a free agent confronted with a choice between doing right and doing wrong and choosing freely to do wrong.' " Glueck, Law and Psychiatry 9 (1962).
3. For a brief but incisive discussion of the relationship postulated by psychoanalysts between guilt and self-punitive behavior, see Alexander, Fundamentals of Psychoanalysis 118–21 (1948).
4. A phrase coined by Freud. See Freud, *Some Character-Types Met With In Psycho-Analytic Work*, in 4 Collected Papers 342–44 (1956).
5. See Jerome Frank's Courts On Trial 159–61 (1950), for a commentary upon these attempts.
6. This belief frequently finds expression in (or is, perhaps, a product of) the view, closely associated with the name of William Blackstone, that law is essentially a sacred mystery: a mystery that may be examined—but reverently, and not too closely. See Boorstin, The Mysterious Science Of The Law (1941).
7. See Carpenter, Foundations of Modern Jurisprudence 206–08, 219–20 (1958).
8. Robinson, Law And The Lawyers 72 (1935).
9. *Id.* at 111.
10. For a resume of some of the achievements of "applied psychoanalysis," see Hendrick, Facts And Theories of Psychoanalysis 301–21 (3d ed. 1958).
11. See, *e.g.*, Brown, Freud And The Post-Freudians (Penguin Books ed. 1961); Shakow & Rapaport, The Influence Of Freud On American Psychology (Meridian Books ed. 1968).
12. N.Y. Times, June 17, 1956, § 7 (Book Reviews), p. 6, col. 4.
13. Robinson, *op. cit. supra* note 8, at 108.

14. Katz, *Psychoanalysis and Law,* 5 U. Chi. L. School Record 13 (1956).
15. Freud, A General Introduction to Psychoanalysis 112 (Permabooks ed. 1957).
16. Clark & Marshall, A Treatise On The Law Of Crimes 398 (6th ed. 1958).
17. See Davidson, *Irresistible Impulse And Criminal Responsibility,* in Nice, Crime and Insanity 30–32 (1958).
18. Freud, New Introductory Lectures On Psychoanalysis 108 (1933).
19. See, *e.g.,* Bromberg & Cleckley, *The Medico-Legal Dilemma—A Suggested Solution,* 42 J. Crim. L., C. & P. S. 729–45 (1952).
20. Glueck, Crime And Justice 180 (1936).
21. Of Freud's five major "case histories," one pertains to a lawyer and another to a judge. See Freud. *Notes Upon A Case of Obsessional Neurosis,* and *Psycho-Analytic Notes Upon An Autobiographical Account Of A Case Of Paranoia (Dementia Paranoides),* in 3 Collected Papers 292–470 (1956).
22. Hurst, The Growth Of American Law 15 (1950).
23. See Schroeder, *The Psychologic Study of Judicial Opinions,* 6 Calif. L. Rev. 89, 95 (1918).
24. Cardozo, The Nature Of The Judicial Process (1921).
25. See Frank, *op. cit. supra* note 5, at 161.
26. Freud to the contrary notwithstanding? See Freud, New Introductory Lectures On Psychoanalysis, *op. cit. supra* note 18, at 248. See also Hall, General Principles Of Criminal Law 455–58 (2d ed. 1960).
27. Hutchins, *The Law And The Psychologists,* 16 Yale Review 678, 689 (1927).
28. Sutherland, Principles of Criminology 3 (5th ed. 1955).
29. Cohen, Reason and Law 187 (First Collier Books ed. 1961).
30. See Hurst, *op. cit. supra* note 22, at 37.
31. Pound, *The Causes Of Popular Dissatisfaction With The Administration Of Justice,* in Trumbell, Materials on the Lawyer's Professional Responsibility 9–25 (1957).
32. *Id.* at 13.

CHAPTER II

1. See Whyte, The Unconscious before Freud 77–176 (1960).
2. Cardozo, The Nature Of The Judicial Process 11–12 (1921).
3. See, *e.g.,* Patterson, Jurisprudence: Men and Ideas of the Law 550 (1953).
4. For thought-provoking suggestions concerning the possible unconscious roots of the ultranationalism that has been "the scourge

of Western civilization for the last century and a half," see Kurth, *Politics: Unconscious Factors in Social Prejudice and Mass Movements*, in Herma & Kurth, A Handbook Of Psychoanalysis 297, 305–09 (Forum Books ed. 1963).

5. Freud, *The Unconscious*, in 4 Collected Papers 98, 119 (1956).
6. A good general account of the influence of unconscious wishes upon behavior is to be found in many standard psychoanalytic texts: for example, in Fenichel, The Psychoanalytic Theory Of Neurosis (1945); Hendrick, Facts And Theories Of Psychoanalysis (3d ed. 1958); Nunberg, Principles Of Psychoanalysis (1955).
7. See, *e.g.*, Malinowski, Sex and Repression in Savage Society (1927), and Jones, *Mother-Right And The Sexual Ignorance Of Savages*, 6 International Journal Of Psychoanalysis 109 (1925).
8. See, *e.g.*, Alexander & Staub, The Criminal, The Judge, And The Public (1956); Abrahamsen, The Psychology Of Crime (First Science ed. 1964); Wittels, Freud And His Time (1931).
9. Wittels, *id.* at 378–83. Zilboorg, The Psychology of the Criminal Act and Punishment 75–76 (1954).
10. The vengeful motives of society and its representatives vis-a-vis criminals are considered at length in Menninger, The Crime of Punishment (1968).
11. See Heller, Polen, & Polsky, An Introduction To Legal Interviewing 18–23 (1960).
12. See Modlin, *The Client and You—What You Are*, 16 N.Y. County B. Bull. 151, 153–54 (1959).
13. For a particularly useful discussion of the problems presented by litigious paranoiacs, see B. Glueck, *The Forensic Phase of Litigious Paranoia*, 5 Journal of the American Institute of Criminal Law and Criminology 371 (1914–1915).
14. Modlin, *op. cit. supra* note 12, at 155.
15. See Heller *et al.*, *op. cit. supra* note 11, at 32.
16. This tendency of lawyers to identify themselves unconsciously with their clients is most easily discernible, perhaps, among defense counsel in criminal cases. See Reiwald, Society and its Criminals 175–79 (1949). For material concerning the unconscious mental mechanism of identification, see, *e.g.*, Hollitscher, Sigmund Freud: An Introduction 63–71 (1947).
17. See generally Frank, Courts On Trial 80–102 (1950).
18. Schroeder, *The Psychologic Study of Judicial Opinions*, 6 Calif. L. Rev. 89 (1918).
19. Frank, *op. cit. supra* note 17, at 250.

20. "One of us once had a judge in psychotherapeutic treatment who had latent homosexual feelings. Every time that he had to judge a case of obvious homosexuality, he fell into a state of enraged indignation." Bergler & Meerloo, Justic and Injustice 69 (1963).

21. Frank, Law and the Modern Mind 147 (6th printing 1949).

22. Bergler & Meerloo, *op. cit. supra* note 20, at 67–85.

23. Reiwald, *op. cit. supra* note 16, at 42–62.

24. *Id.* at 45.

25. See West, *A Psychological Theory Of Law*, in Sayre, Interpretations Of Modern Legal Philosophies 767, 774 (1947).

26. Bergler & Meerloo, *op. cit. supra* note 20, at 67–68; McCarty, Psychology and the Law 177–204 (1960).

27. Borchard, Convicting the Innocent (1932); Frank & Frank, Not Guilty (1957).

28. Bergler & Meerloo, *op. cit. supra* note 20, at 68.

29. Kaufman, Nietzsche 382 (Meridian Books ed. 1956).

30. For an unforgettable description of man's all-too-eager search for opportunities to express the aggressiveness within him, see Freud, Civilization And Its Discontents 85–91 (1930).

31. Smith, *Components Of Proof In Legal Proceedings*, 51 Yale L.J. 537, 575 (1942).

32. Reiwald, *op. cit. supra* note 16, at 13.

33. Weihofen, The Urge to Punish 28 (1956).

34. Barnes & Teeters, New Horizons In Criminology 617 (1945).

35. Menninger, *op. cit. supra* note 10, at 153. Also relevant is R. Eissler, *Scapegoats Of Society*, in K. Eissler, Searchlights On Delinquency 288, 295, 304–05 (1949).

36. Exodus 21:24.

37. See, *e.g.*, Alexander, Fundamentals of Psychoanalysis 102 (1948).

38. See Lunchenbill & Chiera, *The Code of Hammurabi*, in Smith, The Origin And History Of Hebrew Law 181, 209–10 (1931).

39. Abrahamsen, *op. cit. supra* note 8, at 3. See also Reik, The Compulsion to Confess 288–98 (First Evergreen ed. 1961).

40. See Bedau, The Death Penalty in America 40–42 (Anchor Books ed. 1964). See also Laurence, A History Of Capital Punishment (1960).

41. For a discussion of these laws, see Davis v. Berry, 216 Fed. 413 (1914); Mickle v. Henrichs, 262 Fed. 687 (1918), and Stevas, Life, Death and the Law 160–97 (1961).

42. Reiwald, *op. cit. supra* note 16, at 279.

43. Wittels, *op. cit. supra* note 8, at 383.

44. See, *e.g.*, Schoenfeld, *In Defense Of Retribution In The Law*, 35 Psychoanalytic Quarterly 108, 109–111 (1966).

45. For an enumeration and description of these horrible punishments, see Laurence, *op. cit. supra* note 40.

46. Banay, We Call Them Criminals 280 (1957).

47. See, *e.g.*, Menninger, *op. cit. supra* note 10.

48. See, *e.g.*, 4 Stephen's Commentaries On The Laws Of England 12 (Jenks ed. 1925).

49. The classic statement of what may happen if man's desire for vengeance is ignored by society is to be found in Holmes, The Common Law 41 (1881).

50. Cohen, Reason and Law 54 (Collier Books ed. 1961).

CHAPTER III

1. Bergler, The Superego 7 (1952).

2. *Id* at 49.

3. "The entire matter of the inner conscience of the human being has not yet reached the stage of textbook simplicity and finality." Bergler & Meerloo, Justice and Injustice 10 (1963).

4. A number of psychoanalysts make a distinction between the superego and the so-called "ego-ideal" (the standards of conduct towards which a person aspires). See, *e.g.*, Novey, *The Role of the Superego and Ego-Ideal in Character Formation*, in Levitt, Readings In Psychoanalytic Psychology 114, 119 (1959).

5. See Brenner, An Elementary Textbook of Psychoanalysis 125 (Doubleday Anchor Books ed., 1957).

6. White, Ethics For Unbelievers 45 (1948).

7. Klein, The Psycho-Analysis Of Children 195–209 (First Evergreen ed. 1960).

8. Freud, New Introductory Lectures On Psycho-Analysis 89 (1933).

9. See Jones, Hamlet And Oedipus 85 (Doubleday Anchor ed. 1955).

10. Flugel, Man, Morals, And Society 115 (Compass Books ed. 1961).

11. Freud, Group Psychology And The Analysis Of The Ego 88 (1922).

12. Brenner, *op. cit. supra* note 5, at 136. It has been suggested that this demand for retributive punishments ultimately reflects the operation of the instinct of race preservation. See Abrahamsen, The Psychology Of Crime 3 (First Science ed. 1964).

13. Freud, An Outline Of Psychoanalysis 17 (1949).

14. Fromm, Man For Himself 158–59 (1947).

15. See Schoenfeld, *A Psychoanalytic Theory of Juvenile Delinquency*, 17 Crime and Delinquency 469, 473 (1971).
16. See Fuller, The Problems Of Jurisprudence 103–14 (Temporary ed. 1949).
17. Hart, The Concept Of Law 181 (1961).
18. Newman, Equity and Law 26 n.25 (1961).
19. Clark, Equity 28–48 (1954).
20. *Id.* at 41.
21. *Id.* at 31. See also Osborne, The Law Of Mortgages 17 (1951).
22. Clark, *op. cit. supra* note 19, at 33.
23. De Funiak, Modern Equity 84, 101–02 (2d. ed. 1956).
24. Precision Co. v. Automotive Co., 324 U.S. 806, 814 (1945).
25. See the discussion of these defenses in Hall, General Principles of Criminal Law 360–448 (2d ed. 1947).
26. See Clark & Marshall, The Law Of Crimes 620–34 (6th ed. 1958).
27. Holmes, The Common Law 61 (1881).
28. Clark & Marshall, *op. cit. supra* note 26, at 423. See Perkins, Criminal Law 883–909 (1957).
29. See, *e.g.*, the authoritative and incisive discussion of the defense of insanity in Glueck, Law and Psychiatry (1962).
30. Cardozo, *What Medicine Can Do For Law*, in Selected Writings of Benjamin Nathan Cardozo 385 (1947).
31. M'Naghten's Case, 10 Cl. & Fin. 200, 210, 8 Eng. Rep. 718, 722 (1843).
32. See, *e.g.*, Harding, *Individual Responsibility In Anglo-American Law*, in Responsibility In Law And In Morals 69–71 (1960).
33. "Punishment [of such persons] . . . seems to us to be morally wrong because we feel that [they] . . . are not 'guilty' in the usual sense. Since anticipation of legal consequences formed no part of their motivation, we feel that they have not had an adequate chance of guiding their actions according to the standards of the community." Waelder, *Psychiatry And The Problem Of Criminal Responsibility*, 101 U. Pa. L. Rev. 378, 379 (1952).
34. Harding, *op. cit. supra* note 32, at 70–71.
35. Fuller, The Morality Of Law 46 (1964).
36. *Id.* at 59.
37. *Id.* at 49–51, 63–91.
38. *Id.* at 47.
38. In a sense, this definition of law sums up Austin's philosophy of law as expressed in his *magnum opus* Lectures On Jurisprudence.

40. See the discussion of general commands in Austin, Lectures On Jurisprudence 94–98 (4th ed. 1879).

41. See Hart, *op. cit. supra* note 17, at 95.

42. See Stone, Social Dimensions Of Law And Justice 696–728 (1966), for a balanced review of the moral and philosophical problems raised by the growth of administrative agencies during the twentieth century.

43. See, *e.g.*, Bedau, The Death Penalty In America 32–119 (1964), for a summary of the use of the death penalty in the penal codes of the various states. See *e.g.*, Stevas, Life, Death, and the Law 160–97, 294–309 (1961) for a summary of the use of sterilization by the various states as a punishment for rape and other crimes (and as a "eugenic" measure).

44. For a more complete discussion of the relationship between legal certainty, law reform, and the immature superego, see Schoenfeld, *The Superego's Influence On The Law*, 14 De Paul L. Rev. 299, 305–10 (1965).

45. Vanderbilt, The Challenge of Law Reform 40 (1955). See also Pound, Criminal Justice In America 154–64 (1945).

46. Holdsworth, Charles Dickens As A Legal Historian 86 (1928).

47. Dickens, Bleak House 3 (1904).

48. Sunderland, *The English Struggle For Procedural Reform*, 39 Harv. L. Rev. 725 (1926).

49. *Ibid.*

50. Pound, *David Dudley Field: An Appraisal*, in Reppy, David Dudley Field: Centenary Essays Celebrating One Hundred Years Of Legal Reform 3, 9 (1949).

51. Vanderbilt, *op. cit. supra* note 45, at 53.

52. *Id.* at 53–54. For a bird's-eye view of the forms of action and some of their historical complexities, see Morgan, Introduction To The Study Of Law 56–83 (1926).

53. Radin, Anglo-American Legal History 202 (1936).

54. Hurst, The Growth of American Law 72 (1950).

55. *Id.* at 91.

56. See Vanderbilt, *op. cit. supra* note 45, at 55.

57. Morgan, Some Problems Of Proof Under The Anglo-American System Of Litigation 29 (1956).

58. See, *e.g.*, *id.* at 35.

59. See, *e.g.*, Frank, Courts On Trial 80–102 (1950).

60. Of particular interest here is Fowler, *A Psychological Approach To Procedural Law*, 43 Yale L.J. 1254, 1265–66 (1934).

61. Frank, *op. cit. supra* note 59, at 80.

62. For a short but authoritative description of trial by battle as well as other early common-law "trials," see Plucknett, A Concise History Of The Common Law 108–12 (2d ed. 1936).

63. Smith, *Components Of Proof In Legal Proceedings*, 51 Yale L.J. 537, 575 (1942).

64. *Id.* at 575.

CHAPTER IV

1. Freud, A General Introduction to Psychoanalysis 176 (Permabook ed. 1957).

2. Fromm, The Forgotten Language 7 (1951).

3. See, *e.g.*, Rank, The Myth of the Birth of the Hero and Other Writings (Vintage ed. 1959).

4. See, *e.g.*, Friedlander, The Psychoanalytic Approach To Juvenile Delinquency 130 (1960).

5. See, *e.g.*, Abrahamsen, The Psychology of Crime 128–29 (1960).

6. See Jones, Papers On Psycho-Analysis 101 (5th ed. 1948).

7. Freud, *op. cit. supra* note 1, at 160–173.

8. Jones, *op. cit. supra* note 6, at 102.

9. Flugel, The Psycho-Analytic Study Of The Family 117–32 (1950).

10. *Ibid.*; Reiwald, Society and its Criminals 42–62 (1949); Frank, Law and the Modern Mind 18–21 (6th printing 1949); Morris, *The Psychoanalysis of Labor Strikes*, 10 Lab. L.J. 833 (1959).

11. See, *e.g.*, Menninger, Love Against Hate 9–14 (Harvest Books ed. 1942).

12. See, *e.g.*, Balint, The Early Years Of Life 51–54 (1954).

13. See, *e.g.*, Freud, *op. cit. supra* note 1, at 168.

14. Holmes, The Common Law 25–34 (1881).

15. See, *e.g.*, Karpman, *Criminality, Insanity And The Law*, 39 J. Crim. L. & C. 584, 590 (1949).

16. The articles stolen by kleptomaniacs may also represent unconscious phallic substitutes. See, *e.g.*, Abrahamsen, *op. cit. supra* note 5. For a general summary of the law-oriented findings of psychoanalysts concerning kleptomaniacs, see Mannheim, Comparative Criminology 326–27 (1965).

17. See, *e.g.*, Guttmacher & Weihofen, Psychiatry and The Law 57–60 (1952).

18. Abrahamsen, *op. cit. supra* note 5, at 129. A strong connection also appears to exist between pyromania and the urethral eroticism of early childhood. See Ferenczi, *Composite Formations Of Erotic And Character Traits*, in Further Contributions To

The Theory And Technique Of Psycho-Analysis 257, 258 (1951).

19. See the discussion of the "neurotic criminal" in Alexander & Staub, The Criminal, The Judge, And The Public 93–108 (Free Press ed. 1956).

20. See Davidson, *Irresistible Impulse and Criminal Responsibility,* in Crime And Insanity 1 (Nice ed. 1958).

21. For a paean in praise of the efficacy of rehabilitative treatment, see Menninger, The Crime Of Punishment 253 *et. seq.* (1968).

22. For a summary of some of the difficulties that face the psycho-analyst who hopes to treat kleptomania, pyromania, and other so-called "impulse neuroses," see Fenichel, The Psychoanalytic Theory Of Neurosis 385–86 (1945). For a useful evaluation of "treatment" in public mental institutions and of society's reluctance to spend and to do what is necessary to improve this "treatment," see Birnbaum, *The Right To Treatment,* 46 A.B.A.J. 499 (1960).

23. See, *e.g.,* Birnbaum, *id.* at 500. For a particularly egregious example of how punishment and "treatment" in a state institution may prove to be identical (especially in regard to a so-called sexual psychopath), see *In re* Maddox, 351 Mich. 358, 88 N.W.2d 470 (1958).

24. Szasz, Law, Liberty, And Psychiatry 47 (1963).

25. See Morris, *supra* note 10, at 833–842. See also Stagner, Psychology of Industrial Conflict 160 (1956).

26. Morris, *supra* note 10, at 833.

27. The irrationality, emotionalism, and violence that have so often tended to characterize labor relations in the United States are described with particularly telling effect in the writings of Sylvester Petro. See, *e.g.,* Petro, The Labor Policy Of The Free Society (1957), and Petro, The Kohler Strike (1961).

28. Soule, The Strength of Nations 195 (1942).

29. See Morris, *supra* note 10, at 833, 834; Stagner, *op. cit. supra* note 25, at 416.

30. See p. 6 *supra.*

31. As Mr. Justice Oliver Wendell Holmes, Jr., pointed out in typically laconic fashion in his celebrated dissent in Lochner v. New York, 198 U.S. 45, 76 (1905): "General propositions do not decide concrete cases."

32. See the discussion of this latter possibility in Gregory, Labor And The Law 547–51 (2d rev. ed. 1961).

33. Pertinent here is the discussion of power structures in a democracy

in Stone, Social Dimensions Of Law And Justice 626–35 (1966).

34. Arnold, The Symbols Of Government 196 (Harbinger ed. 1962). See also Gabriel, The Course of American Democratic Thought 380, 402, 407 (1940).

35. The psychoanalytic explanation offered in the text (like other comparable psychoanalytic explanations that have been and will be advanced in this book) is a partial explanation that, for completeness, must be supplemented by other explanations. See p. 9 *supra.*

36. This fear of a political revolution was based in part upon the rise of totalitarian regimes in Europe during the depression and the emergence in the United States at this time of such would-be authoritarian leaders as Fritz Kuhn and Huey Long. For a fictional—but surely vivid and engrossing—account of the sort of fascist revolution that many people feared might well occur in the United States during the depression, see the well-known Sinclair Lewis novel It Can't Happen Here.

37. Schwartz, The Supreme Court 13–14 (1957).

38. For a particularly helpful and essentially complete account of the "struggle which began on February 5, 1937, when President Roosevelt disclosed his plan to enlarge the Supreme Court" (p.v), see Alsop & Catledge, The 168 Days (1938).

39. See, *e.g.,* Black, The People and the Court 58 (1960).

40. Gabriel, *op. cit. supra* note 34, at 404.

41. See n.35 *supra.*

42. Of particular interest here is the chapter entitled "The Judge And The Father," in Reiwald, *op. cit. supra* note 10, at 42–65.

43. Hancock, *Conflict, Drama and Magic in the Early English Law,* 14 Ohio St. L.J. 119, 123 (1953).

44. In the unconscious, "there is nothing corresponding to the idea of time, no recognition of the passage of time, and (a thing which is very remarkable and awaits adequate attention in philosophic thought) no alteration of mental processes by the passage of time." Freud, New Introductory Lectures On Psycho-Analysis 104 (1933).

45. Code Of Professional Responsibility, Canon 7, EC 7-22 (1970).

46. *Ibid.*

47. For a brief but sound resume of certain major aspects of the contempt powers of judges, see Perkins, Criminal Law 456–66 (1957). For a more complete analysis of the contempt power, see Thomas, Problems of Contempt of Court (1934).

48. Illinois v. Allen, 397 U.S. 337, 343 (1970).

49. Relevant here are West, *A Psychological Theory Of Law,* in Sayre, Interpretations of Modern Legal Philosophies 767, 774 (1947), and Frank, *Freud And The Law,* 18 The Psychoanalytic Review 247–49 (1931).
50. Code Of Professional Responsibility, Canon 7, EC 7–38 (1970).
51. *Id.,* EC 7–37.
52. Frank, Law and the Modern Mind 18–21 (6th Printing 1949).
53. *Ibid.*
54. *Id.* at 249–50.
55. Of interest here is Hopkins, Father Or Sons? 22, 25 (1927); Flugel, *op. cit. supra* note 9, at 125, 126, 128; Berman, Justice in the U.S.S.R. 16, 28 (Vintage ed. 1963).
56. Clark & Marshall, A Treatise On The Law Of Crimes 675 (6th ed. 1958) (emphasis added).
57. Holmes, *op. cit. supra* note 14, at 108.
58. Berman, *op. cit. supra* note 55, at 6.
59. Szasz, *op. cit. supra* note 24, at 220.
60. See, *e.g.,* N.Y. Domestic Relations Law § 215; Ploscowe & Freed, Family Law 629–56 (1963).
61. See, *e.g.,* Jackson v. Bishop, 404 F.2d. 571 (8th Cir. 1968); Jackson v. Godwin, 400 F.2d. 529 (5th Cir. 1968); Jordan v. Fitzharris, 257 F. Supp. 674 (1966).
62. For a brief—but to the point—discussion of Workmen's Compensation statutes, see Prosser, Torts 518–43 (1941).
63. Giallombardo, Juvenile Delinquency: A Book of Readings 335 (1966).
64. *In re* Gault, 387 U.S. 1, 26 (1967).
65. See, *e.g.,* Lenroot, *The Juvenile Court Today,* in Vedder, The Juvenile Offender: Perspective and Readings 327 (1954); Caldwell, *The Juvenile Court: Its Development and Some Major Problems,* in Giallombardo, *op. cit. supra* note 63, at 355, 360–61.
66. *The Administration of Juvenile Justice—the Juvenile Court and Related Methods of Delinquency Control,* in Task Force Report: Juvenile Delinquency and Youth Crime 1, 7 (1967).
67. Lemert, *The Juvenile Court—Quest And Realities, id.* at 91.
68. See Kent v. United States, 383 U.S. 541 (1966); *In re* Gault, 387 U.S. 1 (1967); In the Matter of Winship 397 U.S. 358 (1970).
69. See *The Administration of Juvenile Justice—the Juvenile Court and Related Methods of Delinquency Control, op. cit. supra* note 66, at 7–9; Vinter, *The Juvenile Court As An Institution,* in Task Force Report: Juvenile Delinquency And Youth Crime 84–90 (1967).

CHAPTER V

1. Dollard, Frustration And Aggression 1 (1939).
2. This doctrine finds particularly subtle expression in the writings of Erich Fromm and other so-called "Neo-Freudians." See, *e.g.*, Fromm, Man For Himself 210–26 (1947).
3. Of interest here is Dollard, *op. cit. supra* note 1, at 23–26, and Freud, New Introductory Lectures On Psycho-Analysis 241–48 (1933).
4. Storr, Human Aggression 109 (1968).
5. *Id.* at 53.
6. James, *The Moral Equivalent Of War,* in Memories And Studies, 267, 272 (1917).
7. See, *e.g.*, Klein, The Psychoanalysis Of Children 185–88 (First Evergreen ed. 1960).
8. See, *e.g.*, Abraham, *A Short Study Of The Development Of The Libido, Viewed In The Light of Mental Disorders,* in 1 Selected Papers Of Karl Abraham 418, 496 (1960).
9. Mao Tse-tung, Quotations From Chairman Mao Tse-tung 61, 63 (2d ed. 1967).
10. Freud, *Why War?,* in 5 Collected Papers 273, 282 (1956).
11. Freud, Civilization And Its Discontents 85 (1955).
12. See, *e.g.*, Menninger, Man Against Himself 372 (1938).
13. See, *e.g.*, Jones, The *Problem of Paul Morphy: a Contribution to the Psychology of Chess,* in 1 Essays In Applied Psycho-Analysis 165, 195 (1951).
14. Bergler, The Psychology of Gambling vii (1957).
15. For a short but particularly helpful source of information concerning the relationship between psychoanalysis and teaching, see Hellman, *Psycho-Analysis And The Teacher,* in Sutherland, Psychoanalysis And Contemporary Thought 58–76 (Evergreen Books ed. 1959).
16. By no means can one safely dismiss the abusive and insulting manner of teaching law attacked in the text as simply an abandoned practice of the past. See, *e.g.*, Peairs, *Essay on the Teaching of Law,* 12 J. Legal Ed. 323–371 (1959–60).
17. See, *e.g.*, St. John-Stevas, Life, Death, and the Law 179 (1961); Menninger, *op. cit. supra* note 12, at 238–39 (n).
18. Mickle v. Hendricks, 262 F. 687, 691 (1918).
19. See, *e.g.*, Menninger, *op. cit. supra* note 12, at 260–62.
20. For a discussion of the concept of sublimation, see Alexander, Fundamentals Of Psychoanalysis 110–13 (1948).
21. See, *e.g.*, Brenner, An Elementary Textbook of Psychoanalysis, 106 (Doubleday Anchor Books ed. 1957).

22. See, *e.g.*, Menninger, *op. cit. supra* note 12, at 317–43.
23. *Id.* at 281–83.
24. Guttmacher & Weihofen, Psychiatry and The Law 48 (1952).
25. Bergler, *Suicide: Psychoanalytic and Medicolegal Aspects*, 8 La. L. Rev. 504, 505 (1948).
26. Menninger, *op. cit. supra* note 12, at 43–44.
27. *Ibid.*
28. West, Conscience And Society 165 (1945).
29. Hobbes, Leviathan 143 (Meridian Books ed. 1963).
30. See, *e.g.*, Morris & Hawkins, The Honest Politician's Guide To Crime Control 5–6, 10 (1970).
31. West, *op. cit. supra* note 28, at 166.
32. Holmes, *The Path of the Law*, 10 Harv. L. Rev. 457, 459 (1897).
33. Fuller, The Law In Quest of Itself 94–95 (1940).
34. Fleming & Dickinson, *Accident Proneness And Accident Law*, 63 Harv. L. Rev. 769, 795 (1950).
35. See, *e.g.*, Stone, Social Dimensions Of Law And Justice 152 (1966).
36. Guttmacher & Weihofen, *op. cit. supra* note 24.
37. Blackstone, IV Commentaries on the Laws of England 189 (various editions).
38. *Id.* at 190.
39. See, *e.g.*, Perkins, Criminal Law 68 (1957).
40. St. John-Stevas, Life, Death and the Law 256 (1961).
41. *Id.* at 232.
42. *Id.* at 261.
43. See, *e.g.*, Pound, *The End Of Law As Developed In Legal Rules And Doctrines*, 27 Harv. L. Rev. 195, 198 (1914).
44. See generally Menninger, The Crime Of Punishment 190–218 (1968).
45. See, *e.g.*, Holmes, The Common Law 37 (1881).
46. Harding, *Individual Responsibility In Anglo-American Law*, in Responsibility In Law And In Morals 41, 73 (1960).
47. Maine, Ancient Law 222 (Everyman ed. 1960).
48. National Commission on Law Observance and Enforcement (1931).
49. Skolnik, Justice Without Trial 3–4 (1966).
50. "the National Commission on Law Observance and Enforcement (the Wickersham Commission), which reported to President Hoover in 1931, found considerable evidence of police brutality. The President's Commission on Civil Rights, appointed by President Truman, made a similar finding in 1947. And in 1961, the U.S. Civil Rights Commission concluded that 'police

brutality is still a serious problem throughout the United States.' " *The Police and the Community,* in Task Force Report: The Police 144, 181 (1967).

51. For an excellent exposition of the changes in the Criminal Law effected by these decisions of the Supreme Court, see George, Constitutional Limitations On Evidence In Criminal Cases (1969).

52. See *The Police and the Community, op. cit. supra* note 50.

53. See, *e.g., The Police,* in The Challenge Of Crime In a Free Society: A Report By The President's Commission On Law Enforcement And The Administration Of Justice 91, 100 (1967).

54. See Skolnik, *op. cit. supra* note 49, at 1–3 for relevant comments regarding the origin of the police.

55. Commonwealth v. Nicely, 130 Pa. 261, 270 (1889).

56. Frank, If Men Were Angels 321–22 (1942).

57. See George, *op. cit. supra* note 51, at 273–319.

58. See, *e.g.,* Schoenfeld, *In Defense of Retribution in the Law,* 35 Psychoanalytic Quarterly 108, 112 (1966).

59. M. Frank, Diary of a D.A. 42 (1960).

60. *Id.* at 42–43.

61. See Kock, The French Code of Criminal Procedure (1964); Schmidt, The German Code of Criminal Procedure (1965). By no means is the statement in the text intended to obscure the fact that criminal procedure in France and West Germany is basically "inquisitorial," whereas in the United States it is basically "accusatorial."

62. See, *e.g.,* Reiwald, *Society and its Criminals* 246–47, 258 (1949).

63. Canons Of Judicial Ethics, Canons 5, 9, 10, 15 (1952).

64. *Id.,* Canon 21.

65. *Ibid.*

66. See, *e.g.,* Wittels, Freud And His Time 381 (1931); Frank, Courts On Trial 249 (1950).

67. Patterson, Jurisprudence: Men and Ideas of the Law 591 (1953).

68. See Thomas, Problems of Contempt Of Court 7–9 (1934).

69. Frank, Courts On Trial, *op. cit. supra* note 66, at 26.

70. For a brief but illuminating discussion of the adversary system of American justice, see Fuller, *The Adversary System,* in Berman, Talks On American Law 30–43 (Vintage Books ed. 1961).

71. Smith, *Components of Proof in Legal Proceedings,* 51 Yale L.J. 537, 575 (1942).

72. Plucknett, A. Concise History Of The Common Law 110–11 (2d ed. 1936).

73. Wittels, *op. cit. supra* note 66, at 382.
74. Frank, Courts On Trial, *op. cit. supra* note 66, at 250.
75. Dawson, *The Functions Of The Judge,* in Berman, *op. cit. supra* note 70, at 18, 27.
76. See, *e.g.,* The Federalist No. 48, at 309–12 (Mentor ed. 1961) (Madison).
77. *Ibid.*
78. These prohibitions appear in U.S. Const. art. I, §§ 9, 10.
79. Calder v. Bull, 3 U.S. (3 Dall.) 386 (1798).
80. *Id.* at 390–91.
81. United States v. Lovett, 328 U.S. 303, 315 (1946).
82. See, *e.g.,* Douglas, A Living Bill of Rights 54–55 (1961).
83. Cummings v. Mo., 71 U.S. (4 Wall.) 277 (1867); *Ex parte* Garland, 71 U.S. (4 Wall.) 333 (1867).
84. United States v. Lovett, 328 U.S. 303 (1946).
85. For a short but perceptive and very useful historical review of what the reaction of the federal government has been to the threat of subversion, see Swisher, The Supreme Court In Modern Role 72–109 (rev. ed. 1965).
86. McCulloch v. Maryland, 17 U.S. (4 Wheat.) 316, 431 (1819). *See generally* Eisenstein, The Ideologies of Taxation (1961).
87. For a brief account of the various punishments that nations have visited upon criminals at different times, see Laurence, A History Of Capital Punishment 1–27 (1960).
88. See, *e.g.,* Menninger, The Crime Of Punishment (1968), for a detailed exposition of this theme.
89. See, *e.g.,* R. Eissler, *Scapegoats Of Society,* in K.R. Eissler, Searchlights On Delinquency 288, 295, 304–05 (1949).
90. Holmes, The Common Law 41 (1881).
91. Of particular interest here is Bikel, The Least Dangerous Branch (1962).

CHAPTER VI

1. Jones, Papers On Psycho-Analysis 499 (5th ed. 1950).
2. Hinsie & Shatzky, Psychiatric Dictionary 458 (1940).
3. See, *e.g.,* Flugel, Man, Morals And Society 291 (Compass Books ed. 1961).
4. For an enlightening—and readable—account of Kant's views regarding punishment and retribution, see Cairns, Legal Philosophy From Plato To Hegel 452–57 (1949).
5. Holmes, The Common Law 45 (1881).
6. Frank, Law and the Modern Mind 31 (6th Printing 1949).

7. Bonham's Case, 8 Co. Rep. 114(1610).
8. 5 U.S.C.A. § 1001.
9. 10 U.S.C.A. § 801.
10. Schmidt, The German Code Of Criminal Procedure 2 (1965).
11. For a perceptive discussion of the difficulties inherent in separating judicial from investigatory and prosecutory functions in administrative agencies, see Davis, Administrative Law And Government 243–60 (1960).
12. 339 U.S. 33 (1950).
13. *Id.* at 44.
14. 349 U.S. 133 (1955).
15. *Id.* at 137.
16. See Goldfarb, The Contempt Power 227–30 (Anchor Books ed. 1971).
17. See, *e.g.*, Fisher v. Pace, 336 U.S. 155 (1948), and Sacher v. U.S., 343 U.S. 1 (1952).
18. Thomas, Problems of Contempt of Court 11 (1934).
19. Illinois v. Allen, 397 U.S. 337, 343–46 (1970).
20. See Goldfarb, *op. cit. supra* note 16, at 229.
21. Thomas, *op, cit. supra* note 18, at 9.
22. Cardozo, The Nature Of The Judicial Process 167 (1921).
23. Frank, *op. cit. supra* note 6, at 111.
24. *Id.* at 103–04, quoting from Hutcheson, *The Judgment Intuitive: The Function of the "Hunch" in Judicial Decisions,* 14 Cornell L.Q. 274 (1929).
25. Schroeder, *The Psychologic Study of Judicial Opinions,* 6 Calif. L. Rev. 89, 93–95 (1918).
26. See, *e.g.*, the appropriate sections of Patterson, Jurisprudence: Men and Ideas of the Law (1953).
27. See Cardozo, *op. cit. supra* note 22, at 30–50.
28. Holmes, *op. cit. supra* note 5, at 1 (emphasis added).
29. Frank, *op. cit. supra* note 6 at 253.
30. *Id.* at 113–14.
31. Cohen, Reason And Law 196 (First Collier Books ed. 1961).
32. *Id.* at 195–96.
33. See, *e.g.*, Frankfurter, *Mr. Justice Holmes And the Constitution,* 41 Harv. L. Rev. 121, 132 (1927); Haines, *General Observations On The Effects Of Personal, Political, And Economic Influences In The Decisions Of Judges,* 17 Ill. L. Rev. 96, 104 (1922).
34. Scepticism concerning rationalization appears, for example, in the work of Felix S. Cohen. See, *e.g.*, F. S. Cohen, *Transcendental Nonsense And The Functional Approach,* 35 Colum. L. Rev. 809, 843–44. (1935).

35. Herma, *The Unconscious,* in Herma & Kurth, Psychoanalysis, 76, 82 (Forum Books ed. 1963).

36. Brenner, An Elementary Textbook of Psychoanalysis 102–03 (Doubleday Anchor Books ed. 1957).

37. Kurth, *Politics: Unconscious Factors in Social Prejudice And Mass Movements,* in Herma & Kurth, *op. cit. supra* note 35, at 297, 301.

38. See, *e.g.,* Flugel, *op. cit. supra* note 3, at 311.

39. *Id,* at 112.

40. West, Conscience And Society 168 (1945).

41. *Id.* at 168–69.

42. For some brutally frank comments upon this gap between the requirements of the law and the sexual practices of the public, see Mueller, Legal Regulation of Sexual Conduct 17 (1961).

43. See, *e.g.,* Kadish, *The Crisis of Overcriminalization,* 374 The Annals of The American Society of Political and Social Science 157, 159–60 (1967).

44. Spencer, Over-Legislation (See Cohen & Cohen, Jurisprudence And Legal Philosophy 484, 485 [1951]).

45. Frank, Courts On Trial 249 (1950).

46. See p. 80 *supra.*

47. See, *e.g.,* the discussion of subversion in Swisher, The Supreme Court in Modern Role 72–109 (Rev. ed. 1965).

48. See, *e.g.,* Schwartz, The Supreme Court 289–93 (1957); Blum, The National Experience 590–92, 704 (1963).

49. Blum, *id.* at 417–41.

50. *Ibid.*

51. "The principal antitrust statutes are the Sherman Act (1890), Clayton Act (1914), Federal Trade Commission Act (1914), and Robinson-Patman Act (1936). . . . The greater part of the 'antitrust laws' are the decisions of the . . . Courts . . . purporting to interpret the statutes. These decisions are not mere interpretation of the statutes, but are, in effect, legislation, since Congress used vague terms in the statutes, leaving it to the Court and the Federal Trade Commission to complete the legislation." Burns, Antitrust Dilemma 205 (1969).

52. For an extraordinarily perceptive analysis of the vital role played by big business in helping to ensure a high standard of productivity and consumption in today's modern industrial sicities, see Galbraith, The New Industrial State (1967).

53. Paradoxically, the likelihood that men may unconsciously identify themselves with big business and its leaders is greatly enhanced by the fear that big business and its leaders tend to engender in the public. See the chapter entitled "Identifica-

tion With The Aggressor," in A. Freud, The Ego And The Mechanisms Of Defense 117–131 (1946).

54. Burns, *op. cit. supra* note 50, at xiii.
55. See, *e.g.,* the authoritative discussion of the antitrust laws in Stone, Social Dimensions Of Law And Justice 433–54 (1966).
56. See Burns, *op. cit. supra* note 50, at 221.
57. See Stone, *op. cit. supra* note 55, at 437.
58. See pp. 80–81 *supra.*
59. West, *op. cit. supra* note 40, at 169.
60. See, *e.g.,* Menninger, The Crime Of Punishment 153–54 (1968); Alexander & Staub, The Criminal, The Judge, And The Public 209–23 (Rev. ed. 1956).
61. See, *e.g.,* West, *op. cit. supra* note 40, at 168–69; Weihofen, The Urge to Punish 138 (1956).
62. Weihofen, *ibid.*
63. Menninger, *op. cit. supra* note 60; R. Eissler, *Scapegoats Of Society,* in K. R. Eissler, Searchlights On Delinquency 288, 295, 304–05 (1949); Glover, The Roots of Crime xiii, 19 (1960).
64. Hinsie & Shatzky, *op. cit. supra* note 2, at 277.
65. Hendrick, Facts And Theories Of Psychoanalysis 374 (3rd ed. 1958).
66. See Noyes, Modern Clinical Psychiatry 29 (3d ed. 1948).
67. Freud, Group Psychology And The Analysis Of The Ego 60–70 (1922).
68. *Id.* at 60.
69. *Id.* at 64–65.
70. *Id.* at 61–62; A. Freud, *op. cit. supra* note 53.
71. See pp. 50–51 *supra.*
72. Klein, The Psychoanalysis Of Children 185–94 (First Evergreen ed. 1960).
73. Jones, Hamlet And Oedipus 85 (Doubleday Anchor ed. 1955).
74. Flugel, *op. cit. supra* note 3, at 190.
75. Glover, *op. cit. supra* note 63, at 8.
76. See pp. 13–14 *supra.*
77. *Ibid.*
78. See, *e.g.,* Abrahamsen, The Psychology Of Crime 3 (First Science ed. 1964).
79. Alexander & Staub, *op. cit. supra* note 60, 215.
80. Abrahamsen, *op. cit. supra* note 78.
81. See pp. 19–20, 69–70 *supra.*
82. Clark, Crime In America 213–14 (1970).
83. See Schoenfeld, *Psychoanalysis, Criminal Justice Planning and Reform, and the Law,* 7 Crim. L. Bull. 313 (1971).

84. See Cahn, *The Consumers Of Injustice,* in London, The Law as Literature 574, 579 (1960).
85. See Cahn, The Sense Of Injustice 14–22 (Midland Book ed. 1964).
86. *Id.* at 24.
87. See p. 35 *supra.*
88. See p. 23 *supra.*
89. See pp. 19, 23 *supra.*
90. See, *e.g.,* Janov, The Primal Scream (1970).
91. See, *e.g.,* Cahn, *The Consumers Of Injustice, op. cit. supra* note 84, at 576–79.
92. See, *e.g.,* Frankfurter, The Case Of Sacco And Vanzetti (1927); Zola, *"J'Accuse! . . .": An Open Letter on the Dreyfus Case,"* in London, *op. cit. supra* note 84, at 229–38; Sholom Aleichem, *Dreyfus in Kasrilevka,* in London, The Law in Literature 199–202 (1960).
93. See, *e.g.,* the examples of Darrow's speeches to juries collated in Weinberg, Attorney for the Damned (1957).
94. *Id.* at 507.
95. *Id.* at 499–500.
96. *Id.* at 252.
97. See Rattigan, *The Winslow Boy,* and Wouk, *The Court-Martial, from The Caine Mutiny,* in London, The Law in Literature, *op. cit. supra* note 92, at 47–132, 341–411.
98. See the discussion of the role of the abolitionists in Blum, The National Experience 251–54 (1963).
99. See Goldstein, The Insanity Defense 15 (1967); Schoenfeld, *Law And Unconscious Mental Mechanisms,* 28 Bull. Menninger Clinic 23, 28–30 (1964).
100. Reiwald, Society and Its Criminals 51 (1949).
101. Frank, *op. cit. supra* note 45, at 80.
102. Morgan, Some Problems Of Proof Under The Anglo-American System Of Litigation 3 (1956).
103. Frank, Court On Trial, *op. cit. supra* note 45, at 82.
104. *Id.* at 84.
105. *Id.* at 85–86.
106. See Modlin, *The Client and You—What You Are,* 16 N.Y. County B. Bull. 151, 155 (1959).
107. See Reiwald, *op. cit. supra* note 100, at 175; Heller, Polen & Polsky, An Introduction To Legal Interviewing 15, 34 (1960).
108. Frank, Court On Trial, *op. cit. supra* note 45, at 374.
109. Modlin, *op. cit. supra* note 106, at 153.
110. Frank, Courts On Trial, *op. cit. supra* note 45, at 5–9; Harding, *Individual Responsibility In Anglo-American Law,* in Harding, Responsibility In Law And In Morals 44–46 (1960).

111. Drinker, Legal Ethics 11 (1953).
112. See Plucknett, A Concise History Of The Common Law 110–12 (2d ed. 1936), for a description of trial by battle at the common law.
113. See p. 31 *supra*.
114. For an incisive thumbnail sketch of the pretrial conference, see Vanderbilt, The Challenge of Law Reform 63–67 (1955).
115. For a brief analysis of the pretrial procedures described in the Federal Rules of Civil Procedure, see Morgan, *op. cit. supra* note 102, at 29–35.

CHAPTER VII

1. Powell, Vagaries and Varieties in Constitutional Interpretation 3 (1956).
2. The Federalist No. 78, at 465 (Mentor ed. 1961) (Hamilton).
3. *Ibid.*
4. Bickel, The Least Dangerous Branch 1 (1962).
5. Rostow, *The Democratic Character of Judicial Review*, 66 Harv. L. Rev. 193, 195–96 (1952).
6. The Federalist, *op. cit. supra* note 2, at 467.
7. Much learning—and, unfortunately, every bit as much disagreement—exists as to the intent of the Founding Fathers regarding judicial review. Some scholars believe that the debates in the Constitutional Convention reveal a desire by many of the ablest of the Founding Fathers that the courts determine the constitutionality of federal legislation. (*E.g.*, Beard, The Supreme Court and the Constitution [1912]). Other Scholars believe that these debates reveal largely the opposite intent. (*E.g.*, Davis, The Judicial Veto [1914]). Still other scholars take what might be described as a "middle view." Charles Grove Haines, for instance, asserts that "the arguments favoring . . . [judicial review] were presented by a few of the ablest members; on the other hand, there was a well-defined opposition to the exercise of such authority by the judiciary." (Haines, The American Doctrine Of Judicial Supremacy 131 [2d ed. 1932]). My own belief is that the Founding Fathers were, by and large, probably undecided regarding judicial review; and in addition, were probably fearful that a decision by them regarding it might well hinder ratification of the Constitution. Hence, they simply left the question unanswered. Whether or not this is so, there can be no doubt that, as is revealed in Max Farrand's authoritative three-volume study of the Constitutional Convention (The Records of the Federal

Convention [1911]), comparatively little concerning the role of the judiciary is to be found in the debates. (Farrand, The Framing Of The Constitution Of The United States 154 [1913]).

8. 12 S. & R. 330 (Pa. Sup. Ct. 1825).

9. 5 U. S. (1 Cr.) 137 (1803).

10. For a study of early American attitudes and practices regarding judicial review, see Thayer, *The Origin And Scope Of The American Doctrine Of Constitutional Law*, 7 Harv. L. Rev. 129 (1893).

11. *E.g.*, Hand, The Bill Of Rights 11 (Antheneum ed. 1964). "The arguments deducing the court's authority from the structure of the new government, or from the implications of any government, were not valid, in spite of the deservedly revered names of their authors." (p. 28) For a comparatively recent, thoroughgoing, and absolutely first-rate dissection of Marshall's reasoning in Marbury v. Madison, see Bickel, *op. cit. supra* note 4, at 1–12.

12. "[Marbury v. Madison] bears many of the earmarks of a deliberately partisan coup. The Court was bent on reading the President a lecture . . . . but at the same time hesitated to invite a snub by actually asserting jurisdiction of the matter." (Corwin, The Doctrine of Judicial Review 9 [1963]).

13. 2 U.S. (2 Dall.) 419 (1793).

14. See Murphy, Congress and the Court 1 (Phoenix ed. 1962); 1 Warren, The Supreme Court in United States History 93–102 (1st ed. 1922).

15. 60 U. S. (19 How.) 393 (1857).

16. A rapid, but certainly clear and enlightening, discussion of the background and influence of the *Dred Scott* case is to be found in Acheson, The Supreme Court 97–124 (1961).

17. Hurst, The Growth of American Law 85 (1950).

18. For a brief description of fatalism, see Hospers, An Introduction To Philosophical Analysis 266–67 (1953). Though fatalism may seem to the reader to be an absurd "philosophy", it has been embraced by a surprisingly large number of well-known thinkers. See, for example, the classic exposition of fatalism in the second epilogue of Tolstoy's War and Peace.

19. Stewart, Modern Forms of Government 140 (Praeger ed. 1961).

20. *Id.* at 137–41. "The example of Switzerland reminds us that a federation, while entrusting review of state authority to a national judiciary, may reserve for the people the function of deciding whether a national law is consistent with the con-

stitution." (Freund, The Supreme Court of the United States 93 [1961]).

21. Stewart, *op. cit. supra* note 19, at 177, 202.
22. *Id.* at 181.
23. *Id.* at 161.
24. This is not to deny, however, that judicial review of national legislation does exist in Canada, Australia, and other nations. See McWhinney, Judicial Review In The English-Speaking World (3d ed. 1965).
25. (pts. 1–2), 42 Harv. L. Rev. 149, 365 (1928–1929).
26. 8 Co. Rep. 114 (1610).
27. *Id.* at 118.
28. Corwin, The Constitution and What It Means Today 141 (12th ed. 1958).
29. Thayer, *supra* note 10, at 133.
30. *Ibid.*
31. For a careful and thoroughgoing study of judicial review in England (and in certain other English-speaking countries) see McWhinney, *op. cit. supra* note 24.
32. By no means is this to suggest or even to imply that a psychoanalytic explanation of judicial review is likely to be a complete explanation. On the contrary, (as has been observed a number of times in earlier chapters), psychoanalytic explanations of legal phenomena (like historical, social, or economic explanations of legal phenomena) are likely to be at best *partial* explanations—and as such, must be supplemented by other (historical, social, economic, etc.) explanations. See Frank, Law and the Modern Mind xxi, 21 n. (6th printing 1949).
33. For an outline of basic psychoanalytic discoveries regarding the unconscious realm of the mind, see Freud, *The Unconscious,* in 4 Collected Papers 98 (1956); *A Note on the Unconscious in Psychoanalysis,* in *id.* at 22. See generally Freud, The Interpretation Of Dreams, in The Basic Writings Of Sigmund Freud 183 (Brill ed. 1938).
34. Particularly useful as an introduction to psychoanalytic material concerning symbolism are Freud, A General Introduction To Psychoanalysis 156–77 (Permabook ed. 1953); Jones, *The Theory Of Symbolism,* in Papers On Psycho-analysis 87 (5th ed. 1950); Fromm, The Forgotten Language (1951).
35. The unconscious relationship between judge and father is explored in considerable detail in Reiwald, Society and Its Criminals 42–62 (1949).
36. *Id.* at 44.

37. Lerner, *Constitution And Court As Symbols*, 46 Yale L.J. 1290, 1292 (1937).

38. Arnold, The Symbols Of Government 196 (1935). See Gabriel, The Course Of American Democratic Thought 396–407 (1940).

39. Further material pertaining to the Supreme Court as an unconscious parent symbol is to be found in Schoenfeld, *On The Relationship Between Law And Unconscious Symbolism*, 26 La. L. Rev. 46 (1965).

40. For an exposition of psychoanalytic theory pertaining to the unconscious meaning of anthropomorphic concepts of God, see Freud, The Future of An Illusion (1928); Jones, *The Psychology of Religion*, in Lorand, Psychoanalysis Today 315 (1944); Schoenfeld, *God The Father—And Mother: Study and Extension of Freud's Conception of God as an Exalted Father*, 19 American Imago 213 (1962).

41. "In 1868, in the difficult days of reconstruction, the Congress took away from the Court the appellate jurisdiction under the Habeas Corpus Act of 1867, the bill being passed over the President's veto. This was done while an appeal in the celebrated *McCardle* case was actually pending in the Supreme Court, in which it was sought to test the validity of the Reconstruction acts. The Court unanimously decided that Congress had deprived it of jurisdiction." (Hughes, The Supreme Court Of The United States 26 [Columbia Paperback ed. 1966]).

42. Gabriel, *op. cit. supra* note 38, at 132.

43. McCloskey, The American Supreme Court 101 (1960).

44. Barker, The Civil War In America 2 (1961).

45. Sometimes a regression may be temporary, as in the case of adults in a panic (caused, for instance, by the cry of "fire" in a crowded theatre), who may push and claw one another; or who may mill about, screaming and crying for help, like children desperately hoping to be rescued by their parents. Or the regression may be more permanent, as in the case of a man who begins to show signs of schizophrenia and who passes through various levels of adaptation formerly lived through by him—until, if the regression is severe enough, he may eventually arrive at a stage resembling intrauterine existence. Pertinent psychoanalytic material concerning regression is to be found in Alexander, Fundamentals Of Psychoanalysis 128–30 (1948); A. Freud, Normality And Pathology In Childhood 93–107 (1965); S. Freud, The Interpretation Of Dreams, *op. cit. supra* note 33, at 485–97; Noyes, Modern Clinical Psychiatry 33–34 (3d ed. 1948).

46. Psychoanalysts have learned that the need of the young child

for parental guidance and control is so strong, that (as was pointed out in Chapter III), he eventually internalizes an image of his parents (called by psychoanalysts the *superego*), which then rules him from within as his parents once ruled him from without. See Brenner, An Elementary Textbook of Psychoanalysis 125–40 (Doubleday ed. (1957); Jones, *The Genesis of the Superego, op. cit. supra* note 34, at 145–52.

47. See note 32 *supra*.

48. For example, an economist who sought to understand why judicial review triumphed after the Civil War might well consider significant the tendency of the propertied classes in the United States during the last third of the nineteenth century to look to the Supreme Court as a bulwark against legislative attacks by the "have nots." See McCloskey, *op. cit. supra* note 43, at 104.

49. Biddle, Justice Holmes, Natural Law, And The Supreme Court 22 (1961).

50. The authoritative biography of Holmes is that written by Mark De Wolfe Howe. For an account of the Civil War experiences of Holmes, see the first volume of this biography: Justice Oliver Wendell Holmes—The Shaping Years 1841–1870 (1957).

51. 1 Fine & Brown, The American Past 574 (2d ed. 1965).

52. Beard & Beard, A Basic History Of The United States 320 (1944).

53. "If we were oppressed, insecure, desperate, and unable to see the reasonable adult solutions to our difficulties, the chances are that numbers of us would try to return to the comfort and security of our infancy, and be tempted by an authoritarian (fascist) state as a father-substitute." (Van Clute, *How Fascism Thwarts The Life Instinct*, 12 American Journal Of Ortho-Psychiatry 335, 337 [1942]).

54. Some of the reasons why so many people seemed eager at this time to renounce freedom and to embrace totalitarianism instead are explored in detail in Fromm, Escape from Freedom (1941).

55. The "standard" history of the furious legislative struggle precipitated by this plan for enlarging the Supreme Court is to be found in Alsop & Catledge, The 168 Days (1938). For a comparatively recent reappraisal of the struggle, see Black, The People and The Court 59–68 (1960).

56. Schwartz, The Supreme Court 12 (1957).

57. See Murphy, *op. cit. supra* note 14, at 53–57; McCloskey, *op. cit. supra* note 43, at 161–69.

58. 2 Bining & Klein, A History of the United States 502 (1952).
59. Schwartz, *op. cit. supra* note 56.
60. "The historic Court (as distinguished from the Court of myth and rhetoric) had very seldom behaved this way, and the exceptions in the record seemed hardly calculated to inspire imitation. Even in the modern period the dominant tendency had been to moderate the regulatory movement without attempting to destroy it, to nudge and advise democracy rather than to frustrate it. The majority had for the time being forgotten this, had forgotten that the Constitution's strength was its flexibility and that the Court's own strength rested on a tradition of judicious self-restraint." (McCloskey, *op. cit. supra* note 49, at 168).
61. See Schoenfeld, *On The Relationship Between Law and Unconscious Symbolism, supra* note 39 at 64.
62. See note 32 *supra*.
63. Gabriel, *op. cit. supra* note 38 at 406.
64. *Ibid.*
65. *Id.* at 407.
66. Judicial supremacy reached its height in the nineteenth century in three cases decided by the Supreme Court in 1895: United States v. E. C. Knight Co., 156 U. S. 1; *In re* Debs, 158 U. S. 564; Pollock v. Farmers Loan and Trust Co., 157 U.S. 429 and 158 U. S. 601. For a brief summary and appraisal of these cases in their historical setting, see Murphy, Congress and the Court 44–45 (Phoenix ed. 1962).
67. See note 40 *supra*.
68. See *e.g.*, Powell, Vagaries and Varieties in Constitutional Interpretation 20 (1956).
69. Rostow, The Sovereign Prerogative xxxiii (1962).
70. See *e.g.*, McWhinney, *op. cit. supra* note 24, at 182. For cogent arguments to the contrary, see Rostow, *op. cit. supra* note 69, at 147–92.
71. Bickel, The Least Dangerous Branch 16–17 (1962).
72. The argument in the text is but one of a variety of objections that can be raised to judicial review from the point of view of democratic theory. One classic argument that immediately comes to mind, for example, is Thayer's contention that judicial review tends to weaken the democratic process by encouraging irresponsibility on the part of legislators and the people who elect them. Thayer contended that if legislators know that a court is standing by ready to correct their mistakes, these legislators will act far less thoughtfully and carefully

than they otherwise might act. Similarly Thayer contended that the knowledge that courts have the final word concerning the validity of legislation tends to make the electorate less prudent than it might otherwise be in selecting legislators. Thayer, John Marshall 103–07 (1901).

73. See Murphy, *op. cit. supra* note 66, at 35–42.

74. *Id.* at 50.

75. *Id.* at 47.

76. *Id.* at 50.

77. *Id.* at 97–223. Paradoxically, perhaps, some scholars have contended that the many attacks upon the Court's power have actually *lent support* to the legitimacy and finality of judicial review. Charles L. Black, Jr., for instance, asserted in 1960 in his book on judicial review—The People and the Court—that "one way of stating the strongest claim of judicial review to historically attested legitimacy would be to point to the fact that it has been under attack almost continuously since the beginning, but that the attacks have always failed. Public acquiescence in a practice not seriously challenged might be taken to evidence no more than indifference; public acquiescence in a practice continually questioned for its very life is a different and altogether more significant matter." (p. 183)

78. Perhaps a good starting point for this thought is a typically laconic comment by Holmes: "I do not think the United States would come to an end if we lost our power to declare an act of Congress void. I do think the Union would be imperiled if we could not make that declaration as to the laws of the several states." (Holmes, Collected Legal Papers 295–96 [1920]).

CHAPTER VIII

1. 198 U. S. 45 (1905).

2. *Id.* at 57–61.

3. *Id.* at 75–76 (dissenting opinion).

4. Laski, The American Democracy 111 (1948).

5. Dred Scott v. Sandford, 60 U.S. (19 How.) 393 (1857).

6. Munn v. Illinois, 94 U.S. 113, 134 (1876). Many students of Constitutional Law regard the difference between judicial activism and judicial self-restraint as one of degree rather than of kind. Samuel J. Konefsky, for instance, contends in The Legacy of Holmes and Brandeis (Collier ed. 1961) that "what separated Holmes from the majority in the *Lochner* case was a matter of degree, a difference of view as to whether

the New York legislature was justified in curtailing freedom of action in the circumstances disclosed by the case." (p. 48) Yet even if the difference between judicial activism and judicial self-restraint is one of degree rather than of kind, still—as those who lived through the Supreme Court's ferocious attack upon New Deal legislation must surely know—the difference between judicial activism and judicial self-restraint is a very real difference indeed.

7. This reluctance of activist judges to admit to their activism has been scathingly ridiculed by T. R. Powell. See, *e.g.,* Powell, *op. cit. supra* note 68, ch. II.

8. 261 U.S. 525 (1923).

9. *Id.* at 544.

10. 297 U.S. 1 (1936).

11. *Id.* at 62. This case is perhaps best remembered for the blistering dissent of Mr. (later Chief) Justice Stone, who inveighed against what he labeled a "tortured construction of the Constitution," warning his colleagues that: "Courts are not the only agency of government that must be assumed to have capacity to govern."

12. 384 U.S. 436 (1966).

13. In Johnson v. New Jersey, 384 U.S. 719, 732 (1966), the Court held that Miranda v. Arizona was not to be applied retroactively.

14. These rules (summarized on pages 478–79 of the majority opinion by Mr. Chief Justice Warren in Miranda v. Arizona) are as follows: "To summarize, we hold that when an individual is taken into custody or otherwise deprived of his freedom by the authorities and it subjected to questioning, the privilege against self-incrimination is jeopardized. Procedural safeguards must be employed to protect the privilege, and unless other fully effective means are adopted to notify the person of his right to silence and to assure that the exercise of the right will be scrupulously honored, the following measures are required. He must be warned prior to any questioning that he has the right to remain silent, that anything he says can be used against him in a court of law, that he has the right to the presence of an attorney, and that if he cannot afford an attorney one will be appointed for him prior to any questioning if he so desires. Opportunity to exercise these rights must be afforded to him throughout the interrogation. After such warnings have been given, and such opportunity afforded him, the individual may knowingly and intelligently

waive these rights and agree to answer questions or make a statement. But unless and until such warnings and waiver are demonstrated by the prosecution at trial, no evidence obtained as a result of interrogation can be used against him."

15. To quote from page 531 of the dissent in Miranda v. Arizona by Mr. Justice White. Note, in addition, that footnote 48 (page 479) of the majority opinion by Mr. Chief Justice Warren reads as follows: "In accordance with our holdings today and in *Escobedo v. Illinois,* 378 U.S. 478, 492, *Crooker v. California,* 357 U.S. 433 (1958) and *Cicenia v. Lagay,* 357 U.S. 504 (1958) are not to be followed."

16. Miranda v. Arizona, 384 U.S. 436, 442 (1966).

17. 291 U. S. 502 (1934).

18. *Id.* at 556 (dissenting opinion).

19. Prohibitions del Roy, 12 Co. Rep. 63, 65 (1607).

20. Pollock v. Farmers Loan and Trust Co., 158 U.S. 601, 607 (1895).

21. Black, *Absolutes, Courts, and the Bill of Rights,* in Westin, The Supreme Court 173–90 (1961).

22. 304 U. S. 144 (1938).

23. *Id.* at 152, n. 4.

24. See Hand, The Bill of Rights 73 (Antheneum ed. 1964). Yet, within only a few years after the Constitution was adopted, the world witnessed a graphic—and still unforgotten—example of the excesses of mob rule: the Jacobin reign of terror during the French Revolution.

25. Thucydides, History (many editions), bk. II, at 66. For a lucid and authoritative description of the political institutions and ideals of Athenian democracy at the time of the Peloponnesian War, see Sabine, A History of Political Theory (2d ed. 1950), ch. I.

26. American Federation of Labor v. American Sash Co., 335 U.S. 538, 553 (1948) (concurring opinion).

27. Tenney v. Brandhove, 341 U.S. 367, 378 (1951).

28. McWhinney, Judicial Review In The English-Speaking World 180 (3d ed. 1965).

29. *Id.* at 181.

30. Sherrer v. Sherrer, 334 U.S. 343, 365–66 (1948) (dissenting opinion).

31. 347 U.S. 483 (1954).

32. 369 U.S. 186 (1962).

33. 384 U.S. 436 (1966).

34. Fromm, Psychoanalysis and Religion 80 (1950).

35. Freud, A General Introduction to Psychoanalysis 345–46 (Perma-book ed. 1953).

36. Fromm, The Art of Loving 51 (1956).
37. For psychoanalytic material pertaining to the tendency to use the State and its leaders as unconscious parent symbols, see Hopkins, Fathers Or Sons? (1927).
38. Flugel, The Psychoanalytic Study Of The Family 236–37 (1950).
39. Van Clute, *How Fascism Thwarts The Life Instinct*, 12 American Journal Of Ortho-Psychiatry 335, 336 (1942).
40. Soule, The Strength Of Nations 241 (1942).
41. Thayer, John Marshall 104 (1901).
42. It ought perhaps be noted here that passivity and femininity are *not* synonymous. Femininity may, as Freud points out, involve "a preference for passive aims . . . [But] a good deal of activity [may be required] . . . to achieve a passive end." (Freud, New Introductory Lectures On Psychoanalysis 157 [1933]) Or, in the words of Herman Nunberg, "The sexual instinct of the male is active, but that of the female is not passive. Only her aim is passive, namely to receive the man, while his aim is active, to subjugate the woman. The aim of an instinct is to achieve gratification by means of an adequate action." (Principles of Psychoanalysis 59 [1955]).
43. See, *e.g.*, the references to activity in Fromm, Man For Himself (1947).
44. Baruch, A Philosophy For Our Time 1 (1954).
45. See the appropriate references in Fenichel, The Psychoanalytic Theory Of Neurosis (1945).
46. *Id.* at 119.
47. Nunberg, *op. cit. supra* note 126, at 99 (italics deleted).
48. See Waelder, Basic Theory Of Psychoanalysis 235 (Schocken ed. 1964).
49. In seeking to explain how activity may serve as a cloak for passive desires, psychoanalysts frequently use the example of the child who is greatly dependent upon maternal care and attention, and who, when his mother is away for any length of time during his waking hours, may avoid going into a panic by identifying with her and vigorously acting out her "mothering" role vis-à-vis a sibling, a pet, or even an inanimate object (a teddy bear, a doll, etc.). See S. Freud, Beyond The Pleasure Principle 13–15 (1950); A. Freud, The Ego And The Mechanisms Of Defence 121–24 (1946).
50. Munn v. Illinois, 95 U.S. 113, 134 (1876).
51. The *ego* and the *id* are the two other psychic agencies identified by psychoanalysts. In a sense, the ego is synonymous with the "executive" aspects of man's personality, the *id* with the "legislative" aspects of the personality. See Freud, New In-

troductory Lectures On Psychoanalysis, *op. cit. supra* note 126, at 82–112; Freud, The Ego And The Id 19–33 (1927).

52. Hall, A Primer Of Freudian Psychology 31 (Mentor ed. 1956).

53. Brenner, An Elementary Textbook of Psychoanalysis 125 (Doubleday ed. 1957).

54. There is some disagreement among psychoanalysts as to whether (as Freud believed) the superego first appears when a child reaches the age of six or so (the time when the child internalizes an image of his parents), or whether—as indicated in the text, and as most psychoanalysts now believe—precursors of the superego appear during the earlier years of a child's life. See Jones, *The Genesis Of The Super-Ego,* in Papers On Psycho-analysis 145–52 (5th ed. 1950). It may prove of interest here to note that the common law uses the age of seven as the dividing line between the stage of life when a child is conclusively presumed to be incapable of harboring a criminal intent (*doli incapax*) and the stage when this presumption may be rebutted. See Perkins, Criminal Law 729–32 (1957).

55. Of particular interest here are Erich Fromm's views regarding the superego. See Fromm, Man For Himself 141–72 (1947). For a more orthodox account of superego development, see Waelder, *op. cit. supra* note 132, at 187–95.

56. A plethora of instances in which judges have, in effect, acted as though they were the conscience of society are, at least in my view, to be found in decisions of the Supreme Court since World War II regarding the rights of persons accused of having committed a crime. See, *e.g.,* Irvin v. Dowd, 366 U.S. 717 (1961), in which the Court reversed a murder conviction on the grounds that prejudicial news coverage had made a fair trial impossible; Gideon v. Wainwright, 372 U.S. 335 (1963), in which the Court overruled Betts v. Brady, 316 U.S. 455 (1942), and contended that "any person haled into court, who is too poor to hire a lawyer, cannot be assured a fair trial unless counsel is provided for him; Rochin v. California, 342 U.S. 165 (1952), in which the Court reversed a narcotics conviction on the grounds that the arresting officers acted in a manner that "shocks the conscience." ("Illegally breaking into the privacy of the petitioner, the struggle to open his mouth and remove what was there, the forcible extraction of his stomach's contents—this course of proceedings by agents of government to obtain evidence is bound to offend even hardened sensibilities.") Not only the Supreme Court, but other

courts as well, have acted at times as though they were society's conscience. A classic example is provided by the celebrated case of Riggs v. Palmer, 115 U.S. 506 (1889), in which the New York Court of Appeals refused to permit a legatee who murdered his testator to collect under the testator's will, even though (in the court's words): "It is quite true that statutes regulating the making, proof and effect of wills, and the devolution of property, if literally construed . . . give this property to the murderer." In ruling against the legatee's claim, the Court declared that "all laws as well as all contracts may be controlled in their operation and effect by general, fundamental maxims of the common law. No one shall be permitted to profit by his own fraud, or to take advantage of his own wrong, or to found any claim upon his own iniquity, or to acquire property by his own crime. These maxims are dictated by public policy, have their foundation in universal law administered in all civilized countries, and have nowhere been superseded by statutes." Perhaps it also ought to be recalled here that Courts of Equity have traditionally acted as "courts of conscience," and that many a rule promulgated by these courts was, certainly at first, largely a product of conscience. (As an example, consider the so-called "equity of redemption": the rule originated by the Court of Chancery that permitted a mortgagor to redeem mortgaged land by paying the mortgage debt within a reasonable time after the due date had passed, even though—technically—the mortgaged land became the property of the mortgagee when the mortgagor failed to make payment on the due date. See Osborne, The Law Of Mortgages 16–20 [1951]).

57. A phrase repeatedly used by Bernard Schwartz when commenting upon Supreme Court decisions in Schwartz, The Supreme Court 13, 23, 192, 312, 347 (1957).

58. See the extended discussion of this matter *supra*. Quite outspoken on the point is Alpheus Thomas Mason, whose book The Supreme Court From Taft To Warren (Norton ed. 1964) begins with the words: "With disarming candor Justice John Marshall Harlan (grandfather of the present Justice Harlan) told a class of law students: 'I want to say to you young gentlemen that if we don't like an act of Congress, we don't have much trouble to find grounds for declaring it unconstitutional.'"

59. See, *e.g.*, Fromm, Escape From Freedom (1941).

60. See p. 40 *supra*.

61. It is of interest to recall here that back in 1835, Alexis de Tocque-

ville observed in his classic and extraordinarily perceptive study—Democracy In America—that: "Hardly any question arises in the United States that is not resolved sooner or later into a judicial question."

CHAPTER IX

1. Bander, Mr. Dooley On The Choice Of Law 52 (1963).
2. Gray, The Nature And Sources Of The Law 125 (2d ed. 1921).
3. Surprising, perhaps, a careful reading of Marbury v. Madison (5 U.S. [1 Cr.] 137 [1803]) reveals that even Mr. Chief Justice John Marshall himself may, for some time during his early judicial career, have believed that the Constitution ought to be interpreted literally. See Murphy & Pritchett, Courts, Judges, And Politics 433 (1961).
4. For an authoritative introduction to and analysis of the view (identified with Roscoe Pound and Julius Stone) that the law reflects a balancing of diverse interests, see Stone, Social Dimensions Of Law And Justice 164–98 (1966).
5. See Black, *Absolutes, Courts, and the Bill of Rights* in Westin, The Supreme Court 173–90 (1961).
6. Smith v. California, 361 U.S. 147, 157 (1959). For a devastating critique of Black's insistence on the existence of "absolute" prohibitions in the Bill of Rights, see Hook, *Commentary on Mr. Justice Black,* in Mendelson, The Supreme Court: Law And Discretion 484–89 (1967).
7. 300 U. S. 379 (1937).
8. *Id.* at 402 (dissenting opinion).
9. 290 U.S. 398 (1934).
10. *Id.* at 450 (dissenting opinion).
11. Adkins v. Children's Hospital, 261 U. S. 525, 560 (1923). Sutherland was exceedingly distrustful of majority rule. See Paschal, *Mr. Justice Sutherland,* in Dunham & Kurland, Mr. Justice 203, 206 (First Phoenix ed. 1964).
12. Home Building And Loan Association v. Blaisdell, 290 U.S. 398, 483 (1934) (dissenting opinion).
13. See, *e.g.,* McCloskey, The American Supreme Court 158–61 (1960). As Holmes had put it years earlier in Lochner v. New York (118 U.S. 45, 75 [1905] [dissenting opinion]), such judges were seeking to enact into law "Mr. Herbert Spencer's Social Statics."
14. 60 U.S. (19 How.) 393 (1857).
15. *Id.* at 426.

16. Taney's decision was, in the words of T. R. Powell, "a monstrous piece of judicial effrontery." Powell, Vagaries and Varieties in Constitutional Interpretation 20 (1956).

17. *Id.* at 28.

18. Anderson, *The Intention Of The Framers: A Note On Constitutional Interpretation,* in Murphy & Pritchett, *op. cit. supra* note 3, at 440, 441.

19. *Id.* at 440.

20. *Id.* at 441.

21. To quote in part from Benjamin Franklin's short but remarkably persuasive address on the closing day of the Convention: "Mr. President, I confess that there are several parts of this constitution which I do not at present approve, but I am not sure that I shall never approve them: For, having lived long, I have experienced many instances of being obliged by better information or fuller consideration to change opinions even on important subjects, which I once thought right, but found to be otherwise. It is therefore that the older I grow, the more apt I am to doubt my own judgment, and to pay more respect to the judgment of others. . . . I agree to this Constitution with all its faults, if they are such, because I think a general Government necessary for us and there is no form of Government but what may be a blessing to the people if well administered, and believe farther that this is likely to be well administered for a course of years, and can only end in Despotism as other forms have done before it, when the people have become so corrupted as to need despotic Government, being incapable of any other. I doubt too whether any other Convention we can obtain may be able to make a better Constitution. For when you assemble a number of men to have the advantage of their joint wisdom, you inevitably assemble with those men, all their prejudices, their passions, their errors of opinion, their local interests, and their selfishness. From such an Assembly can a perfect production be expected? It therefore astonishes me, Sir, to find this system approaching so near to perfection as it does and I think it will astonish our enemies who are waiting with confidence to hear that our councils are confounded like those of the Builders of Babel; and that our States are on the point of separation, only to meet hereafter for the purpose of cutting one another's throats. Thus I consent, Sir, to this Constitution because I expect no better, and because I am not sure it is not the best. . . . I cannot help expressing a wish that every member of the Con-

vention who may still have objection to it, would with me, on this occasion doubt a little of his own infallibility—and to make manifest our unanimity, put his name to this instrument." See Hand, The Bill Of Rights 75–77 (Antheneum ed. 1964).

22. Anderson, *op. cit. supra* note 3, at 443–44.

23. *Id.* at 444.

24. 1 Crosskey, Politics and the Constitution in the History of the United States 5 (1953).

25. Murphy & Pritchett, *op. cit. supra* note 3, at 435.

26. Professor Crosskey charges that "the Justices [of the Supreme Court], over the years since 1789, have very generally done things they ought not to have done, and, quite as generally, left undone the things they ought to have done; and, further to pursue the language of the Book of Common Prayer, it does truly seem that, in their discharge of this important function, there has been no health in them. . . . there cannot be a doubt that the Court's long record has been one, pervasively of failure." 2 Crosskey, *op. cit. supra* note 24, at 1161.

27. McCloskey, *op. cit. supra* note 13, at 240. Professor Crosskey asserts, among other things, that "if the Constitution were allowed to operate as the instrument was drawn, the American people could, through Congress, deal with any subject they wished, on a simple, straightforward, nationwide basis. . . ." 2 Crosskey, *op. cit supra* note 24, at 1172.

28. " (T)here is a fundamentally non-empirical quality about Crosskey's work: at crucial points in the argument he falls back on a type of divination which can only be described as Kabbalistic. He may be right, for example, in stating (without any proof) that Richard Henry Lee did not write the 'Letters from a Federal Farmer,' but in this country spectral evidence has not been admissible since the Seventeenth Century." Roche, *The Founding Fathers: A Reform Caucus in Action,* in Levy, American Constitutional Law: Historical Essays 10, 44 n. 75 (1966).

29. For example, Professor Crosskey discerns a consensus among the Convention's delegates that, he believes, reveals as unwarranted the distinction between *interstate* commerce and *intrastate* commerce that the Supreme Court has traditionally made when interpreting the commerce clause of the Constitution. 2 Crosskey, *op. cit. supra* note 24 at 49.

30. Roche, *op. cit. supra* note 28, at 44.

31. *E.g.,* Levy, *Introduction,* in Levy, *op. cit. supra* note 28, at 1, 3.
32. *Id.* at 2.
33. Mendelson, Justices Black And Frankfurter viii (1961).
34. Hood v. Dumond, 336 U.S. 525, 535 (1949).
35. *Ibid.*
36. McCloskey, *op. cit. supra* note 13, at 5.
37. 17 U. S. (4 Wheat.) 316 (1819).
38. *Id.* at 407.
39. Levy, *op. cit. supra* note 28, at 1.
40. See Frankfurter, *The Judicial Process and the Supreme Court,* in Mendelson, The Supreme Court: Law and Discretion, *op. cit. supra* note 6, at 489, 495.
41. Bickel, The Least Dangerous Branch 194 (1962).
42. McCloskey, *op. cit. supra* note 13, at 15.
43. "No State shall . . . pass any . . . Law impairing the Obligation of Contracts. . . ." U.S. Const. art. I, § 10.
44. 10 U.S. (6 Cranch) 87 (1810).
45. 17 U.S. (4 Wheat.) 518 (1819).
46. See, *e.g.,* Lerner, *John Marshall And The Campaign Of History,* in Levy, *op. cit. supra* note 28, at 47, 66. In Trustees of Dartmouth College v. Woodward (17 U.S. [4 Wheat] 518, 644 [1819]), Marshall himself admits that he is using the contract clause of the Constitution in a way "not in the mind of the Convention."
47. "The Congress shall have Power. . . . To regulate Commerce with foreign Nations, and among the several States, and with the Indian tribes." U.S. Const. art. I, § 8.
48. 22 U.S. (9 Wheat.) 1 (1824).
49. See, *e.g.,* Forkosch, Constitutional Law 192–241 (1963). For a brief but incisive summary of Gibbons v. Ogden (22 U.S. [9 Wheat.] 1 [1824]) and of subsequent highlights of the judicial history of the commerce clause, see Griswold, Law and Lawyers In The United States 82–89 (1964).
50. Douglas, *Stare Decisis,* in Westin, The Supreme Court 122, 132 (1961).
51. 347 U.S. 483 (1954).
52. 163 U.S. 537 (1896).
53. 304 U.S. 64 (1938).
54. 41 U.S. (16 Pet.) 1 (1842).
55. 157 U.S. 429 (1894).
56. 158 U.S. 601 (1894).
57. 79 U.S. (12 Wall.) 457 (1871).

58. 75 U.S. (8 Wall.) 603 (1870).

59. Bickel, *op. cit. supra* note 41, at 107 (quoting Mr. Justice Brandeis).

60. Gompers v. United States, 233 U.S. 604, 610 (1914). See Frankfurter, Mr. Justice Holmes And The Supreme Court 59, 97 (Antheneum ed. 1965).

61. Levy, *op. cit. supra* note 28, at 3 n. 6.

62. Missouri v. Holland, 252 U.S. 416, 433 (1920).

63. Home Building and Loan Association v. Blaisdell, 290 U.S. 398, 442 (1934).

64. Schwartz, The Supreme Court 47 (1957).

65. Levy, *op. cit. supra* note 28, at 3.

66. Bickel, *op. cit. supra* note 41, at 107 (quoting Mr. Justice Brandeis).

67. 17 U.S. (4 Wheat.) 316 (1819).

68. Powell, *op. cit. supra* note 16, at 28.

69. A particularly helpful discussion of the need for stability and certainty in the law is to be found in Sprecher, *The Development Of The Doctrine Of Stare Decisis And The Extent To Which It Should Be Applied,* 31 A.B.A.J. 501 (1945).

70. For a short but useful discussion of the growth of "the cult of the Constitution," see Gabriel, The Course of American Democratic Thought 397–407 (1940).

71. See the discussion of this matter in Chapter I.

72. See, *e.g.,* Fenichel, *Early Stages of Ego Development,* in The Collected Papers of Otto Fenichel: Second Series 25–48 (1954).

73. "Everything points to the conclusion that the child passes through an *animistic period* in the apprehension of reality, in which every object appears to him to be endowed with life, and in which he seeks to find again in every object his own organs and their activities." Ferenczi, *Stages In The Development Of The Sense Of Reality,* in Sex In Psycho-Analysis (Contributions to Psycho-Analysis) 181, 193 (Dover ed. 1956).

74. Blum, Psychoanalytic Theories Of Personality 64–65 (1953).

75. Frank, Law and the Modern Mind 89 (6th printing 1949).

76. See Nunberg, Principles Of Psychoanalysis 121–26 (1955); Fenichel, The Psychoanalytic Theory of Neurosis 46–47, 294–96 (1945).

77. "Since the time when we recognized the error of supposing that ordinary forgetting signified destruction or annihilation of the memory-trace, we have been inclined to the opposite view that nothing once formed in the mind could ever perish, that

everything survives in some way or other, and is capable under certain conditions of being brought to light again, as, for instance, when regression extends back far enough. . . . Perhaps we are going too far with this conclusion. Perhaps we ought be content with the assertion that what is past in the mind *can* survive and need not necessarily perish. . . . We can only be sure that it is more the rule than the exception for the past to survive in the mind." Freud, Civilization And Its Discontents 15–20 (1930).

78. The way in which the ideas and feelings of early childhood may influence adult behavior constitutes a basic theme of psychoanalytic psychology and is explored in depth in psychoanalytic texts such as Fenichel, The Psychoanalytic Theory Of Neurosis, *op. cit. supra* note 76. For a particularly suggestive treatment of the relationship between the events of early childhood and the conduct of adults, see Silverberg, Childhood Experience and Personal Destiny (1952).

79. See Nunberg, *op. cit. supra* note 76, at 121–26; Fenichel, The Psychoanalytic Theory Of Neurosis, *op. cit. supra* note 76, at 295–96, 312–13, 437; Freud, Totem And Taboo 85–86 (1950).

80. See, *e.g.*, Fenichel, The Psychoanalytic Theory of Neurosis, *op. cit. supra* note 76, at 47, 296. Of especial interest here is Ferenczi's pioneer study *On Obscene Words* in Ferenczi, *op. cit. supra* note 73, at 112–130.

81. The possible benefits to be derived from psychoanalytic studies of jurists and their judicial decisions are suggested (and, I believe, exaggerated) in a landmark article by Theodore Schroeder, *The Psychologic Study of Judicial Opinions*, 6 Calif. L. Rev. 89 (1918). See also Frank, Courts On Trial 248–50 (1950).

82. See note 33 of Chapter VII for references to psychoanalytic material pertaining to the influence of "the unconscious" in man's life.

83. See, *e.g.*, Williams, *Philosophy and Psychoanalysis,* and Flew, *Philosophy and Psychopathology,* in Hook, Psychoanalysis, Scientific Method, And Philosophy 157–79, 180–97 (1959).

84. Patterson, Jurisprudence 550 (1953).

85. See, *e.g.*, Holmes, *The Path Of The Law,* 10 Harv. L. Rev. 457 (1897); Cardozo, The Nature Of The Judicial Process 11, 167 (1921); Frankfurther, *Mr. Justice Holmes And The Constitution,* 41 Harv. L. Rev. 121 (1927).

86. Frankfurter, *id.* at 132.

87. See *e.g.,* Freud, *Notes Upon A Case Of Obsessional Neurosis,* and *Psycho-Analytic Notes Upon An Autobiographical Case Of Paranoia (Dementia Paranoides),* in 3 Collected Papers 293–383, 387–470 (1956); Modlin, *The Client And You—What You Are,* 16 N.Y. County B. Bull. 151, 155 (1959).

88. West, *A Psychological Theory Of Law,* in Sayre, Interpretations Of Modern Legal Philosophies 767, 774 (1947).

89. See Frank, Law And The Modern Mind, *op. cit. supra* note 75, at 82–83, 91: Schoenfeld, *Law and Childhood Psychological Experience* 17 Clev.-Mar. L. Rev. 139 (1965).

90. Frank sums up much of this type of legal thinking under the labels "Scholasticism," "Bealism," and "Wousining." See Law And The Modern Mind, *op. cit. supra* note 75, at 48–92.

91. Schroeder, *op. cit. supra* note 226, at 81.

92. Id. at 95. A far more plausible description of the influence of "personal" factors upon judicial opinions is to be found in Haines, *General Observations On The Effects Of Personal, Political, And Economic Influences In The Decisions Of Judges,* 17 Ill. L. Rev. 96, 104–05 (1922–1923): "Psychological motives and influences have been subjected to analysis in their effects upon political conduct to some extent, and it is conceded that these motives and influences are not altered when one assumes the role of judge. Just as is the case with other opinions of individuals, judicial opinions necessarily represent in a measure the personal impulses of the judge, in relation to the situation before him, and these impulses are determined by the judge's lifelong series of previous experiences. The psychologists recently have emphasized the fact that all of us have predispositions which unconsciously attach themselves to the conscious consideration of any question."

93. See especially Cardozo, *op. cit. supra* note 85.

94. See Cohen, Reason And Law 195 (Collier ed. 1961).

95. Back in 1928, Dean Leon Green pointed out that: Word ritual under one guise or another has always been one of the primary methods of law administration. . . . We can scarely realize the part which . . . magic words, continue to play in our law." (Green, *The Duty Problem In Negligence Cases,* 28 Colum. L. Rev. 1014, 1016 [1928]).

96. Cribbet, Principles Of The Law Of Property 41 (1962).

97. *Ibid.*

98. See Tiffany, A Treatise On The Modern Law Of Real Property And Other Interests In Land 260–80 (Zollmann ed. 1940).

99. As W. Barton Leach (a leading authority on the Rule Against

Perpetuities) has pointed out: "Many perfectly reasonable dispositions are striken down because on some outside chance not foreseen by the testator or his lawyer it is mathematically possible that the vesting might occur too remotely." (Leach, *Perpetuities In A Nutshell,* 51 Harv. L. Rev. 638, 643 [1938]). For a short and simple—but devastating—critique of the pitfalls for the unwary in the Rule Against Perpetuities, see Leach, Property Law Indicted! 69–92 (1967).

100. Kubie, *To Break the Hold of the Past,* 16 N.Y. County B. Bull. 139, 142 (1959).

101. See Keeton, Trial Tactics And Methods 191 (1954). Or as Judge Jenks put it almost seventy years ago: "No effort of will can shut out memory; there is no art of forgetting. We cannot be certain that the human mind will deliberate and determine unaffected by that which it knows, but which it should forget in that process." People v. Haas, 105 App. Div. 119, 122 (1905).

102. See Vanderbilt, The Challenge Of Law Reform 44 (1955).

103. For a short authoritative resume of the more important forms of action at the common law, see Morgan, Introduction To The Study Of Law 56–83 (1926).

104. See Pound, Criminal Justice In America 161 (1945).

105. Frank, Courts On Trial, *op. cit. supra* note 81, at 117.

106. *Id.* at 116.

107. Though defined somewhat differently at different times, the judicial oath is essentially a pledge of truthfulness coupled with an appeal to God taken in a judicial proceeding or in connection with some matter related to a judicial proceeding. (See Black's Law Dictionary 1268 [3d. ed. 1933]). Historically, the judicial oath appears to be derived from an ancient method of trying to ascertain truth by invoking supernatural help—the ordeal (See Radin, Anglo-American Legal History 35–36 [1936]); and confidence in the oath may have reached its zenith in the common law procedure known as "wager of law," in which a defendant could successfully defend himself by getting a number of persons to swear that his oath was trustworthy (See Plucknett, A concise History Of The Common Law 109–10 [2d ed. 1936]). Today, confidence in the judicial oath has been seriously eroded, possibly because of a decline in religious belief, coupled with what appears to be the widespread commission of perjury in judicial proceedings. (See Frank, Courts On Trial, *op. cit. supra* note 81, at 85). Nevertheless, the judicial oath still seems to retain its old

magic for a considerable number of people: its use is usually defended on the grounds that it has "a distinct, salutary effect upon the tongues of the great majority of persons." (Moreland, Modern Criminal Procedure 17 [1959]).

108. Hendrick, Facts And Theories Of Psychoanalysis 191–92 (3d ed. 1958).

109. See the discussion of this point in Chapter I.

CHAPTER X

1. The landmark cases that immediately come to mind are, of course, Baker v. Carr, 369 U.S. 186 (1962), Brown v. Board of Education of Topeka, 347 U.S. 483 (1954), and Miranda v. Arizona, 384 U.S. 436 (1967). So significant are these three cases, that, in a sense, they may be said to constitute the essence of the Warren Court's contribution to Constitutional Law.

2. 367 U.S. 643 (1961).

3. 338 U.S. 25 (1949).

4. See Maguire, Evidence of Guilt 5, 170 (1959).

5. Allen, *Federalism And The Fourth Amendment: A Requiem For Wolf,* in Kurland, The Supreme Court And The Constitution: Essays in Constitutional Law from the Supreme Court Review 121 (1965).

6. See Byrnes, *Usurpation by the Court,* in Westin, The Supreme Court 113–21 (1961).

7. *Report of the Committee on Federal-State Relationships as Affected by Judicial Decisions, Adopted by the Conference of Chief Justices at Pasadena, August 1958,* in We The States: An Anthology of Historic Documents and Commentaries thereon, Expounding the State and Federal Relationship 400 (1964).

8. *Id.* at 401.

9. See *e.g.,* Jackson, The Supreme Court In The American System of Government 65–72 (Harper Torchbooks ed. 1963).

10. "The Constitution drafted in 1787 was actually the second American constitution. The first was the Articles of Confederation, drawn up in 1777 and adopted in 1781." Pritchett, The American Constitutional System 3 (1963).

11. The Articles of Confederation consisted of thirteen articles. Article II provided that each of the signatory states was to retain its sovereignty, and Article IX set forth the powers that were to be exercised by the central government.

12. McLaughlin, The Confederation And The Constitution 1783–1789 45–46 (Collier Books ed. 1962).
13. Forkosch, Constitutional Law 3 (1963).
14. 3 Farrand, Records Of The Federal Convention 13 (1911).
15. 2 Madison, Writings 398 (Hunt ed. 1901).
16. U.S. Const. art. 1, § 8. See McLaughlin, *op. cit. supra* note 12, at 45.
17. See, *e.g.,* McCloskey, The American Supreme Court 240 (1960).
18. See Roche, *The Founding Fathers: A Reform Caucus in Action,* in Levy, American Constitutional Law: Historical Essays 10, 45 (1966).
19. 2 U.S. (2 Dall.) 419 (1793).
20. 2 U.S. (2 Dall.) 402 (1792).
21. To quote from the opinion of Mr. Justice Wilson in the case: "This is a case of uncommon magnitude. One of the parties to it is a state; certainly respectable, claiming to be sovereign. The question to be determined, is whether this state, so respectable, and whose claim soars so high, is amenable to the jurisdiction of the supreme court of the United States. . . . I find nothing, which tends to evince an exemption of the state of Georgia, from the jurisdiction of the court." (pp. 453–58).
22. The emotional reaction to the Supreme Court's decision in Chisholm v. Georgia, and to certain other decisions of the Court, will be considered *infra.*
23. The full text of the applicable part of section twenty-five of the Judiciary Act of 1789 reads as follows: "And be it further enacted, That a final judgment or decree in any suit, in the highest court of law or equity of a State in which a decision in the suit could be had, where is drawn in question the validity of a treaty or statute of, or an authority exercised under the United States, and the decision is against their validity; or where is drawn in question the validity of a statute of, or an authority exercised under any State, on the ground of their being repugnant to the constitution, treaties or laws of the United States, and the decision is in favour of such validity, or where is drawn in question the construction of any clause of the constitution, or of a treaty, or statute of, or commission held under the United States, and the decisions is against the title, right, privilege or exemption specially set up or claimed by either party under such clause of the said constitution, treaty, statute or commission, may be re-examined and reversed or affirmed in the Supreme Court of the United States . . . ."

24. 14 U.S. (1 Wheat.) 304 (1816).
25. 11 U.S. (7 Cr.) 603 (1813).
26. A short but excellent discussion of the "Fairfax-Martin" case is to be found in McCloskey, The American Supreme Court 59–64 (1960).
27. Martin v. Hunter's Lessee, 14 U. S. (1 Wheat.) 304, 351 (1816).
28. 19 U.S. (6 Wheat.) 264 (1821).
29. To quote from Marshall's opinion in Cohen's v. Virginia: "It is most true that this Court will not take jurisdiction if it should not; but it is equally true, that it must take jurisdiction if it should . . . . We have no more right to decline the exercise of jurisdiction which is given, than to usurp that which is not given. The one or the other would be treason to the constitution." (19 U.S. [6 Wheat] 264, 404 [1821]).
30. "In 1821, in *Cohen's v. Virginia*, Marshall not only reiterated Story's basic points but interpreted the Eleventh Amendment, that supposed warranty of states' rights, so as to permit individuals to appeal to the Supreme Court even though a state was the other party in the litigation. The Amendment, said Marshall, prevents individual suits against states only if the action is 'commenced' by the individual; if the state has initiated the action (for instance, by arresting a person), the person can still bring the state into the Supreme Court to defend itself against an appeal." McCloskey, *op. cit. supra* note 26, at 64. It also ought to be noted here that Supreme Court decisions have, over the years, limited even further the purview of the Eleventh Amendment. See Corwin, The Constitution And What It Means Today 241 (12th ed. 1958).
31. U.S. Const. art. 1, § 10.
32. 10 U.S. (6 Cr.) 87 (1810).
33. The background and significance of Fletcher v. Peck (a case which arose as a result of the scandalous Yazoo land frauds, and which has been described as "a corner-stone of legal structure laid in mud") is vividly described in Lerner, *John Marshall and the Campaign of History*, in Levy, *op. cit. supra* note 272, at 66–67.
34. 17 U.S. (4 Wheat.) 418 (1819).
35. Those persons who may sometimes doubt the power of "mere words" to move men's hearts and minds would do well to read Daniel Webster's famous argument for Dartmouth in this case before Chief Justice Marshall, an argument which concluded with the words: "Sir, you may destroy this little institution. It is weak. It is in your hands! I know it is one of the lesser

lights in the literary horizon of the country. You may put it out. But if you do so, you must carry through your work. You must extinguish, one after another, all those great lights of science, which, for more than a century, have thrown their radiance over our land. . . . . It is, Sir, as I have said, a small college and yet, there are those who love it. . . . Sir, I care not how others feel, but, for myself, when I see my Alma Mater surrounded like Caesar in the senate house, by those who are reiterating stab on stab, I would not, for this right hand, have her turn to me, and say, *et tu quoque, mi fili.*"

36. 17 U.S. (4 Wheat.) 122 (1819).
37. 17 U.S. (4 Wheat.) 316 (1819).
38. In 1928 (more than one hundred years after McCulloch v. Maryland was decided), Mr. Justice Holmes supplied the *coup de grace* to this supposed truism by declaring in a decision rendered by the Supreme Court that: "The power to tax is not the power to destroy while this Court sits." (Panhandle Oil Oil Co. v. Miss. 277 U.S. 218, 223).
39. McCulloch v. Maryland, 17 U.S. (4 Wheat.) 316, 433 (1819).
40. *Id.* at 436.
41. *Id.* at 421.
42. See, *e.g.,* *Report of the Committee on Federal-State Relationships as Affected by Judicial Decisions, op. cit. supra* note 7, at 398.
43. 22 U.S. (9 Wheat.) 1 (1824).
44. Gibbons v. Ogden, 22 U.S. (9 Wheat.) 1, 196 (1824).
45. *Id.* at 194.
46. *Id.* at 189.
47. *Id.* at 189–90.
48. *Id.* at 197.
49. Frankfurter, The Commerce Clause Under Marshall, Taney And Waite 20 (Quadrangle Books ed. 1964).
50. For a comparatively recent and authoritative discussion of Gibbons v. Ogden, see Benson, The Supreme Court and the Commerce Clause, 1937–1970, 9–25 (1970).
51. 25 U.S. (12 Wheat.) 419 (1827).
52. The term *implicitly* is used here advisedly. There can be little doubt that the restriction upon local taxation of imports in their original packages in the hands of the original importers—the "original package" doctrine (which "still remains the law of the subject, a unique instance of longevity in this general field" [Corwin, The Constitution And What It Means Today, *op. cit. supra* note 30, at 47]—was read into the federal statute by Marshall. See, *e.g.,* Powell, Vagaries and Va-

rieties in Constitutional Interpretation 54 (1956); Frankfurter, The Commerce Clause Under Marshall, Taney And Waite, *op. cit. supra* note 49, at 20, 36.

53. 27 U.S. (2 Pet.) 245 (1829).

54. Admittedly, it would hardly be appropriate here to debate at any great length the usefulness of the much-mooted concept of the "police power" of the states. Still, note ought to be taken (albeit in passing) of the ease with which this concept can be used as a substitute for reasoned analysis. For example, instead of a judge deciding that for reasons A to Z a state ought to be permitted to pass laws concerning a certain matter, he may all too easily avoid analysis by simply asserting that the matter involved comes within the ambit of the state's police power and (assuming that no conflicting federal statute exists) that the state may "therefore" regulate the matter. Of course, instead of *presuming* that the matter comes within the state's police power, the judge may advance reasons one to a hundred to *prove* that this is so. But even if the judge were to advance such proofs, the fact remains that *a reasoned analysis of whether or not a matter comes within the ambit of a state's police power is not at all the same thing as a reasoned analysis of whether or not a state ought to be permitted to pass laws concerning the matter.*

55. "Marshall was, after all, a Virginian; he recognized that the effective regulation of local problems belongs to the state. And so, at the same time that he evolved from the commerce clause drastic restrictions upon state power, he felt his way towards another doctrine . . . [the police power concept] which would be available to meet the diverse local conditions of a sprawling federal society." Frankfurter, The Commerce Clause Under Marshall, Taney And Waite, *op. cit. supra* note 49, at 27.

56. 53 U.S. (12 How.) 299 (1851).

57. *Id.* at 319. As T. R. Powell has pointed out, the dichotomy advanced by Mr. Justice Curtis is assailable on a number of grounds. For example, it fails to take into account those subjects of the commerce power that "do not imperatively demand either uniformity or diversity of regulatory rules." Powell, *op. cit. supra* note 52, at 153.

58. See, *e.g.*, Stern, *The Problems of Yesteryear—Commerce and Due Process,* in Levy, *op. cit. supra* note 18, 193, 199–211.

59. T. R. Powell has contended that in the light of cases decided since Cooley v. Board of Port Wardens, the *Cooley* rule has proven to be "not an absolute prohibition of state power over the com-

merce that is national in character, but only a qualified one. The states must leave national commerce alone *unless by the consent of Congress.*" Powell, *op. cit. supra* note 306, at 161. (Emphasis added.)

60. 118 U.S. 557 (1886).
61. "There were some fourteen cases between 1877 and 1886 in which state regulations of commerce were held invalid, most of them on the ground that the subject in question was national in character and required a uniform rule which only Congress could provide." McCloskey, *op. cit. supra* note 26, at 124–25.
62. Federal regulatory agencies did, of course, exist before the Interstate Commerce Commission was created in 1887. Indeed, the first such federal agency was created by Congress in 1789 to estimate the duties payable on imports and to perform related functions. See Davis, Administrative Law And Government 25 (1960). For a brief—but very useful and authoritative—outline of the major reasons for the growth of modern federal regulatory agencies, see *id.* at 32–39. See also Stone, Social Dimensions Of Law And Justice 696–728 (1966).
63. 156 U.S. 1 (1895).
64. *Id.* at 12–13.
65. 208 U.S. 161 (1908).
66. *Id.* at 180.
67. 247 U.S. (1918).
68. *Id.* at 271–72.
69. *Id.* at 280 (dissenting opinion).
70. *Id.* at 281 (dissenting opinion).
71. 295 U.S. 495 (1935).
72. Schechter Poultry Corp. v. United States, 295 U.S. 495, 528 (1935). These linguistic niceties paraded by Hughes are less than clear—and are certainly less than convincing. As Edward S. Corwin pointed out in 1936 in a critical analysis of the *Schechter* case: "If 'extraordinary conditions may call for extraordinary remedies' and this fact has to be considered 'when the exercise of power is challanged,' then to people unacquainted with legalistic jargon, or not disposed to be unduly impressed thereby, it would seem that 'extraordinary conditions' do 'enlarge constitutional power.'" (*The Schechter Case—Landmark or What?*, 13 N.Y.U.L.Q. Rev. 151, 155 [1936]). Unfortunately, quite a few of the judicial opinions rendered by Hughes contain "dialectics" comparable to the passage from the *Schechter* case quoted in the text and criticized by Corwin. See, for example, the decision of Hughes

in Home Building and Loan Association v. Blaisdell (290 U.S. 398 [1934]), in which he asserts in one paragraph that: "Emergency does not create power. Emergency does not increase granted power or remove or diminish the restrictions imposed upon power granted or reserved"; and in the very next paragraph he concludes that: "While emergency does not create power, emergency may furnish the occasion for the exercise of power. 'Although an emergency may not call into life a power which has never lived, nevertheless emergency may afford a reason for the exertion of a living power already enjoyed.'" (pp. 425–26) In a penetrating chapter concerning Hughes in The Supreme Court From Taft To Warren 70–118 (Norton ed. 1964), A. T. Mason not only points to the repeated appearance of such dialectics in the judicial opinions of Hughes, but also notes that Hughes learned early in life to employ deliberately confusing and misleading language so as to be able to seem to be conforming to the wishes of his incredibly demanding parents, while actually maintaining some independence of judgment and action. (A particularly vivid sketch of the influence that the parents of Hughes sought to exert upon him is to be found in Glad, Charles Evans Hughes And The Illusions Of Innocence 11–47 ([1966], in which the author emphasizes that even when Hughes was away in college, his parents "instructed him on every conceivable matter—the care of his bed, his stove, his flannels; how to take his medicines, schedule his work, say his prayers, act in the classroom; whether or not to join a college society or take a roommate.") Hopefully, a future biographer of Hughes (perhaps someone with both legal and psychoanalytic training) will be able to build upon the materials already adduced concerning the life of Hughes (especially the very fine two-volume biography—Charles Evans Hughes—by Merlo J. Pusey), and will be able to explore in depth the possibility that meaningful connections exist between the extraordinarily demanding upbringing Hughes received and his behavior later in life as a jurist.

73. 297 U.S. 1 (1936).

74. 301 U.S. 1 (1937).

75. In a sense, the Court's new attitude had been revealed late in March of 1937, when the Court in West Coast Hotel v. Parrish (300 U.S. 379) had upheld a Washington state statute establishing minimum wages and maximum hours of work for women.

76. National Labor Relations Board v. Jones & Laughlin Steel Corp., 301 U.S. 1, 37 (1937).

77. *Id.* at 41.

78. 312 U.S. 100 (1941).

79. *Id.* at 116–17.

80. 334 U.S. 111 (1942).

81. In the words of Mr. Justice Jackson in Wickard v. Filburn: "It can hardly be denied that a factor of such volume and variability as home-consumed wheat would have a substantial influence on price and market conditions. This may arise because being in marketable condition such wheat overhangs the market and, if induced by rising prices, tends to flow into the market and check price increases. But if we assume that it is never marketed, it supplies a need of the man who grew it which would otherwise be reflected by purchases in the open market. Home-grown wheat in this sense competes with wheat in commerce. The stimulation of commerce is a use of the regulatory function quite as definitely as prohibitions or restrictions thereon. This record leaves us in no doubt that Congress may properly have considered that wheat consumed on the farm where grown, if wholly outside the scheme of regulation, would have a substantial effect in defeating and obstructing its purpose to stimulate trade therein at increased prices." (pp. 128–29)

82. Schwartz, The Supreme Court 41 (1957).

83. Levy, American Constitutional Law: Historical Essays 188–89 (1966).

84. 2 U.S. (2 Dall.) 419 (1793) See the comments upon this case *supra.*

85. One of the reasons for the shock generated by the Court's decision in Chisholm v. Georgia was that the decision violated "a positive assurance" by Alexander Hamilton in The Federalist that a state could not be sued by another state in the Supreme Court. See Corwin, The Twilight Of The Supreme Court 4 (1934).

86. 1 Warren, The Supreme Court In United States History 96 (1st ed. 1922).

87. *Id.* at 100.

88. These laws, four in number, were: a Naturalization Act that lengthened the period of residence required for naturalization from five to fourteen years; an Enemy Alien Act that enabled the President to deport enemy aliens during wartime; an Alien

Act that empowered the President to deport any foreigner he considered "dangerous to the peace and safety of the United States," and a Sedition Act (described in the text).

89. The generally accepted view today is that the Sedition Act "was one of the most flagrantly unconstitutional laws ever enacted in American history in that it was a direct violation of the First Amendment to the Constitution." Acheson, The Supreme Court 42 (1961). Nevertheless, before the Act expired in 1801, its validity had been repeatedly sustained in the lower federal courts (see Rice, Freedom Of Association 123 [1962]); and every member of the Supreme Court from 1798 to 1800, when ruling on circuit, considered it to be constitutional. See Levy, Legacy Of Suppression: Freedom Of Speech And Press In Early American History 246 (1960).

90. Under the Sedition Act, the Federalists secured about twenty-five arrests, at least fifteen indictments, and ten convictions. See Rice, op. cit. supra note 89.

91. See Pritchett, The American Constitutional System 24–25 (1963).

92. See Acheson, op. cit. supra note 89, at 34–35. For a sketch of the trial of Mr. Justice Chase, see Murphy, Congress and the Court 12–15 (Phoenix ed. 1962).

93. 10 U.S. (6 Cr.) 87 (1810). See the discussion of this case, supra.

94. McKay, Georgia Versus The United States Supreme Court, 4 J. Pub. L. 285, 292 (1955).

95. Warren, op. cit. supra note 86, at 398.

96. McKay, op. cit. supra note 94.

97. 17 U.S. (4 Wheat.) 316 (1819). See the discussion of this case, supra.

98. Warren, op. cit. supra note 86, at 520.

99. Id. at 519.

100. Id. at 516.

101. For an account of this incident and its aftermath, see Acheson, op. cit. supra note 89, at 72–75.

102. See Lerner, John Marshall and the Campaign of History, in Levy, American Constitutional Law: Historical Essays, op. cit. supra note 83, at 82.

103. Marshall went so far as to write and have published a long article defending the decision reached by the Court in McCulloch v. Maryland. (Ibid.)

104. 19 U.S. (6 Wheat.) 264 (1821).

105. See the discussion of this matter, supra.

106. "Had Marshall's chair been vacted during Jefferson's administration, Roane would probably have become Chief Justice of the United States." Murphy, op. cit. supra note 92, at 19.

107. 2 Warren, *op. cit. supra* note 86, at 15.

108. Murphy, *op. cit supra* note 92, at 18.

109. Lerner, *John Marshall And The Campaign Of History*, in Levy *op. cit. supra* note 83, at 83.

110. Elliott, *Court-Curbing Proposals In Congress,* 33 Notre Dame Law. 597, 607 (1958).

111. Possibly because Calhoun's name is associated in American history with concepts that seem to belong irrevocably to the past—nullification and secession—his views have been largely neglected. This is unfortunate, for Calhoun was an extremely able and thoughtful student of public affairs, and his views on such matters as the rights of minorities, the attractiveness of violence for many Americans, and the nature of a truly democratic society are not only of interest in themselves, but are particularly relevant to some of today's most troublesome social problems. For a pithy examination of some of Calhoun's fundamental views, see Gabriel, The Course Of American Democratic Thought 103–10 (1940).

112. A more detailed summary of these concepts is to be found in Blum, The National Experience (1963).

113. Bowers, The Party Battles of the Jackson Period 256 (Anniversary ed. 1928).

114. Jackson's proclamation is quoted and considered in its historical context in Haines, The Role of the Supreme Court in American Government and Politics 1789–1835 (1944).

115. Blum, *op. cit. supra* note 112, at 225.

116. Bowers, *op. cit. supra* note 113, at 265.

117. In 1848, for example, the so-called "Wilmot Proviso" (a bill introduced in the House of Representatives by Congressman David Wilmot of Pennsylvania that prohibited slavery in territory acquired by the United States from Mexico) aroused considerable apprehension in the South. See Blum, *op. cit. supra* note 112, at 275.

118. Pritchett, *op. cit. supra* note 91, at 25.

119. See the discussion of this matter in Chapter VII.

120. Gabriel, *op. cit. supra* note 111, at 132.

121. See Barker, The Civil War In America 9–18 (1961).

122. 74 U.S. (7 Wall.) 700, 725 (1869).

123. McCloskey, The American Supreme Court 103 (1960).

124. An example that immediately comes to mind is President Eisenhower's use of troops in 1957 to force the state of Arkansas to comply with a court order integrating the schools. See Murphy & Pritchett, Courts, Judges, And Politics 228–35 (1961).

125. 94 U.S. 113 (1876).

126. The Court insisted that the regulation of grain warehouses in Chicago was "a thing of domestic concern, and, certainly, until Congress acts in reference to . . . [a State's] inter-state relations, the State may exercise all the powers of government over them even though in so doing it may indirectly operate upon commerce outside its immediate jurisdiction." *Id.* at 135.

127. See 2 Warren, The Supreme Court In United States History 582 (Rev. ed. 1926).

128. During the last third of the nineteenth century, American farmers (especially in the Midwest) banded together in "granges" and other organizations in an attempt to improve their desperate economic plight. For material pertaining to the precarious economic situation of American farmers at this time and their organizational attempts to help themselves, see 2 Hofstadter, Great Issues in American History 131–77 (1958); Blum, *op. cit. supra* note 110, at 482–83.

129. McCloskey, *op. cit. supra* note 123, at 104.

130. 2 Warren, *op. cit. supra* note 127, at 582.

131. See 2 Hofstadter, *op. cit. supra* note 128, at 142–43.

132. Munn v. Illinois, 94 U.S. 113, 140 (1876) (dissenting opinion).

133. 198 U.S. 45 (1905). See the discussion of this case in Chapter VIII.

134. A considerable portion of the reasoning in the majority opinion by Mr. Justice Peckham is in terms of the "police power" concept. (See note 54 *supra* regarding this concept.) Mr. Justice Peckham notes that there are "certain powers, existing in the sovereignty of each state in the Union, somewhat vaguely termed police powers." He then points out that the Court had tried in the past to interpret these police powers broadly enough so as to enable a state to protect the health, safety, and morals of its inhabitants. He warns, however, that there must be "a limit to the valid exercise of the police power by the state. . . . Otherwise . . . the legislatures of the states would have unbounded power, and it would be enough to say that any piece of legislation was enacted to conserve the morals, the health, or the safety of the people." In such cases, he concludes, the "claim of the police power would be a mere pretext . . . another and delusive name for the supreme sovereignty of the state . . . exercised free from constitutional restraint." These observations by Mr. Justice Peckham may well be true. Yet as Mr. Justice Holmes observes in typically laconic fashion in his dissent: "General propositions do not decide concrete cases."

135. N. Y. Times, April 18, 1905, p. 1.
136. See Konefsky, The Legacy of Holmes and Brandeis 48–49 (Collier ed. 1961).
137. 208 U.S. 412 (1908).
138. 243 U.S. 426 (1917).
139. Jackson, The Struggle For Judicial Supremacy 86 (1941).
140. Murphy, *op. cit. supra* note 92, at 57.
141. *Ibid.*
142. United States v. Butler, 297 U.S. 1, 87 (1936) (dissenting opinion).
143. *Ibid.*
144. Mason, The Supreme Court From Taft To Warren 92 (Norton ed. 1964).
145. Alsop & Catledge, The 168 Days, 73 (1938).
146. *Id.* at 69.
147. 2 Hofstadter, *op. cit. supra* note 128, at 376–81.
148. "Two years after the . . . fight, the President claimed that he had lost the battle but won the war. Without the appointment of a single new member the Court had radically changed its course. On the contrary, a biographer of Roosevelt concluded in 1956 that the President had lost the battle, won the campaign, but lost the war. The mighty New Deal coalition that had triumphantly swept forty-six states in November, 1936, had splattered like Humpty Dumpty the next spring. After the Court fight FDR got through Congress only one more major piece of domestic New Deal legislation. . . ." Murphy, *op. cit. supra* note 92, at 62.
149. See the discussion of the Court's post-1937 interpretation of the Commerce Clause *supra.*
150. 347 U.S. 483 (1954).
151. See, *e.g.,* West Virginia State Board of Education v. Barnette, 319 U.S. 624 (1943), in which the Supreme Court invalidated a West Virginia requirement that students attending public schools participate in flag salute ceremonies.
152. In a series of cases beginning in 1938, the Supreme Court had raised objections to segregation in higher education. See Missouri *ex rel.* Gaines v. Canada, 305 U.S. 337 (1938); Sipuel v. Oklahoma, 332 U.S. 631 (1948); Sweatt v. Painter, 339 U.S. 629 (1950); and McLaurin v. Oklahoma State Regents 339 U.S. 637 (1950).
153. 163 U.S. 537 (1896).
154. "Laws permitting, and even requiring . . . separation [of races] in places where they are liable to be brought into contact . . . have been generally, if not universally, recognized as within

the competency of the state legislatures in the exercise of their police power. The most common instance of this is connected with the establishment of separate schools for white and colored children, which has been held to be a valid exercise of the legislative power. . . ." *Id.* at 544.

155. The Court's saying this does not, of course, make it so. For a perceptive and balanced discussion of the Court's declaration that separate educational facilities are inherently unequal, see Swisher, The Supreme Court In Modern Role 166–70 (Rev. ed. 1965).

156. Brown v. Board of Education of Topeka, 347 U.S. 483, 495 (1954).

157. Brown v. Board of Education of Topeka, 349 U.S. 294, 301 (1955). For a useful discussion of the phrase "all deliberate speed," see Bikel, The Least Dangerous Branch 247–54 (1962).

158. See Bikel, *id.* at 254–55.

159. *Id.* at 255.

160. 2 Hofstadter, *op. cit. supra* note 128, at 66.

161. See A. Freud, The Ego And The Mechanisms Of Defence 117–31 (1946).

162. For a short but most enlightening discussion of the concept of "anomie" as originally formulated by Durkheim and later extended by R. K. Merton—a discussion that repeatedly calls to mind the post-1964 disturbances noted in the text—see Mannheim, Comparative Criminology 501–06 (1965). For a more detailed presentation of such material, see Durkheim On The Division Of Labour In Society 353–73, 396–436 (Ed. 1933), and Merton, Social Theory And Social Structure 131–94 (Ed. 1957).

163. 369 U.S. 186 (1962).

164. For a thoroughgoing analysis of Baker v. Carr and some of the later cases based upon it, see Neal, *Baker v. Carr: Politics In Search Of Law,* in Kurland, These Supreme Court And The Constitution: Essays in Constitutional Law from The Supreme Court Review 187–262 (1965).

165. See, *e.g.,* Mapp v. Ohio, 367 U.S. 643, discussed *supra.*

166. See, *e.g.,* Miranda v. Arizona, 384 U.S. 436, discussed in Chapter VIII.

167. This increase in crime is catalogued with doleful regularity in the yearly Uniform Crime Reports for the United States issued by the Federal Bureau of Investigation, U.S. Department of Justice, Washington, D.C.

168. See, *e.g.*, the discussion of federalism in Forkosh, Constitutional Law 62–88 (1963).

169. For a clear and comparatively recent presentation of the states' rights point of view, see Goldwater, The Conscience Of A Conservative (1960). For a useful (albeit somewhat dated) historical study of this point of view, see Pierce, Federal Usurpation (1908).

170. Pritchett, The American Constitutional System 111 (1963). See also Jaffa, *The Case For A Stronger National Government,* in Goldwin, A Nation Of States: Essays on the American Federal System 106 (1961).

171. See, *e.g.*, Byrnes, *Usurpation by the Court,* in Westin, The Supreme Court: Views from Inside 113–21 (1961); Bloch, States' Rights: The Law Of The Land (1958); Kilpatrick, the Sovereign States (1957).

172. See the states' rights arguments detailed early in this chapter.

173. See the discussion of the influence of such unconscious material in Chapter VII.

174. Jones, Hamlet And Oedipus 85 (Doubleday Anchor ed. 1955). See Klein, The Psychoanalysis Of Children 185–87 (First Evergreen ed. 1960); A. Freud, Psychoanalysis for Teachers and Parents 55 (Emerson Books ed. 1954); Menninger, Love Against Hate 9–10 (Harvest Books ed. 1942).

175. Freud, Civilization And Its Discontents 102 (1955). Freud's views regarding aggression have found considerable support during the past number of years in studies based upon the research of Konrad Lorenz. See, *e.g.*, Human Aggression, published in 1968, in which Anthony Storr declares that aggression is "a necessary part of our biological inheritance," and that it is "a drive as innate, as natural, and as powerful as sex." (pp. 3, 109). See also Chapter V.

176. See Jones, Hamlet And Oedipus, *op. cit. supra* note 174.

177. See, *e.g.*, Abraham, *A Short Study Of The Development Of The Libido, Viewed In The Light Of Mental Disorders,* in 1 Selected Papers of Karl Abraham 418, 496 (1960).

178. "When a child tears off the legs and wings of butterflies and flies, kills or tortures birds or vents his rage for destruction on his playthings or articles in daily use, his elders excuse it on the ground of lack of capacity to feel for a different living creature, or his slight comprehension of the money value of things. But our observation teaches us something different. We hold that the child tortures animals, not because he does not understand that it adds to their suffering, but just be-

cause he wants to add to their sufferings, and small, defenseless beetles are the least dangerous of creatures." A. Freud, Psychoanalysis for Teachers and Parents, *op. cit. supra* note 174.

179. Psychoanalysts also point out that the birth of a brother or sister may serve as a stimulus for a young child to begin what Freud believed ought to be described as an "infantile sexual investigation." In Freud's words: "[M]any, perhaps most children . . . go through a period beginning with the third year, which may be designated as the period of *infantile sexual investigation.* As far as we know, this curiosity is not awakened spontaneously in children of this age. It is aroused through the impression of an important experience, through the birth of a little brother or sister, or through fear of the same engendered by some outward experience, wherein the child sees a danger to his egotistic interests. The investigation directs itself to the question whence children come, as if the child were looking for means to guard against such an undesirable event." S. Freud, Leonardo Da Vinci: A Study In Psychosexuality 27 (Random House ed. 1947).

180. Balint, The Early Years Of Life: A Psychoanalytic Study 53–54 (Basic Books ed. 1954). See also Flugel, The Psychoanalytic Study Of The Family 19–20 (1950).

181. For a resume of psychoanalytic discoveries concerning the Oedipus complex and its influence upon man's behavior, see such standard psychoanalytic texts as Fenichel, The Psychoanalytic Theory Of Neurosis (1945); Hendrick, Facts and Theories of Psychoanalysis (3d ed. 1958); Nunberg, Principles Of Psychoanalysis (1955); and Brenner, An Elementary Textbook of Psychoanalysis (Doubleday Anchor ed. 1957). Possibly because of the huge amount of evidence adduced by psychoanalysts concerning the Oedipus complex, debates concerning its existence no longer occupy a significant place in psychological writings. Indeed, even among cultural anthropologists (many of whom have persistently refused to acknowledge the universality of the Oedipus complex), there is a growing acceptance of the view that "the best evidence which is available at present speaks for the existence of incestuous and parrenticidal impulses and conflicts about them in every culture we know of (Roheim, 1950)." [Brenner, *id.* at 118.] See, *e.g.* Stephens, The Oedipus Complex: Cross-Cultural Evidence (1962). Indisputably, however, the existence or ubiquity of the Oedipus complex is still occasionally challenged: and, sooner or later, the challenge is usually met.

\

See, *e.g.*, Schoenfeld, *Erich Fromm's Attacks Upon The Oedipus Complex—A Brief Critique*, 141 Journal of Nervous and Mental Disease 580 (1965).

182. Freud, The Interpretation Of Dreams, in The Basic Writings Of Sigmund Freud 308 (Brill ed. 1938).

183. See, e.g., Balint, *op. cit. supra* note 180, at 36–39.

184. *Id.* at 62.

185. *"Si le petit sauvage était abandonné à lui-même, qu'il conserva toute son imbécilité et qu'il réunit un peu de raison de l'enfant au berceau la violence des passions de l'homme de trente ans, il torderait le cou à son père et coucherait avec sa mère."* The very free translation in the text is by Ernest Jones. Jones, Hamlet And Oedipus, *op. cit. supra* note 174, at 90.

186. Historically—or more accurately, phylogenetically—this may not have always been so. For an admittedly speculative suggestion concerning the origin of Oedipal desires and feelings, see Schoenfeld, *God The Father—And Mother: Study and Extension of Freud's Conception of God as an Exalted Father*, 19 American Imago 219 (1962).

187. See the discussion of the mental mechanism of identification in Chapter VI.

188. See Balint, *op. cit. supra* note 180, at 109.

189. See the discussion of the superego in Chapter III.

190. For a resume of various psychic changes at about the age of five and six that seem to contribute to the disappearance of Oedipal desires and feelings from consciousness, see Freud, *The Passing Of The Oedipus Complex*, in 2 Collected Papers 269–76 (1956).

191. Freud, Three Contributions To The Theory Of Sex, in The Basic Writings Of Sigmund Freud, *op. cit. supra* note 182, at 581.

192. Id. at 582–83.

193. See the discussion of repression in Chapter II.

194. Freud, Three Contributions To The Theory Of Sex, in The Basic Writings Of Sigmund Freud, *op. cit. supra* note 182, at 582–83.

195. Schachtel, *On Memory And Childhood Amnesia*, in Mullahy, A Study Of Interpersonal Relations 9–10 (Grove Press ed. 1949).

196. *Id.* at 10. Schachtel points out, among other things, that "it is not sufficiently clear why a repression of sexual experience should lead to a repression of all experience in early childhood." Further, Schachtel notes that the "term and concept of repression suggest that material which *per se* could be recalled is excluded from recall because of its traumatic

nature. If the traumatic factor can be clarified and dissolved, the material is again accessible to recall. But even the most profound and prolonged psychoanalysis does not lead to a recovery of childhood memory; at best it unearths some incidents and feelings that had been forgotten." *Id.* at 9–10.

197. See note 33 of Chapter VII for appropriate references. See also the relevant sections of Fenichel, The Psychoanalytic Theory Of Neurosis, *op. cit. supra* note 181.

198. See Chapter II.

199. See Chapters II, III, IV, V, and VI.

200. See Morris, *The Psychoanalysis of Labor Strikes,* 10 Lab L. J. 833, 834, 841 (1959), and Soule, The Strength of Nations 195 (1959).

201. See Schoenfeld, *Law and Childhood Psychological Experience,* 14, Cleve,-Mar. L. Rev. 139, 150 (1965).

202. *Id.* at 148.

203. *Id.* at 152–53.

204. *Id.* at 151–52.

205. See the discussion of symbolism in Chapters IV and VII.

206. See the discussion of this matter in Chapter VIII.

207. J. C. Flugel, for instance, has pointed out that many of us tend "to regard our native land as a great mother who brings into being, nourishes, protects and cherishes her sons and daughters and inspires them with respect and love for herself and her traditions, customs, beliefs and institutions; in return for which her children are prepared to work and fight for her— and above all, to protect her from her enemies." Flugel, *op. cit. supra* note 180, at 126. See Soule, *op. cit supra* note 200, at 241; Van Clute, *How Fascism Thwarts The Life* Instinct, 12 American Journal Of Ortho-Psychiatry 336 (1942). See generally Schoenfeld, *Psychoanalytic Guideposts For The Good Society,* 55 Psychoanalytic Review 91, 106–09 (1968).

208. Favoring this possibility is the very limited number of ideas or themes with which the unconscious is basically concerned. These fundamental ideas or themes—as revealed in unconscious symbolism—are birth, love (sex), death, concepts of self and of close blood relatives (or their surrogates). See Jones, *The Theory Of Symbolism,* in Papers On Psychoanalysis 87, 102–04 (5th ed. 1950).

209. 367 U.S. 643 (1961). See the discussion of Mapp v. Ohio at the beginning of this chapter.

210. 347 U.S. 483 (1954). See the discussion of Brown v. Board of Education of Topeka earlier in this chapter.

211. It is difficult to overestimate the influence of unconscious vestiges of the Oedipus complex during adulthood. These vestiges may, for example, find reflection in such diverse and significant matters as political theory (see, *e.g.*, Hopkins, Fathers Or Sons? xi, 6, 22, 25), labor relations (see, *e.g.*, Soule, *op. cit. supra* note 200, at 195), attitudes towards private property (see, *e.g.*, Silverberg, Childhood Experience And Personal Destiny 182 [1952]), regicide (see *e.g.*, Flugel, *op. cit. supra* note 180, at 110–20), and, of course, in man's love life (see *e.g.*, Freud, *Contributions to the Psychology of Love* in 4 Collected Papers 192–235 [1956]).

212. See p. 198 *supra.*

213. See the discussion of Marshall's judicial decisions earlier in this chapter.

214. 304 U.S. 64 (1938). The essence of the Supreme Court's ruling is distilled in masterly fashion in Griswold, Law And Lawyers In The United States 72–74 (1964).

215. The considerable influence exerted by unconscious traces of the desires and emotions of early childhood upon the words and deeds of adults has, of course, been stressed repeatedly in this book (see, *e.g.*, note 211 *supra*). This emphasis upon the role of the unconscious in adult life has by no means been accidental, however, for the essence of psychoanalysis may be said to lie in its elucidation of the many different and often significant ways in which unconscious forces affect man's behavior. In fact, Freud believed that the emphasis placed by psychoanalysis upon the part played in man's life by unconscious ideas and emotions—and particularly the resultant knowledge that man, in effect, "it not even master in his own house, but . . . must remain content with . . . scraps of information about what is going on unconsciously in his own mind" (Freud, A General Introduction To Psychoanalysis 296 [Permabook ed. 1953])—proved to be such grave blows to man's self-love, that they (coupled with the psychoanalytic stress upon sexuality) were in large measure responsible for the great opposition psychoanalysis encountered from its inception. See Freud, *One Of The Difficulties Of Psycho-Analysis,* in 4 Collected Papers, *op. cit. supra* note 211, at 347–56; Shakow & Rapaport, The Influence Of Freud On American Psychology 14–32 (Meridian Books ed. 1968).

216. See the end of Chapter IX.

CHAPTER XI

1. Munroe, Schools Of Psychoanalytic Thought 54 (1955).
2. Mendelson, Justices Black and Frankfurter: Conflict in the Court 31 (1961).
3. See the distinction drawn between "fixed" and "expendable" psychoanalytic theories in Bergler, The Superego 1–3 (1952).
4. See, *e.g.*, Morgan, Some Problems Of Proof Under The Anglo-American System Of Litigation (1956), for a powerful and authoritative indictment of the rules of evidence. For material pertaining to the relevance of psychoanalytic psychology to the law of evidence, see Goldstein, *Psychoanalysis And Jurisprudence,* in 23 The Psychoanalytic Study of the Child 459, 467–71 (1968).
5. Miller v. United States, 320 F.2d 767, 770 (1963).
6. Morgan, *op. cit. supra* note 4, at 164.
7. See Schoenfeld, *Law And Unconscious Motivation,* 8 How. L.J. 15, 23–24 (1962).
8. See, *e.g.*, Saxe, *Psychiatry, Psychoanalysis, And The Credibility Of Witnesses,* 45 Notre Dame Lawyer 238 (1970); Silving, *Testing Of The Unconscious In Criminal Cases,* 69 Harv. L. Rev. 683–705 (1956); Skolnick, *Scientific Theory And Scientific Evidence: An Analysis Of Lie-Detection* 70 Yale L.J. 694, 724–25 (1961).
9. See Freud, New Introductory Lectures On Psychoanalysis 188–89 (1933).
10. Jones, 2 The Life and Work of Sigmund Freud 108–09 (1955).
11. Rieff, Freud: The Mind Of The Moralist xi (1959).
12. Eysenck, Uses and Abuses of Psychology 241 (1955). See also Murphy, Historical Introduction to Modern Psychology (Rev. ed. 1949).
13. See Patterson, Jurisprudence: Men and Ideas of the Law 550 (1953).
14. See, *e.g.*, *Seminar on Psychiatry and Psychology as a Tool for Lawyers,* 16 N.Y. County B. Bull. 129–57 (1959); *Symposium—Psychology and Law,* 14 Ohio St. L.J. 117–212 (1953); Silving, *Psychoanalysis And The Criminal Law,* 51 J. Crim. L.C. & P.S. 19–33 (1960); Mueller, *The Law Of Public Wrongs—Its Concepts In The World Of Reality* 10 J. Pub. L. 203–60 (1962); Katz, Goldstein, & Dershowitz, Psychoanalysis, Psychiatry, and Law (1967).
15. Story, Miscellaneous Writings 460 (1835).

INDEX

A

Abraham, Karl, 222, 263
Abrahamsen, David, 91, 213–215, 218, 228
Accident-prone individuals, 54, 56–57
Acheson, Patricia C., 231, 258
Activity, preference for, 131–133
Adair v. United States, 172, 175
Adams, Henry, 113
Adams, John, 179
Adkins v. Children's Hospital, 123, 242
Administrative agencies, arbitrariness of, 28
Administrative Procedure Act of 1946, 74
Admiralty Law, 35–36
Adults
  aggressiveness of, 51
  projection by, 80
  unconscious, role of, 267
Adversary system of litigation
  abuses of, 96–101
  identification, 97–99
Aethelberht, Laws of, 59–60
Aggression, 50–71, 195, 263
  accident-prone individuals, 54, 56–57
  achievements resulting from, 52
  ancient laws, 59–60
  big business legislation, 83–86
  classrooms, 52–53
  criminal law, 69–70, 86–87
  district attorneys, 61–63
  extra-legal approaches to, 55–56
  games, 52
  judges, 63–66
  law as means of controlling, 54–71
  legislators, 66–71, 81–82
  police brutality, 60–61
  prosecutors, 61–63
  revengeful nature of law, 59–60
  self-directed, 53–54, 56–57
  sports, 52
  sterilization of habitual criminals, 53
  sublimation of, 53
  subversives, laws dealing with, 83
  suicide, 54, 57–58
  trials as outlets for, 64
  unconscious, 52–53
  undesirable results of, 51
Agricultural Adjustment Act, 116, 174, 176
Aleichem, Sholom, 229
Alexander, Franz, 81, 211, 213–214, 219, 222, 228, 233
Alien Act, 257–258
Alien and Sedition Laws, 179
Allen, Francis A., 159, 250
Alsop, Joseph W., 220, 261
American Federation of Labor v. American Sash Co., 238
Anal-sadistic period of infancy, 51, 195
Analytic jurisprudence, 28
Ancient Law, 12
Anderson, William, 243–244
Animistic period, 150, 246
Anomie, 190, 262
Anti-Semitism, 80
Antisocial urgencies and desires, 81, 86–87, 89–91
Antitrust legislation, 84–86, 227
Aristotle, 131
Arnold, Thurman W., 112, 220, 233
Articles of Confederation, 161–162, 177–178, 250
Austin, John, 24, 28, 55, 216–217
Australia, 232

B

"Bad man," influences of, 56
Baker v. Carr, 128, 132, 135, 191, 193–194, 250, 262